THE DAY OF
THE LIBERALS IN SPAIN

THE DAY OF
THE LIBERALS IN SPAIN

BY

RHEA MARSH SMITH
Associate Professor of History
Rollins College

Philadelphia

UNIVERSITY OF PENNSYLVANIA PRESS

LONDON: HUMPHREY MILFORD: OXFORD UNIVERSITY PRESS

1938

CONTENTS

v

PREFACE

THERE are interesting similarities between the Spanish Revolution which began in 1931 and other revolutions which history records. In many instances the course of events appears almost identical with certain phases of the French Revolution, which moved from idealism through a reign of terror to empire; to the German Revolution which led to the framing of the model contemporary Constitution of Weimar; and to the Mexican Revolution of 1910 and the Constitution of 1917. In the latter case, especially, the problems are very like those which confronted the leaders of the Second Spanish Republic.

To a large extent, however, these similarities may be attributed to the influence of unchanging human factors, and they are less important than the differences between the trend of the Spanish Revolution and other such movements. It is trite to repeat that the evolution of each nation is conditioned by economic, geographic, and human factors which impart to its historical vicissitudes peculiarities of their own. The varied nature of the Iberian Peninsula, the invasion and settlement of many peoples, the era of Moslem domination, the reconquest, the development of the Spanish Empire, and the individuality of the Spanish temperament have all had special significance in the evolution of Spain. The Revolution of 1931, therefore, could have followed its special course in no other nation in the world.

It is essential to delve deep into the historical background of the problems which faced the Spanish idealists and politicians in 1931 in order to comprehend them. It is important to gain not only a perspective of their origin and evolution but the relation of the solution to each problem and the reaction to that solution as well. The evolution of Spain from medievalism to modernity was so delayed and so peculiarly

related to the strength of tradition and the individuality of
the Spanish temperament that Spain became an anachronism
in the modern world. Even the idealism of the reformers of
1931 as embodied in their measures scarcely ruffled the placid
depths of rural Spanish life or materially changed the evolution of the nation.

Unfortunately, the opportunity for the solution of the
problems of Spain was violently wrested from Spanish hands
by military insurrection and foreign intervention. It is an
interesting paradox that in Spain, Fascism and National
Socialism, which began as national movements, have become
international in scope, while Spanish Socialism, which was
international in origin, became national in its tendencies.
This was perhaps inevitable. The nations which have intervened in the Spanish Civil War had solved their national
problems and sought foreign exercise not only as a testing
ground for imperial ambitions and as diversion from concentration on national difficulties, but for such economic reasons
as German interest in the mineral wealth of Spain and Italian
ambition as a Mediterranean power. These were even more
important than the reputed and proclaimed hostility toward
their Communist rivals. The Spanish Socialists, on the other
hand, were more intent on the solution of their national problems, and, as the pressure of conservative traditions forced
them to compromise, became more particularly national in
their aims.

While the scope of this volume is restricted to the specific
problem of tracing the evolution of the Constitution of 1931
in its formulation, it is to be hoped that some understanding
of the subsequent trends in the Second Spanish Republic may
be derived from it. For this reason five chapters have been
devoted to the summarizing of the historical background of
the problems of Spain, although the remainder of the work
has been definitely limited to the actual framing of the constitution, from the establishment of the republic to its promulgation.

However incomplete the execution of this intent, the first

year of the republic appears to have been the decisive one. In that year the bloodless change of régime was effected. In that year a compromise between individual liberties and their social obligations was attempted. In that year the re-action of vested interests and the impatient violence of the radicals of the other extreme had already sharply divided public opinion. In 1931, the future of the compromise and the reforms of the liberals already appeared precarious. Never-theless, buoyant in its idealism and bright in its promise, this appears to have been the day of the liberals in Spain.

Although the responsibility for the content of this volume and any errors that may appear rests solely on the author, I wish to take this opportunity of expressing my appreciation to the many persons who have so kindly given their time and assistance in various capacities during its preparation. Dr. William E. Lingelbach, of the University of Pennsylvania, to whom this work was presented as a doctoral dissertation, was not only an inspiration as a guide into the intricacies of history, but was more than generous with his time and advice. Dr. James A. Robertson, Dr. Alfred E. Hasbrouck, Dr. Albert Shaw, and Professor W. A. Rhea rendered invaluable assist-ance in reading the manuscript and advising me both as to style and content. I am indebted to Dr. Fernando de los Ríos, Dr. Salvador de Madariaga, Professor J. B. Trend, and Señor Alberto Jiménez for suggestions received in interviews with each of them. Various members of the *Sección de Florida del Instituto de las Españas* have encouraged and assisted me in many ways, including my colleagues, Professor Alfred J. Hanna and Professor Angela Paloma Campbell, Señor An-tonio Flores, Mrs. William C. Bowers, and Señor Celestino C. Vega, Jr. I wish to express my appreciation for the valuable assistance rendered by my wife in the encouragement and criticism she gave during the preparation of this volume. Finally, I wish to thank Lord Davies of the Royal Institute of International Affairs for giving me an introduction to the Chatham House Library of that organization; Miss Maynell Cleeve, the Librarian of Chatham House; Señor Luis M. de

Yrujo, former Chargé d'Affaires of the Spanish Embassy; and
the staffs of the British Museum, the Manuscript Division of
the Library of Congress, the Library of the University of
Pennsylvania, the Philadelphia Free Library, and the Library
of Rollins College for their assistance in the collection of the
material out of which this volume has grown.

R.M.S.

Winter Park, Florida
April 27, 1938

I

THE CHURCH AND THE LAND

THE PEACEFUL transition from the rule of the Bourbons to the Second Spanish Republic belied the gravity of the problems confronting the men who, in 1931, assumed the direction of the government of Spain. These problems were deeply rooted in the national history, and the long delay in their solution was in a large measure responsible for the loss of the imperial grandeur of Spain and her decline to a second-rate power. They had perplexed the statesmen of the monarchy for more than a century and had grown more complex as successive politicians had ignored increasing demands for their solution. The internal peace and progress of the new republic depended on the success of the Provisional Government and the Constituent Cortes in satisfying the various sections of public opinion with reforms that would prove real and permanent.

Their task was rendered difficult by the strength of the vested interests which were opposed to any attack on their rights and were oblivious of their obligations. The great obstacle, however, lay in the individualism of the people whose soverignty was then proclaimed. The intensity of this characteristic led the Spaniard to follow personal criteria rather than national considerations, and to demand his rights more vigorously than he fulfilled his obligations. His political experience in the exercise of the suffrage had been meager, and even that experience had been abused by the influence of political bosses and the intrigue of managed elections.

The most serious problem was that involved in the religious question. It was not primarily or exclusively a question of religion but was concerned rather with the political and economic position and influence of the Catholic Church

1

in Spain. The people were devoutly religious. There was a mystic appeal in the universal element in the Catholic Church, and the unity of Spain had been a religious rather than a racial or geographical unity. The devotion of the *conquistadores* had been an important factor in the conquest and establishment of an empire in the New World.[1]

An alliance between the Church and the state had developed during the Middle Ages, when Spain was being reconquered from the Moors. In one of the medieval coronation oaths the king swore to protect the Catholic faith and defend the churches and their ministers. The Church sanctified the coronation with a theory of divine right, that God had conceded the king the territory to rule and govern.[2] The king, therefore, received the support of the Church in his struggle to consolidate his elective position into an hereditary one. In return, the clergy were granted privileges over which the Castilian kings always exercised a superior power. A strict dependence of the Church on the royal power developed, despite the efforts of Gregory VII to extend papal authority in Spain. The king exercised the right to choose bishops both directly and indirectly, but the latter assumed independent jurisdiction within their dioceses after they were elected. They were subject to papal authority only in religious matters.[3] Under the impetus of Gregory VII, however, the clergy developed their own ecclesiastical councils in which royalty did not intervene and in which they formulated their own policies.[4] Gregory VII also extended his authority to Spain through the persons of his legates, who presided over the general councils and intervened in ecclesiastical matters.[5]

Ferdinand and Isabella emerged triumphant from the struggle between the theory of the coördination of the civil

---

[1] Salvador de Madariaga, *España. Ensayo de historia contemporánea,* 2nd edition. Madrid, 1934. 154.

[2] Antonio Ballesteros y Beretta, *Historia de España y su influencia en la historia universal.* 8 vol. Barcelona, 1925-1934. II, 488.

[3] Rafael Altamira y Crevea, *Historia de España y de la civilización española.* 4 vol. Barcelona, 1928-1929. I, 454-455.

[4] Ballesteros, II, 506.

[5] Altamira, I, 455.

and ecclesiastical power and the supremacy of the latter. Despite their piety and religious zeal, which won them their title, Ferdinand and Isabella made a careful distinction between the spiritual and temporal relations of the Church and the state. They maintained the preponderance and freedom of action of the crown, employing the Inquisition to unify the state in matters of doctrine and limiting clerical jurisdiction when it tended to interfere with the absolute sense of the monarchy. They retained the approval of papal nominations and were conceded the right of patronage over the Church in Granada and America.[6]

The Hapsburgs accentuated the sense of the independence of the royal power because of their absorbing interest in absolute monarchy. One of the results of the religious unity attained in Castile and Aragon under the early Hapsburgs was the exaltation of the religious sentiment which had served as a basis for that unity. Likewise, the reaction of the Catholics to the Reformation was evident under Charles I and Philip II who were the champions of religious unity. The Inquisition became increasingly more rigorous and the Company of Jesus was founded. An immediate consequence of this reaction was the increased power and social influence of the clergy.[7] The Hapsburgs, however, continued to wield their power over the Church. The Royal Council held the right of inspection of the ecclesiastical courts, and royal intervention in the life of the Church was exercised through the principle that no assembly could be convened without the consent of the king and the attendance of a royal delegate.[8]

The Bourbons were also preoccupied with the affirmation of civil supremacy and the emasculation of any power considered dangerous to civil authority. They viewed the problem as a political one and followed a policy of secularization in order to make the state preponderant, extend its sphere of action, and destroy every privilege that threatened their abso-

[6] *Ibid.*, II, 488.
[7] *Ibid.*, III, 340.
[8] *Ibid.*, III, 415, 417.

lutism. Pope Clement XI had declared in favor of the Arch-duke of Austria during the War of the Spanish Succession and the zeal of the Bourbons was increased by the continued intervention of the Roman *curia* in the affairs of the Spanish Church.[9] Charles III enacted various measures to subject the Spanish clergy to the crown and improve their economic and professional conditions. In 1773 he approved a bull for the expulsion of the Jesuits. The Bourbons, nevertheless, con-tinued to pursue the ideal of religious unity through the persecution of heresy.[10]

Thus the union of Church and state, with the political subordination of the Church, had become a tradition by the beginning of the nineteenth century. All of the constitutions during that century sanctioned the establishment of the Cath-olic Church and recognized the universality of that faith in Spain by restricting or prohibiting other creeds. There was a gradual diffusion of the idea of tolerance and a decline of the fear of the Inquisition, but the kings were pious and the majority of the country and the clergy continued to be zealous and fundamentally Catholic. It was not until the promulga-tion of the Constitution of 1876 that a limited degree of toler-ation was extended to other sects. Article 11 provided that no person should be molested for his religious opinions or for the exercise of his respective creed, but public worship for all sects besides the Catholic Church was still prohibited.[11]

A principal source of the power of the Church lay in its vast wealth. At the beginning of the nineteenth century the clergy possessed an income of 1,101,753,430 *reales* and, in 1787, there were 3,148 cities, villages, and smaller communi-ties which contributed feudal dues to the clergy.[12] By the twentieth century the wealth of the Church had far exceeded that mark, although it is impossible to compute its total in-come because of the nature of its interests in various indus-trial enterprises and other profitable pursuits. In addition,

[9] *Ibid.,* IV, 211-212.
[10] *Ibid.,* IV, 216, 236, 240.
[11] *Constitución de la monarquía española promulgada en 30 de Junio de 1876.*
[12] Altamira, IV, 236-237.

the state contributed 67,773,495 *pesetas* to the support of the clergy, buildings, and other expenses of the Church in 1929.[13] At the time of the Revolution of 1931, the Jesuits are reported to have controlled a third of the national wealth, while the capital of their enterprises was over a billion *pesetas*.[14]

A policy of restricting the religious orders was adopted by the Spanish government in the eighteenth century. In 1623 there were 200,000 members of these orders in Spain. They exercised a preponderant influence as educators, confessors, and censors of all Christians. The Church was one of the first proprietors of the nation, and the rapid increase in its wealth in property and rents led the government to attempt to free some of the land held in mortmain through a policy of *desamortización*.[15] This policy was continued in the nineteenth century by the liberals, who became the principal opponents of the clergy, and was enforced or suspended as they gained or lost control of the government.[16]

The Inquisition and the Jesuits had long been special objects for the attack of the liberals. Charles III had expelled the Jesuits; Napoleon had extended this policy to the other orders, reducing the convents by two-thirds; and Joseph had suppressed them. The Constitution of 1812 abolished the Inquisition, suppressed certain religious houses, and prohibited the establishment of new ones. The effect of these measures, however, varied with the power of the liberals during the reign of Ferdinand VII and the political strife under Isabella II.[17] The Inquisition was not reëstablished but the Jesuits returned. They were again suppressed after the Revolution of 1868, but reëntered Spain during the period of reaction following the restoration of Alfonso XII and became more powerful than ever.[18]

[13] *The Statesman's Yearbook*, M. Epstein, ed. London, 1931. 1278.
[14] Sir George Young, *The New Spain*. London, 1933. 24.
[15] Altamira, III, 340-343.
[16] Pío Zabala y Lera, *Historia de España y de la civilización española*. 2 vol. Barcelona, 1930. I, 198-202; II, 146-154.
[17] Ballesteros, VII, 641-645.
[18] Zabala y Lera, II, 111.

Relations between the Church and the state were settled
by the Concordat of 1851, which was far more favorable to
the Vatican than the arrangement had previously allowed. It
recognized the right of the Church to hold legitimate titles
to property and guaranteed that the title to propery acquired
and to be acquired would be respected. It thus sanctioned
the sale of church lands and at the same time provided that
the state should grant an annual subsidy for the support of
the clergy.[19]

The effort of the state to restrict the lands held in mortmain
continued, but in 1902 the religious orders were given a legal
basis. The opportunity had been presented by the passage of
the Law of Associations, in 1887. They had only to be authorized by the Concordat of 1851 or to fulfil the formality of
civil registration, which could hardly be denied.[20] As a result,
the number of religious houses increased. Between 1787 and
1833 there was a definite agitation for their diminution. In
the first year there were 3,189 houses with 133,000 members,
while in 1833 there were only 2,743 houses with 55,279 members.[21] A hundred years later, in 1928, there were 4,267
houses. There were 12,000 men in 866 houses, of which 465
were devoted to education, 200 to the training of priests, 128
to charity, 67 to a contemplative life, and six to industry.
There were 52,000 women in 3,401 houses, of which 1,410
were devoted to education, 1,385 to charity, and 606 to a
contemplative life.[22]

Liberal hostility to the Catholic Church in Spain rose from
its established position under the protection of the political
authority, the intolerance of its effort to preserve the religious
unity of Spain, and the accumulation of its great wealth.
They claimed that the Church did not wholly recognize its
spiritual responsibilities and was primarily concerned with
the exploitation and extension of its privileges and properties.

[19] *Ibid.*, II, 110; Ballesteros, VII, 646-647.
[20] Zabala y Lera, II, 153; Young, 21.
[21] Zabala y Lera, I, 325.
[22] *Statesman's Yearbook*, 1278.

On the other hand, as a result of the attacks on their vested political and economic interests, the clergy generally followed a reactionary policy. They were largely responsible for the reaction of Ferdinand VII and supported the absolutist theories of the Carlists. Even Gregory XVI was sympathetic with this party because the liberals opposed the exercise of his spiritual authority and the temporal interests of the clergy.[23] With this antagonism, it is not surprising that throughout the disorder of the nineteenth century members of the clergy were frequently killed and convents were sacked and burned.

The entrance of the Church into the field of capitalism, at a period when the struggle between capital and labor for the improvement of working conditions was intense, widened the breach between the people and the clergy. They incurred further unpopularity by competing with merchants and man-ufacturers. One observer reported that monks made confec-tionery out of scraps that had been collected for the poor, while some of the religious orders used child labor from their schools to undersell laundries and lace manufacturers.[24] In its essence, then, in a country where the majority of the peo-ple were Catholic, the hostility to the Church was not anti-religious but anti-clerical.

There were two problems closely related to the religious question because they were controlled by the clergy. One was the question of marriage. The canonical form of matri-mony was the only one existent in Spain until 1870. Prior to the passage of this law the sacrament of the Church was a matrimonial contract in civil law. Its enactment subjected all Spaniards, whether Catholic or Protestant, to the norms of civil marriage. A royal decree in 1875, however, excused Catholics from this obligation and two forms of marriage were provided, canonical for Catholics and civil for non-Catholics. The civil code conceded all civil rights to canonical marriage.[25] The liberals held that civil matrimony was really

[23] Zabala y Lera, II, 146-147.
[24] Young, 24.
[25] Zabala y Lera, II, 106.

impossible because the people were largely Catholic. Clerical influence succeeded in obtaining the promulgation of a decree, in 1900, which declared all civil marriages void, unless they were celebrated after hearing the opinion of a priest on the religion of the couple. The liberal Count of Romanones had this decree abrogated nine years later, but not without a violent protest from the episcopate.[26]

The question of education was also closely related to the religious question because of the great influence of the Church in that field. The state had supported schools since 1902, and in 1928 contributed 112,323,690 *pesetas* to 23,690 primary schools. There were, in addition, 6,000 private schools and sixty-five secondary schools which prepared students for the universities. Nevertheless, 45.46 per cent of the people of Spain were illiterate in 1920.[27] Half of the children were therefore uneducated and half of the remainder were educated in clerical schools. There was also a strong clerical influence in the public schools. The religious orders had tried to secure control of the education of those who were destined to form the ruling class in Spain, particularly after the Restoration of 1875. They opened colleges and forced many private institutions to close. In the course of time the majority of the teachers were recruited from these monastic institutions, and the various professions of Spain were filled with men who had been educated in the shadow of the Church. The conservative Catholics had rejected all educational reforms advocated in the nineteenth century, such as the imitation of foreign models and the study of science. The latter was held to be the enemy of religion.[28] The liberals consequently considered the policy of the Church in regard to education as calamitous. They charged that the Church reserved education as far as possible to the religious and restricted it to religion for others.[29]

[26] Madariaga, 150.
[27] *Statesman's Yearbook*, 1279.
[28] Young, 28-29; J. B. Trend, *The Origins of Modern Spain*. New York and Cambridge, England, 1934. 81.
[29] Trend, 73.

Universities were so regulated that all initiative was killed. They had had an illustrious tradition in the Middle Ages, but declined as a result of the domination of the Bourbons and the Hapsburgs and the unity imposed through the influence of the Church. The rebirth of the national spirit in Spain had revived the universities as centers of culture and a source of most of the liberal thought. The struggle for academic freedom against clerical reaction was led by Madariaga and Unamuno. There was an increase in student strikes and riots and in the dismissal and deportation of professors who sinned from liberalism during the early part of the twentieth century, especially in the period of the Directory.[30]

In the latter part of the nineteenth century, the liberals recognized that the real problem of Spain was an educational one and that it consisted primarily in adapting the national psychology to the conditions of the modern world. They thought that this could best be achieved through the secondary schools, where there was a need for the reformation and improvement of teaching methods. Francisco Giner de los Ríos became the leader of the liberal university group after the death of Sanz del Río. Realizing the futility of struggling against the reactive tendencies of the Restoration, he turned his energy into the field of teaching. He was dismissed from the university because of his resistance to the efforts of the Minister of Public Instruction to restrict academic freedom. Then, in 1876, with a small group of associates, he formed the *Institución Libre de Enseñanza,* or Free Educational Institute, as a protest against state and clerical control of education.[31] It was a private association, independent of any religious or political party. It received no state subsidies and was financed by shares which paid a low rate of interest. The Institution was organized as a day school, and in 1884 had two hundred boys enrolled. The methods of teaching were progressive. It gained European fame, stimulated other in-

[30] *Ibid.,* 74; Young, 29-31.
[31] Madariaga, 88-91; Trend, 71-73.

stitutions, and helped to secure greater freedom for Spanish teaching.[32]

As a result of the decline of the universities, many Spanish families sent their children abroad to study in the universities of France, England, Germany, Switzerland, and Belgium. Many deserving students, however, did not have the funds to take them abroad, and the *Junta para Ampliación de Estudios* was formed in 1907. This Board for the Expansion of Studies aimed primarily to enable students to undertake foreign study with adequate means. It received an annual subsidy from the government which also delegated certain powers of organization and administration to this autonomous group. The eminent Dr. Ramón y Cajal was chosen as its president in order to insure its independence of political interference. José Castillejo, however, was its great administrator and defender. He served as secretary. The board sent carefully chosen students abroad for the next quarter of a century, organized laboratories and centers of research, and in many ways tried to stimulate a more active interest in the improvement of teaching methods and learning.[33]

The agrarian question was another important problem that had to be solved if the Second Spanish Republic was to endure. Spain was a poor country, with an income of only 250 billion *pesetas* in 1930.[34] Her natural resources were undeveloped and her forest lands had been recklessly abused. Industrial development had been retarded by internal instability, and agriculture remained more important than the fertility of the soil and the poverty of the farmers justified. Yet its annual value was only 9,615,000,000 *pesetas*.[35] Spain was backward in agriculture. The peasants had an aversion to the introduction of machinery and modern methods. The geography of the country was varied and there were climatic differences and variations in the fertility of the soil in the several sections.

---

[32] Trend, 67-70.
[33] *Ibid.*, 85; Madariaga, 95-96.
[34] Carlos Araujo García and Kenneth G. Grubb, *Religion in the Republic of Spain*. London and Toronto, 1933. 5.
[35] *Ibid.*

A principal cause of the poverty of Spanish agriculture, however, arose from the survival of medieval conditions. There were two classes of landed properties. The small properties and those near the towns were generally cultivated by their owners. In Catalonia, for example, ninety-seven per cent of the owners cultivated their own lands. Many such properties, however, were too small to yield an adequate living to their owners as a result of the excessive subdivision. This condition existed primarily in Alava, Coruña, Santander, Segovia, and parts of Huesca and Madrid. The solution lay in the adoption of measures which would result in the concentration of the scattered parcels.[36]

Excessive subdivision of the land was produced by the development of the institution known as the *foro*. This was a lease contracted for three generations, under which a rent, usually low and little more than the recognition of a right, was paid by the tenants or *foreros*. When the *foro* expired, the land and the improvements made by the tenant reverted to the landlord in full ownership. Consequently there were frequent conflicts and many peasants emigrated. In 1763 a decree of Charles III ruled that no *foros* should be reclaimed by the landlords until the whole form of the tenure was settled. The problem was never solved and the tenants remained on their properties to enjoy a tacit property right. It was exercised to sublet the holdings and produced a sharp rise in the price of land and a ridiculous subdivision. Some of the holdings in the Cantabrian provinces included only 130 to 140 square yards and the owners cultivated forty or fifty scattered parcels. In Santa María de Ordáx, farmers worked from eighty to 120 plots with an aggregate area of sixteen to seventeen acres, scattered over a radius of three miles. There were many parcels of thirty-five, twenty-five, or even twelve square yards in Vigo. Two continuous acres in the tenure of a single farmer constituted a large holding.[37]

The larger properties were located primarily in lower

[36] International Labour Office, *Studies and Reports,* Series K, No. 2, "Agrarian Conditions in Spain," November 10, 1920. 1-3.
[37] *Ibid.*, 3-4.

Andalusia and Extremadura, the region of the *latifundia,* but there were also large holdings in Asturias and Galicia. They were generally cultivated by tenants. The evils in this system resulted from the neglect of the absentee landlords, the unsatisfactory nature of the contracts, and the failure to improve much land which might have been rendered productive. In 1914, in a total area of 121,632,000 acres, 164 persons owned an average of 6,875 or a total of 1,003,294 acres.[38]

Cáceres was typical of the region of extensive pasture lands held by absentee landlords who were interested only in the rents which their property produced. In that province, 230,116 of the total area of 4,906,880 acres was held by twelve owners, or an average of 19,176 acres for each. It was a cattle country par excellence, with a privileged climate and a fertile soil. An interest in irrigation would have multiplied the yield from the breeding of cattle a hundred-fold. The failure of these landlords to interest themselves in progressive improvements represented a survival of medieval conditions.[39]

During the crusade against the Moors stock raising had been much more actively pursued than agriculture. It had become important because of the ease with which the herds could be removed from the hazards of war and because it was a tradition in the country. The kings of Castile protected the stock raisers, at times to the detriment of agriculture, while they took advantage of this royal favor to appropriate common lands and even to enter and despoil cultivated fields. Conflicts between farmers and herders frequently arose, and both groups organized associations in defense of their respective interests.[40]

In the thirteenth century Alfonso X recognized the associations of stock raisers and extended them special jurisdiction in their own affairs and in their quarrels with the farm-

[38] *Ibid.,* 2.

[39] *Ibid.,* 2-3.

[40] Altamira, I, 514-515; Charles E. Chapman, *A History of Spain.* New York, 1927. 104-105.

ers. Under Alfonso XI, in 1347, these local *concejos de mesta* formed a single *mesta* which proved a formidable corporation.[41] Ferdinand and Isabella favored the *mesta* with various measures in order to prevent the decline of stock raising and to supply the textile factories with abundant raw material. The farmers complained, but the Catholic Sovereigns confirmed the privileges granted by Alfonso XI. At the same time, they levied a special tax on the corporation and subjected it to the crown by appointing a royal agent as a member of the association.[42]

The privileges of the *mesta* hindered the development of agriculture. Fields lay uncultivated and the inhabitants were generally indifferent to this important occupation. Many regions like Castile failed to produce the necessities for their own use, much less for export.[43] Such conditions continued throughout the rule of the Hapsburgs. Abundant protection was extended to the *mesta* to prevent pasture lands from being reduced to cultivation, but agriculture was not legally protected.[44] Charles III, however, checked the power of the *mesta* by encouraging the farmers to fence lands for their own use. In 1795, the separate jurisdiction of the corporation of the *mesta* was abolished, but the legislation was not effectively enforced and agriculture was not greatly improved.[45]

There was a great deal of uncultivated land on which settlement could have been effected and the land improved. The origin of the concentration of these great *latifundia* in the hands of a few owners was also medieval. The noble families which had acquired possession of them had conquered them from the Moslems. The institution of the *mayorazgo* (entail) prohibited the division of the lands and their alienation. In this manner lands were not only accumulated in the hands of the family heir but were withdrawn from circulation. The policy was begun in the time

[41] Altamira, II, 210.
[42] *Ibid.*, II, 492, 496-497.
[43] *Ibid.*
[44] *Ibid.*, III, 447-449.
[45] *Ibid.*, IV, 262, 271.

of Alfonso X. When the political power of the nobles declined, their landed possessions prevented them from losing their economic and social power and feudalism was perpetuated. They not only failed to develop their lands to their full productive capacity, but wasted the produce in luxury. *Latifundia* became the rule in Andalusia, and the day laborers who cultivated a portion of the estates were employed only at certain seasons and lived in great misery the rest of the year.[46]

At the beginning of the nineteenth century, the nobility possessed about 45 million acres and the middle class some 27,300,000 acres. The majority of these lands were held under the *mayorazgo,* however, and accumulated in the possession of their owners. They were inalienable and impeded the creation of a class of small proprietors.[47] The lands in the southern part of Spain were subjected to mercenary exploitation, and the majority of the people were wage earners.[48] The wars of the nineteenth century caused a decrease in the population of Spain and the farmer became a soldier. Agricultural life was interrupted.[49] Toward the end of the century, however, there was some progress in agriculture. Modern implements were introduced, soil conditions were studied, fertilizers were used, and granges were organized. At the close of the century an agricultural machine factory was established, and a decade later there were twenty such factories.[50]

Feudalism had never been important in Spain, but there were *señorios* or noble estates in which property rights were fused with sovereignty. In fact, of the 25,230 territories in Spain, 13,309 were in the possession of private lords at the opening of the nineteenth century. Some 3,013 of the 4,716 small towns were also subject to some noble.[51] The decree of August 6, 1811, incorporated all jurisdictional estates of every

[46] I.L.O., 3; Altamira, II, 7-8; III, 504; IV, 268-269; Chapman, 522.
[47] Altamira, IV, 268; Ballesteros, VI, 132.
[48] Ballesteros, VI, 132, 134-135.
[49] *Ibid.,* VII, 624.
[50] Zabala y Lera, II, 164.
[51] *Ibid.,* I, 168-169.

class in the nation and abolished vassalage. In 1820 the *cortes*
abolished all *mayorazgos*. These decrees were annulled during the period of reaction but were finally restored by 1841.[52]
Nevertheless, conditions had not been improved by 1920.
In Málaga, 39,266 of the 1,799,680, acres belonged to six landlords. In Cádiz, 147,710 of the 3,324,920 acres belonged to
thirty-one and in Jaen, 117,224 acres to twenty proprietors.[53]
Despite the efforts at reform, property accumulated in the
hands of negligent proprietors and enormous tracts continued
to be unimproved.

Another feature of the agrarian question was the unsatisfactory nature of the contracts for tenants. A form of perpetual tenancy in Catalonia, the *rabassa morta*, was provided
in an agreement for a term of two hundred years. Likewise,
in Valencia, the quitrent tenants acquired permanent and
hereditary tenure. Agreements such as these, however, tended
to lose importance in other sections of Spain. Land was generally let for money or for a share of the produce. The common lease was usually for a very short term and was ruinous
to the tenant. The tenure was uncertain, the rent was high,
and no compensation for improvements was provided at the
expiration of the lease. Annual leases of this type were customary in Aragón. The perpetual or hereditary lease in
Asturias had been superseded by short-term leases for four
to six years. The terms of the leases tended to diminish and
the rents to rise on the large properties of the south. The
evils were further aggravated by the agents, who profited at
the expense of the tenants. These middlemen were often
money lenders to whom an exorbitant proportion of the
crop was pledged as interest on loans.[54]

Ɫ The common lease in Catalonia was that for a fixed term
with the possibility of its being extended. Payment was rendered in kind with a fixed share of the produce of the holding. Some forms of lease harmonized the interests of the land-

[52] *Ibid.*, II, 109.
[53] I.L.O., 3.
[54] *Ibid.*, 4-5.

lord and the tenant. The ancient and hereditary *caserías* of the Basque provinces, regulated by custom, and the *masoverías* of Catalonia were the most important of these. The *casería* was held by families for several centuries and the small rent consisted of a pair of fowls, a dozen eggs, and one-half of the produce sold during the year, after the needs of the tenant's household had been provided. If the tenant had cows he supplied the proprietor with milk at the current market price. If he had stock, the landlord supplied the animals and received half of the price of the young animals. These agreements were not written, but the terms were faithfully fulfilled. The Catalan *masover* lived in part of the house, which the landlord (*mos*) owned. He hired the necessary day labor and paid the cost of cultivation. The landlord paid the direct taxes and the tenant the indirect taxes. The landlord then received a half, a third, or a fourth of the produce.[55]

There were few agricultural day laborers in the northern provinces. The farmer and his family cultivated the land with the aid of neighbors. There was a surplus of labor in these regions, and the unemployed migrated to the central and southern provinces. The large holdings there were managed by agents or farmers who employed gangs of day laborers. The latter were lodged, fed, and paid in money, but the wages were too low to provide savings and the lodgings were deplorable, consisting of sheds, outhouses, and cellars. The diet was insufficient and often unhealthy. As a result there was much unemployment in Castile, Andalusia, and Extremadura, where the landlords exploited the land and labor for profit and many were deprived of their lands at the expiration of the leases.[56]

The liberals regarded the existence of the numerous peasant class, which the government had been unable to save from misery, as one of the most serious evils of Spanish life. Many measures had been proposed in an effort to improve the situation, but they had rarely been incorporated into the

[55] *Ibid.*, 5.
[56] *Ibid.*, 6.

law of the land. The *Junta Central de Colonización* was established in 1907 and reorganized in 1917. It was a semi-autonomous body which administered the funds appropriated by the state for the acquisition of lands to be distributed among the poorer tenants. An attempt had also been made to limit the excessive division of the lands by the reform of the inheritance laws. The general tendency of these efforts, however, had been toward the study of the problem rather than toward the execution of any policy through legislation. The political influence of the landlords and the instability of Spanish politics were effective bars to active reform. The power of the landlord over the ballot of the tenant, even in the zone of the smaller properties, was well demonstrated in the elections for the Constituent Cortes of 1931.[57]

A Land Settlement Decree of 1918 aimed to restrict rural emigration, populate the countryside, and make uncultivated lands productive. It provided for the settlement of inalienable lands of the state which were unused, of the common lands of the villages, and those which were officially classed as lands of public utility. Individual owners might cede their lands to the state for land settlement, and the new agricultural colonies were to be provided with the necessary public services and coöperative institutions of production, consumption, and mutual aid. The commission encouraged experimental farming and financed the coöperative associations. In 1920 the powers of the commission were extended and it was attached to the Ministry of Labor.[58]

Some consideration had also been given to the problem of rural credit. The establishment of the *Junta del Crédito Agrícola* was a step toward the provision of credit for the small farmer. The Catholic Church also created rural associations to extend credit which proved rather successful, particularly after their federation, in 1912, as the *Confederación Nacional Católicoagraria.*[59]

The official inquiries into the agrarian problem recom-

[57] Madariaga, 127; *ABC*, July 24, 1931.
[58] I.L.O., 6-8.
[59] Madariaga, 129.

mended that the government eliminate the middlemen, establish rural banks, form legally recognized trade unions,
and appoint joint commissions to settle disputes, redistribute
the large properties, and expropriate uncultivated lands. The
situation, however, was not improved. The discontented peasants turned to trade unionism and great numbers of the day
laborers became members of socialist or syndicalist unions.
An international congress of the organized workers of Andalusia and Extremadura, shortly before the advent of Primo
de Rivera, included thirty delegates from 147 sections, representing 62,177 organized workers.[60]

[60] I.L.O., 9-10.

II

THE CATALANS AND THE ARMY

SPAIN had never become a united nation. It had been colonized by the Phoenicians, Greeks, and Carthaginians; erected into a prosperous and important province of the Roman Empire; invaded by the Suevi, Vandals, and Alans; and had become the center of the Visigothic kingdom. Then, for eight centuries, it was dominated by the Moslem Arabs and their Berber allies from North Africa. During that period the reconquest absorbed the energy of the Spaniards and resulted in the erection of petty states, separated by geographical, linguistic, and traditional barriers. It was the work of feudal lords who struggled among themselves when they were not fighting the Moors. Asturias and León were united under the hegemony of Castile through feudal warfare and intermarriage, while Aragón gained control of Valencia and Catalonia in a similar manner. Thus the union of Castile and Aragón through the marriage of Ferdinand and Isabella produced a dyarchy, and the conquest of Granada, in 1492, gave Spain her position as a territorial unit in the sixteenth century.

A fundamental regional diversity, however, persisted, despite the centralizing efforts of the Catholic Sovereigns. The prospect of the evolution of a real unity was wrecked by the dynastic marriages arranged by Ferdinand. Spain lost her national identity and became a part of the Hapsburg empire of Charles V. True, this empire was divided in 1556, but Philip II ruled a colonial empire in the New World and a dynastic one in Europe. For a short time he brought Portugal into that empire and ruled the whole of the Iberian Peninsula, but Spain remained a dynastic monarchy rather than a unified state similar to those evolving in England and

France. The dynastic continuity was broken when the Bourbons upset the balance of power and Philip V, the grandson of Louis XIV, replaced the Hapsburgs on the Spanish throne. Shortly after the close of the War of the Spanish Succession, Spain became a satellite of France under the Family Compact.

The first real opportunity for the creation of a unified Spanish state occurred in the first quarter of the nineteenth century. The penetration of French revolutionary ideals in Spain, followed by the betrayal of Napoleon, aroused the national feeling of the people and a spontaneous resistance to French domination more intense than that of the crusade against the Moors. The basis for a democratic government as a limited monarchy was laid in the Constitution of 1812, but the victory over Napoleon also brought back the Bourbon Ferdinand VII, and the misplaced loyalty of the liberals was rewarded with a fierce reaction and the abrogation of the constitution.

During the following half century there was a dual struggle. On the one hand, a dynastic civil war raged between the Carlists and those who rallied to the support of Isabella II. On the other, the adherents of Isabella II were divided into two political factions, the Progressives and the Moderates, whose interest in democratic government produced a succession of constitutions as they alternately gained power, but provided no solution for the fundamental problems of a modern state.

This political fiasco was broken in 1868, by a brief interlude. Isabella II was overthrown and Amadeo of Savoy tried vainly to rally the liberals to the support of the Constitution of 1869. When he abdicated the Republicans had their first opportunity and failed miserably. Four provisional presidents in less than a year were unable to maintain order, and the effort to formulate a constitution foundered on the rock of federalism. The military leaders intervened, the Bourbons were restored, and Alfonso XII and his son ruled Spain until the Revolution of 1931.

The fiction of monarchical unity and the theory of absolutism advanced by the Bourbons did not satisfy the aspirations of various regions for an autonomous existence. The Basques and Galicians demanded local autonomy on the basis of linguistic differences from the other parts of Spain. The strongest and most typical center of regionalism, however, was in Catalonia. The desire of the Catalans for home rule was based on tradition, culture, and language. They demanded local autonomy within the state, but this involved the surrender of regional sovereignty by the national government to an autonomous government in Catalonia.[1]

The Catalans had a local history of which they were proud. In the eighth century, the Moslems had overrun all of the Catalan territory. Toward the end of the century, Charlemagne sent his son, Louis the Pious, who reconquered the territory and created the Spanish March. It included the region between the Pyrenees and the Llobregat, and was ruled by governors of Frankish or Visigothic origin. Upon the decay of the Carolingian Empire the counts of Barcelona declared their independence and obliged the other Catalan counts to recognize their sovereignty. The name Catalonia was derived from *castellanus* and was applied to this region because of the numerous castles. By the end of the ninth century the region was free from Moslem domination and independent of any foreign power. Even the clergy abandoned the custom of asking the Frankish kings for protection.[2]

Count Ramón Berenguer IV extended the bounds of Barcelona and increased its political importance. In 1150 he married Petronila, daughter of the King of Aragón, and fourteen years later their son, Alfonso, united Catalonia and Aragón. The Catalan-Aragonese monarchy became a Mediterranean sea power and occupied territories in Italy and the East. The commercial prosperity of Barcelona rivaled that of Venice, Genoa, and Marseilles, and it became a center of medieval industry.[3]

[1] Ballesteros, VIII, 581.
[2] Altamira, I, 253-254; L. Martín Echeverría, *Geografía de España*, Barcelona, 1932. III, 33-34.
[3] Altamira, I, 404, 626-628; Echeverría, III, 33-34.

The union of Castile and Aragón did not smother the personality of Catalonia. The Catalans rebelled against Don Juan, the father of Ferdinand, in the middle of the fourteenth century, and were the leaders of successive protests against the centralizing policies of the Catholic Sovereigns and the Hapsburgs.[4] In the seventeenth century the Catalans rebelled against Philip IV and were assisted by the French. Their allies, however, deserted them and the Treaty of the Pyrenees deprived them of Roussillon.[5] As a result of this treachery and their disapproval of the policy represented by the Bourbons, the Catalans supported the Archduke of Austria against the grandson of Louis XIV during the War of the Spanish Succession.[6]

This action may, in part, explain the repressive attitude which became a characteristic policy of the Bourbons toward Catalonia. Philip V dissolved the ancient Council of the Hundred as soon as Barcelona had capitulated, replacing it and other regional organs with agencies representing the royal authority.[7] The "New Plan" of 1716 extended the laws and customs of Castile to Catalonia and prohibited the use of the Catalan language in the administration of justice.[8] This policy was followed throughout the nineteenth century despite the valiant defense of their territory by the volunteer corps which prevented the French from subduing Catalonia during the Peninsular War.[9] Soon after the restoration of Ferdinand VII further steps in the interests of uniformity and centralization were taken. The special courts and regional penal and commercial codes were abolished, while the use of the Catalan language was again suppressed.[10] In 1833 the old regional organization was abandoned and Spain was redivided on an artificial basis for administrative purposes.[11]

[4] Altamira, I, 638-640; Echeverría, III, 34.
[5] Altamira, III, 143-151; Echeverría, III, 34.
[6] Altamira, IV, 14-22.
[7] Ibid., 155.
[8] Ballesteros, VII, 91.
[9] Altamira, IV, 156 ff.
[10] Zabala y Lera, II, 130; Young, 173.
[11] Zabala y Lera, II, 119.

Nevertheless the Catalan spirit survived the tendencies toward centralization and absolutism and was revived in the latter part of the nineteenth century. The Catalans rebelled against Espartero, Isabella II, and Amadeo and forced federalism on the First Republic. The renaissance began with the revival of the use of the Catalan language as a medium of literary expression and was followed by political agitation for the restoration of the ancient Catalan rights. The Catalan, Pí y Margall, was president of the First Republic.[12]

After the restoration of Alfonso XII the Catalan movement divided into two groups. The radical elements formed the *Centre Catalá* in 1882, while the conservative elements formed the *Lliga de Catalunya* five years later. The memorials presented to the throne during this decade were not heeded, and in the next ten years regionalism developed into the separatism of Prat de la Riba. The program of this group, the *Unió Catalanista*, was formulated by the Congress of Manresa, in 1892.[13] The "Bases of Manresa" proposed that Spain should be organized on a federal basis, which would allow Catalonia complete freedom in internal administration, including coinage and the means of her coöperation in national defense. Such powers as foreign relations, the customs, and the relations between the regions were to be reserved to the federal government. The leaders of this and the succeeding assemblies of Reus, Balaguer, and Olot were academic and theoretical rather than practical politicians.[14]

A more realistic group was formed in 1900, under the leadership of Francisco Cambó. He was a disciple of Prat de la Riba and organized the *Lliga Regionalista,* following the fusion of the *Centre Catalá* and the *Unió Catalanista* after an electoral victory in which the two groups had coöperated. At first Cambó refused to participate in national elections but he soon abandoned this policy. At Gerona, in 1906, all factions were merged in the *Solidaritat Catalana,* with the aim

[12] Young, 173-174.
[13] *Ibid.,* 174.
[14] Madariaga, 207; Young, 174.

of obtaining representation in the *cortes*. This group over-
threw the power of Alejandro Lerroux in Barcelona in the
following year and within a few years held forty-one of the
forty-four Catalan seats in the *cortes*. It revived the "Bases of
Manresa" as a political program.[15]

A period of increasing regional agitation, complicated by
anarchist outrages and disorder in Barcelona, ensued. Then,
in December 1913, a royal decree conceded a measure of
regional autonomy through the association of provincial
councils. The first *Asamblea de la Mancomunitat* in Barcelona was celebrated less than two months later. The four
Catalan provinces thus had a representative assembly, elected
for two years by males over twenty-five years of age and of
two years' residence. This body elected an executive committee of which Prat de la Riba was president and which was
endowed with powers over health, factory legislation, local
education and finance, roads, forests, and mines. These organs functioned until they were abolished by Primo de
Rivera, but the autonomy was too restricted to satisfy the
Catalans.[16]

During the World War there was an insistent demand in
Catalonia for the further extension of the regional powers
which reached the extreme of bidding for French or German
assistance.[17] The problem became even more involved in
politics when the Republicans, in 1918, asked for an integral
autonomy for the regions. They urged that free and autonomous regional states were compatible with the existence of a
central power and with the unity of Spain. The fact that all
of the Republicans, as well as the Federalists, supported this
maneuver does not indicate that they were entirely sincere.
It was probably a political move to gain the support of the
Catalan deputies in national politics. Three days later, the
Catalan municipalities voted for an integral autonomy for

[15] Madariaga, 211 ff.; Young, 174-175; Ballesteros, VIII, 507-516; Zabala y
Lera, II, 349.
[16] Zabala y Lera, II, 375; Young, 175.
[17] Madariaga, 211.

Catalonia. Cambó argued in the *cortes* that the Catalan problem was one of sovereignty and that its extension could be discussed but not its intensity. The request of the Catalan cities that they be represented by a regional government with full sovereignty for purely local matters was presented to the government. They desired a bicameral parliament and a responsible executive power.[18]

The Catalan movement had meanwhile aroused resentment in other sections of Spain and had been partly confused with the activity of the Anarchists in Barcelona. Various provincial deputations and mercantile and industrial groups protested the Catalan petition. When the question was raised in the *cortes,* Antonio Maura, former Conservative leader and prime minister, praised the advantages of unity and was warmly applauded. The regional deputies and some Republicans thereupon resolved to withdraw, and Cambó declared in Barcelona that regardless of the cost or under either a republic or a monarchy, Catalonia had chosen her course. This determined attitude led to concessions, and the Catalans began to formulate a statute. A special parliamentary commission was appointed to study the problem.[19] The military opposed the grant of Catalan autonomy, there were constant clashes between Castilians and Catalans, and the Anarchists began to take advantage of the disorder and unrest in Barcelona. The Catalans approved a statute and submitted it to the government, but it decided that the solution should be based on a policy of decentralization rather than the extension of sovereignty.[20]

Primo de Rivera initiated the *coup d'état* which made him Dictator of Spain from Barcelona. He had been Captain-General of Catalonia and relied upon the support of the garrison and leading Catalans. They expected him to reciprocate by assisting them in realizing their aspirations but were soon undeceived. They became the first victims of the Direc-

[18] Ballesteros, VIII, 584-585.
[19] *Ibid.*
[20] *Ibid.*, VIII, 585-586; Zabala y Lera, II, 410.

tory. Primo de Rivera suppressed the rights which they had regained with such difficulty. Their centers were closed. The provincial and municipal councils were suspended and replaced by a more centralized local authority. The *Mancomuintat* was packed with the nominees of Primo de Rivera and finally suppressed. The display of the Catalan flag or the use of the Catalan language was prohibited.[21]

The reaction to this policy was immediate and definite. The Catalan movement was driven into separatism. The *Acció Catalana* took over the leadership from the *Lliga Regionalista* and then surrendered that control to the separatist party of Francisco Maciá, which aimed at the establishment of a Catalan state through a policy of armed insurrection. The Catalans refused to coöperate with the dictator in his Consultative Assembly and with the succeeding Berenguer government, even when the latter repealed the repressive measures. One Catalan, Ventosa, ventured to participate in the Aznar cabinet and Cambó joined with the Conservatives in trying to rally a party to save the monarchy. This split the solidarity of the Catalans,[22] but they were resolved. The Pact of San Sebastian had resulted in the alliance of the Republicans, Socialists, and Catalans in August 1930. The Catalan republicans agreed to collaborate in the overthrow of the monarchy in return for the recognition of their right to establish an autonomous government. Maciá's Catalan Left party defeated the *Lliga* in the municipal elections which effected the overthrow of the monarchy, and the Catalan Republic was proclaimed.[23]

A strong enthusiasm for military exploits had prevailed in Spain since the beginning of the Crusade against the Moors. The *Cid Campeador* may well be regarded as the personification of the military hero whose feats of arms delighted his followers, whether he was fighting Christians or Moors. Under the Catholic Sovereigns and the early Hapsburgs, the

[21] Ballesteros, VIII, 605-606; Young, 176.
[22] Ballesteros, VIII, 609, 614-615.
[23] *Ibid.*, VIII, 637, 647; Young, 177.

military spirit found expression in the daring exploits of the *conquistadores*. Both the Hapsburgs and the Bourbons gave it an outlet on the battlefields of Europe. When Napoleon placed Joseph Bonaparte on the throne of Spain he awakened a nation to arms in defense of their country and their hereditary sovereign, Ferdinand VII. In all of these wars, however intrepid in battle against the savage or national enemy, whether mercenary or guerrilla, the Spanish soldier was always loyal to his king.

With the restoration of Ferdinand VII and the reaction against the liberal movement which had found expression in the Cortes of Cádiz, the soldier began to intervene in the civil life of the nation. The liberals, who had neither the patience to curb their desire to liberalize Spain before they died, nor the necessary support of the masses to effect that desire, called on the liberal military leaders to set up a régime of reason. The disastrous habit of military intervention in civil affairs developed and in its very use of force defeated the aims of the liberals who initiated it.

The military leaders wished to express their own wills and as strong individualists contributed to the development of the excessive influence of personal ambition. They were generally reactionary in temperament and, desiring to establish order in a purely mechanical way, they suspended individual liberties in an effort to prevent reprisals and establish their own authority. They had little regard for such civil rights as the freedom of the press and speech, which the liberals sought to establish. They were usually well disposed toward education and favored a moderate policy of religious liberty, but their governments often adopted policies of toleration or stimulation of clerical reaction.[24]

Generals who imposed their wills on the government relied on the armed forces for support. They were generally concerned with professional grievances or ambitions, although they could also "be mobilized into direct action for an idealist cause." The twenty thousand officers were more

[24] Madariaga, 75-77.

conservative than the soldiers, but in the nineteenth century they were recruited from the liberal middle class and many of them were revolutionary in sentiment. The armed forces, moreover, formed the only effective representation for the progressive elements in Spain and their desire for reform. Without their support the constitutionalists and the reformers would have quickly been eliminated by the forces of reaction.[25]

The first intervention of the army in the political affairs of Spain occurred in 1820. Upon his restoration in 1814, Ferdinand VII had abrogated the liberal Constitution of 1812 and inaugurated a severe policy of reaction. The liberals used the secret Masonic societies to conspire for the restoration of the constitutional régime. Several military revolts were suppressed before the liberals found, in 1819, a more opportune occasion. The Masonic lodge in Cádiz contained many active partisans of the Constitution of 1812. They took advantage of the fact that an army, destined for the suppression of the revolt in the American colonies, was stationed in lower Andalusia. General Enrique O'Donnell failed to co-operate in the first effort to inspire a liberal revolt in the army. The second effort of Colonel Antonio Quiroga and Major Rafael Riego was nearly crushed when the cities of La Coruña, Zaragoza, Barcelona, Pamplona, and Cádiz proclaimed the Constitution of 1812 and it was restored for three years.[26]

Spain was torn by civil strife after the death of Ferdinand VII. During this period nearly fifty years before the Carlists were finally defeated, the intervention of the general as a civil dictator was confirmed. It was a simple solution for the maintenance of order but it was a dangerous precedent. The generals usually followed their own personal interests as politicians and used the political idealism of the army to achieve political ambitions. The followers of Don Carlos refused to recognize the right of Isabella II to the throne and the liberals rallied to the support of the Regency of María

Cristina. As has already been indicated, they were divided into two factions and in such circumstances ambitious military politicians found ample opportunity for their manifestoes and *coups d'état*.

The next activity of the army in behalf of liberalism occurred in the Mutiny of La Granja, in 1836. The soldiers forced the Queen Regent to restore again the Constitution of 1812, until a *cortes* could formulate a document that would express the will of the nation.[27] In 1840 Baldomero Espartero forced María Cristina to renounce the regency, and assumed her powers a year later. Within three years, however, Espartero was overthrown by a coalition of Moderates and Progressives, and Isabella II was declared to have reached her majority.[28] Her reign was dominated by two military politicians who relied upon the army to suppress opposition and support their domination of Spanish affairs, namely, Ramón Narváez and Leopoldo O'Donnell. The period was characterized by factional politics, broken now and again by the intervention of the armed forces in behalf of one general or the other.

The reign of Isabella II was brought to a timely end by the Revolution of 1868, in which the army again participated. It was led by General Juan Prim, assisted by a group of officers who had been exiled, and the liberals gained control of the government. General Prim finally found a suitable sovereign in Amadeo of Savoy, but Prim was assassinated while the new king was on his way to Spain and Amadeo lost his most valuable ally. He tried loyally to govern Spain for two years, but, unable to win the support of the various political factions, he abdicated in 1873. The Republicans seized this opportunity to establish the First Spanish Republic. They were unable, however, to unite upon a positive program and their *cortes* was dissolved by an armed force sent by General Pavía.[29]

[27] Zabala y Lera, I, 344-347; Ballesteros, VII, 509-514.
[28] Zabala y Lera, I, 384-395, 414-416; Ballesteros, VII, 549-557, VIII, 1-6.
[29] Zabala y Lera, II, 1-32 *passim*.

The restoration of Alfonso XII, the son of Isabella II, inaugurated an era of comparative internal peace, broken only by the successful conclusion of the campaign against the Carlists and the defeat in the Spanish-American War. The intervention of the generals became less important and the armed forces were organized on a more professional basis. They returned to their traditional rôle of supporting the crown and the Church under Alfonso XII, the Regency of María Cristina, and Alfonso XIII. The *cortes*, with two parties, the Conservatives and the Liberals, assumed the rôle of governing Spain under the Constitution of 1876, in a parliamentary manner. The liberal element, especially, attempted to subject the armed forces to the will of the *cortes*. Sagasta was important for the partially successful reforms which made the rôle of the general as a politician less attractive by requiring his resignation of his commission and pay when he entered politics. Meanwhile, public opinion began to regard the intervention of the army in politics as an unconstitutional menace to the political evolution of the state. Nevertheless the excessive number of officers led to their assumption of an undue influence in administrative affairs. They used their power for the profit and the prestige of their own profession. In attempting to establish rigid standards, they became less progressive. The regimental officers were organized into *Juntas de Defensa,* representing the politics of the middle class. The non-commissioned officers and conscripts served for short terms and could be aroused to revolt only by severe suffering or socialist propaganda.[30]

The collapse of the Spanish empire, following the maladministration of the military governors and the resultant Spanish-American War, flooded Spain with unemployed soldiers. The officers hoped for employment in return for their political activity in resenting any criticism of the armed forces. In addition, they were influential enough to secure the passage of a Law of Jurisdictions which placed all cases of attack on military institutions, by word or writing, in the

[30] Young, 56-57.

hands of military tribunals. Alfonso XIII maintained close relations with the *Juntas de Defensa* and the commanding officers. He controlled army appointments in an effort to subordinate the army completely to the royal will.[31]

These *Juntas* had been organized during the World War with the aim of improving conditions of service and promotion. The government was forced to recognize these committees in 1917. In the same year the army was employed as an ordinary police force to suppress the general strike. Their power to mutiny, however, had not been crushed, as was indicated in the mutiny of the rank and file at Zaragoza in 1917. Nevertheless, the armed forces became a force of conservatism and a power behind the throne under the domination of the *Juntas de Defensa*.[32]

The incompetence of the army was soon revealed in Morocco. It was overweighed with officials, with 219 generals and 19,906 officers for 207,000 soldiers. The Moroccan War was not popular in Spain, and the defeats which the army suffered did not increase its prestige in the popular estimation, despite the valor of individual soldiers.[33] The most serious reverse was the disastrous defeat of General Silvestre at Annual by Abd-el-Krim, with the loss of some fourteen thousand men.[34] The public immediately demanded an investigation of the causes. Some blamed the Allendesalazar government; some attributed the disaster to the lack of accord between Silvestre and General Berenguer, High Commissioner of Morocco; some concentrated their attack on the *Juntas de Defensa*, because of the suppression of the merit system in promotion; while others declared that the whole nation was responsible because of the failure to support the war.[35]

The most difficult question, however, was that of the responsibility of Alfonso XIII. It was rumored that he had inspired Silvestre to disobey the commands of Berenguer.

[31] *Ibid.*, 58; Madariaga, 161, 163-164.
[32] Young, 58-59; Ballesteros, VIII, 565-580.
[33] Madariaga, 161; Ballesteros, VIII, 711.
[34] Ballesteros, VIII, 594-595; Zabala y Lera, II, 423.
[35] Zabala, II, 425.

While Alfonso had passed the summer pleasantly at Deauville, his soldiers had borne the hardships of the Moroccan outposts. He evidently did not share the anxiety of the country and his popularity began to wane.[36] The popular demand for an investigation of the responsibilities caused the resignation of Berenguer, and he was replaced by Burguete. General Miguel Primo de Rivera, who had advised the abandonment of the Moroccan project, was relieved of his position as Captain-General of Madrid.[37] The question also produced a heated debate in the *cortes*. Finally a parliamentary commission was named to investigate the matter and assess responsibility for the disaster.[38]

Meanwhile many had become convinced that the only means of rescuing the country from the reigning anarchy and confusion was the establishment of a government of force. The African forces and the *Juntas de Defensa* were antagonistic, and Alfonso condemned the policy of the latter at a military banquet. In the midst of this clamor, General Primo de Rivera established the military directory. He was undoubtedly provoked by the ineffectual procedure of parliamentary government as well as by the desire to vindicate the honor of the army. The participation of the sovereign in the *coup d'état* was a disputed point, but he accepted it as a *fait accompli*.[39] The fact remained, however, that the army had again asserted itself and intervened in civil matters. It was the habit acquired in the course of the past century, a habit which the years of tranquillity and the efforts at reform had not been sufficient to eradicate.

[36] Ballesteros, VIII, 597.
[37] Zabala y Lera, II, 426, 430.
[38] *Ibid.*, II, 438.
[39] Ballesteros, VIII, 606.

III

THE CONSTITUTIONAL EVOLUTION
OF SPAIN

THE EXPERIENCE of the Spanish people in popular government was an inheritance from the Middle Ages. Their political evolution had followed a course which diverged from that of the other nations of Europe. Their embryonic democratic institutions had been smothered by centralization, absolutism, and the necessities of governing a dynastic empire. Representative government developed, decayed, and was revived in the nineteenth century in an era of written constitutions.

The medieval *municipio* was a profoundly democratic institution. It was the first agency for the protection of individual and political rights in Spain. According to some authorities, it originated in the application of the judicial agencies of the Teutonic invaders to the sphere of the city. The interests of the heterogeneous urban population were regulated in the *concilium* or assembly of freemen. The municipal magistrates represented the city in its exterior relations and governed it internally. The *fuero* or charter of privileges provided the juridical basis of the rights and was the first fundamental charter or constitution known in Spain. In it the king or lord granted the land to the inhabitants of the municipality, who in turn swore to maintain the precepts of the *fuero* and remain faithful to the crown. Such a régime was effective in securing the improvement of the condition of the lower classes and their civil and political emancipation. Its period of greatest importance occurred in the later Middle Ages, particularly in the thirteenth century, when it had a frankly democratic character and an absolute independence.[1]

[1] Ballesteros, II, 515-518; Altamira, I, 435-436, 471, 484.

Meanwhile, the kings had not only granted the *municipios* privileges in local government, but had also extended them a voice in the affairs of the several Spanish states. The assemblies of the feudal lords and ecclesiastics were expanded to include representatives of the towns. They were earlier known as *concilios,* but an assembly convoked at Nájera by Alfonso VII, in 1137, received the new name of *cortes.* The special characteristic of the *cortes* was the inclusion of popular representatives. This occurred for the first time at León in 1188, under Alfonso IX. According to some authorities, this assembly was the first in Europe and the Spanish Peninsula in which the representatives of the privileged cities met with the king.[2] The Cortes of León, however, was important for another reason. It promulgated a real political constitution, restricting the authority of the monarch and providing guarantees for persons and property. It recognized the inviolability of the home and proclaimed the principle of the right of judicial protection against injustice.[3]

An evolution similar to that in Castile extended representation of the cities of Aragón, Navarre, and Catalonia in the thirteenth century. The intervention of these municipal *procuradores,* however, was not a municipal right but a concession from the crown to gain the financial support of the middle class. Although the king could legislate without the *procuradores* he could not impose new taxes or extraordinary services without their approval. The granting of money and the approval of taxes, however, was not the only object of the assemblies. They often legislated on matters of internal government and dictated principles in economic laws. They had no direct and regular participation in the government of the realm, but their influence in general administration was important. Their action was considered a reflection of popular sentiment and their petitions had the force of legislative acts when approved by the monarchs.[4]

[2] Altamira, I, 431.
[3] Ballesteros, II, 511-512.
[4] *Ibid.,* III, 331-338.

For many years the *cortes* was a restraining force on the royal power and its ally against the turbulent aristocracy. The Cortes of Madrid, 1391, was the last with a great concurrence of municipal representatives, and the decline of the institution accompanied the decay of the municipalities. The cities had flourished during the period of the conquest and received their *fueros* for their services as valuable allies against the Moors. They began to decline in the fifteenth century. Many causes have been advanced for their loss of political significance. The authority in the cities became concentrated in the hands of their representatives as it passed from the democratic *cabildo abierto* or popular assembly to the *ayuntamiento* or municipal council. The monarch also began to intervene in the choice of magistrates, the appointment of *procuradores,* and finally in naming the members of the councils. This suppressed the independent authority of the cities which was further restricted by royal administrative officials. As the cities became more class conscious with maturity, the offices in the municipal councils were gradually monopolized by gentlemen and the rival noble families. The municipality was democratic in its origin but was slowly subjected to the domination of the urban aristocracy. Finally, as the power of the king increased, the number of officials was arbitrarily increased to reward favorites or courtiers, and the cities had to bear this increased financial responsibility.[5]

There was a change in the constitutional basis of the Spanish monarchy under Charles V. The Catholic Sovereigns had introduced absolute government but the *cortes* still influenced the royal decisions. Under their successor, however, the several royal councils began to function, and replaced the *cortes* as advisory organs. In addition, Charles V was not as dependent on financial aid from the *cortes* as were his contemporaries in England. The resources of the crown from the dynastic empire of the Hapsburgs and the treasure from the New World placed the Spanish sovereign in a far more independent position. This period was also one

[5] *Ibid.,* III, 341-343.

of great commercial prosperity, and the customs which poured into the royal treasury decreased the necessity of further extraordinary exactions.[6] The discontent of the middle classes in the cities was evident in the attitude of the representatives of Salamanca, Córdoba, and León. They refused to take the oath of allegiance in the Cortes of Santiago-Coruña until the king conceded what they asked. This attitude anticipated the revolt of the cities against the policies of Charles V. The suppression of their opposition hastened the decay of municipal independence.[7]

The *cortes* had a precarious and decadent existence under the House of Austria. It did not represent all the interests of the respective kingdoms. The Castilian nobility, for example, withdrew because they had little interest in assessing or denying impositions which they did not have to pay. The nobles were not convoked after the Cortes of 1538. On the other hand, the clergy, protected by the pope, assembled in their own councils and defended their privileges through interdict and excommunication. They were, therefore, not very zealous in the defense of their legislative rights. The *procuradores* were the only true representatives in the *cortes* and they incarnated a privilege because few cities enjoyed the right of representation. The towns which petitioned for representation were systematically opposed by the privileged cities. The latter even threatened to refuse grants to the crown if the petitions received royal approval. There were also cases when the cities refused to pay their representatives and the latter received gifts from the crown. In addition, since the powers of the *procuradores* terminated with the end of the session for which they had been conferred, the king could adjourn the assembly if he did not consider its members sufficiently docile. Thus the king gained control of the will of the *cortes* and it lost its independence.[8]

Despite this decadence, the Castilian *cortes* had a constitu-

[6] Altamira, III, 454-458; Ballesteros, IV, Pt. 2, 2.
[7] Altamira, III, 13-37.
[8] Ballesteros, IV, Pt. 2, 34-35.

tional value as its reason for existence. It recognized the sovereign, who appeared before it to swear to conserve the integrity of his dominions and the rights of the crown, and to maintain the laws of the kingdom and the immunities and privileges of the municipalities. The most substantial prerogative, however, was that of approving every new tax introduced by the government and voting the direct taxes. In 1525 Charles V promised that no direct tax would ever be solicited without the consent of the *cortes,* and that the returns would be dedicated entirely to the expenses of the administration of the Castilian provinces.[9]

The triumph of the *cortes* would have been assured if its members could have united on economic matters. The convocations, however, were generally hurried and the representatives were unable to agree on the defense of their collective interests. They suffered from the vigilance of agents of the crown and could not organize an effective opposition. They were easily intimidated because of their economic dependence on the crown. In addition, the places were often bought and were sometimes assigned by the crown. In the end, therefore, the *procuradores* had little freedom in the exercise of their powers.[10]

In Navarre, Aragón, Valencia, and Catalonia, however, the *cortes* resisted the encroachment of the royal authority more vigorously. They maintained their participation in the work of legislation and continued to present their grievances. Financial necessity rendered regular convocations more necessary, but the representatives tenaciously resisted all requests for subsidies. At times the sum requested was reduced to such an extent that it barely sufficed to pay for the royal journey.[11]

Characteristic notes of the administration of the Bourbons were centralization and uniformity. During this period the *cortes* barely merited its name. Nevertheless, the memory of

[9] *Ibid.,* 37.
[10] *Ibid.,* 38-39.
[11] *Ibid.,* 43.

its ancient privileges was preserved and the *cortes* revived in the nineteenth century. Philip V did not desire to give it any importance, but one important change occurred during his reign. There was an assembly in 1701 which included the Spanish grandees and prelates and representatives of the towns of Aragón, Valencia, and Navarre as well as of Castile. This assembly was not considered a *cortes,* but eight years later the first general *cortes* of Castile and Aragón was convoked and the two kingdoms were united politically. Otherwise, the dependence of the municipal authorities and representatives on the crown was maintained.[12]

The importance of the middle class, however, increased although the decline of the *cortes* threatened its political influence. The Bourbons stimulated this development as a result of their desire to protect and assist bourgeois interests in an effort to destroy the barriers between the wealthy and the aristocratic.[13] The bourgeoisie moreover, was sympathetic toward the liberal ideas introduced from France. Floridablanca, the minister of Charles IV, sought to prevent the introduction of French revolutionary propaganda, but palace intrigue produced his dismissal and that of his successor, Aranda. Thus Manuel Godoy, the favorite of Queen María Luisa, became the principal minister of Spain. He pursued a vacillating policy in an effort to evade an alliance with France or the other alternative, a declaration of war. Finally, the decapitation of Louis XVI produced a reaction in Spain against the French revolutionaries, and Charles IV signed a treaty of alliance with England. The breach with France was popular, but within three years the war was concluded and Spain became the ally of the French Directory against her ancient enemy and recent ally.[14]

Nevertheless liberalism had already penetrated into Spain. French influence had become very strong in the seventeenth century and naturally increased during the eighteenth cen-

---

[12] *Ibid.,* VI, 29, 31.
[13] *Ibid.,* VI, 51-52.
[14] Altamira, IV, 70-76, 79.

tury, as a result of the close political relations between the two countries and the fame of the French literary celebrities at a time when Spanish literature was declining.[15] It was natural, therefore, that the ideas of the French Encyclopedists and revolutionaries should be popular in Spain among a minority, especially in the Basque provinces. The works of Voltaire, Rousseau, Mirabeau, Montesquieu, and many English authors of liberal tendencies were translated and circulated, even among the nobility and clergy. The radical *Real Seminario de Vergara* was established and secret revolutionary societies were formed.[16]

Floridablanca tried to prohibit the importation of inflammatory literature and the entrance of agitators, while the Inquisition extended its list of prohibited books. Such efforts, however, were of little avail because of the indecision of the government and the benevolence of certain public officials toward liberal ideas. The majority of the Spanish people continued to be centralists, realists, and partisans of the absolutist régime. The effect of the liberal activity on the Spanish government was slight. The agitation continued among the younger generation, and men like the Abbot Marchena, Vicente María Santibañez, and Martínez Balleteros were openly sympathetic with the French Revolution. Some of them fought in the French Republican armies, while others remained in Spain as fervent partisans of the new ideas and even conspired with revolutionary aims. The policy of the government, which aimed to suppress any public manifestations in behalf of reform or revolution, did not eradicate the seed of liberalism which had been sown and which was soon to bear fruit.[17]

The influence of Napoleon was shortly felt in Spain. It was necessary for him to dominate the peninsula in order to enforce his Continental System, and the opportunity for his intervention was presented in the factional intrigue in the

[15] *Ibid.*, IV, 382.
[16] *Ibid.*, IV, 148-151.
[17] *Ibid.*, IV, 151-153.

court of Charles IV. Ferdinand, Prince of Asturias, had been offended by the opposition of Godoy to his marriage to Marie Antoinette of Naples and was ambitious to succeed his father. An anti-Godoy or *fernandista* faction therefore gathered around the prince, under the leadership of Escoiquiz, an ambitious canon. Both factions sought to win the support of Napoleon, who played one against the other.[18]

Napoleon's first move was to enter into the Convention of Fontainebleau with Godoy, on November 27, 1806. It provided for the definitive conquest and dismemberment of Portugal, a power traditionally friendly to Great Britain. Ten days later Junot led a French army into Spain and, following the subjugation of Portugal, demanded the cession of all of that country to France with the right of access through northern Spain. Charles IV realized the duplicity of Napoleon and the increasing popularity and ambition of his son, and fled from Madrid to Aranjuez. The followers of Ferdinand then seized their opportunity, provoked a riot, and forced Charles IV to abdicate.[19]

The Spanish people were jubilant at the elevation of Ferdinand VII to the throne. Napoleon, however, quickly undeceived them as to his designs. The French had been received as friends in Madrid, but their Emperor refused to recognize the new sovereign and offered the Spanish crown to Louis Bonaparte, then King of Holland. Ferdinand was lured to Bayonne, Charles IV arrived a few days later, and Napoleon had the whole royal family in his power. In the ensuing negotiations Ferdinand renounced the throne in favor of his father, who again abdicated, this time in favor of the Emperor, May 5, 1808.[20] Napoleon, however, had not foreseen the reaction that such a policy would produce in Spain. There were outbreaks in Burgos, Toledo, and other centers. The agitation came to a head in Madrid, on May 2, when the mob attacked the French troops quartered in the

[18] *Ibid.*, IV, 83-95 *passim*
[19] *Ibid.*, IV, 100-103.
[20] *Ibid.*, IV, 103-108; Zabala y Lera, I, 8-11.

city. Then all of Spain rose against the French, animated by
hatred for Napoleon and a misguided loyalty to Ferdinand.
Juntas were organized throughout the country and began the
struggle to regain their independence.[21]

Meanwhile Napoleon had named his brother, Joseph, King
of Spain and declared his desire to renew the ancient Spanish
monarchy by the promulgation of a constitutional code. He
had a blind confidence in written constitutions and desired
to reconcile the authority of his brother with the traditional
liberties and privileges of the country. Consequently on June
15, 1808, an assembly of 150 representatives was convoked to
meet at Bayonne two months later. Only eighty-three of the
representatives were to be freely elected, and the general disorder not only interfered with the elections but prevented
many of the members from attending. Some of the representatives of the privileged classes refused to appear and there
were only sixty-five deputies at the opening session. Three
weeks later, when the oath of allegiance to the constitutional
charter was administered, less than a hundred members had
arrived.[22]

This assembly at Bayonne, therefore, was hardly a constituent *cortes*. It was convoked by an unrecognized authority
and did not represent the nation. The document that it formulated was a charter rather than a true constitution, representing the will of Napoleon rather than that of the nation.
The approval of the Spanish representatives was necessary to
give it an aspect of legality. Joseph Bonaparte was recognized
as king, after which the constitutional project was read to
the deputies. It had been drafted by Napoleon and, after a
preliminary revision, had been submitted to the *Junta de
Gobierno* and the Council of Castile. Neither of these bodies
had any conception of the currents of European ideology and
no experience in the drafting of constitutions. Nevertheless
some modifications were introduced, the project was submitted to a commission, and the deputies were invited to sub-

[21] Zabala y Lera, I, 16-20.
[22] *Ibid.*, I, 20-24; Ballesteros, VII, 590-591.

mit their observations in writing. Three weeks later they swore an oath of allegiance to their first constitutional document.[23]

The Constitution of Bayonne consisted of 146 articles. It provided for the establishment of the Roman Catholic Church. A senate of princes and royal appointees was given the power of suspending the constitution in cases of armed rebellion or threats to the security of the state. This body was also entrusted with the protection of individual liberties and the freedom of the press through special committees. A Council of State was endowed with the examination and drafting of civil projects and the supervision of administrative bodies. The *cortes* consisted of three chambers or *estamentos,* consisting of 172 members: twenty-five archbishops, twenty-five grandees, and 122 deputies. Sixty-two of the latter were to represent the provinces, including the American colonies, which were conceded equality with the natives of Spain. Thirty deputies represented the principal cities, and fifteen were appointed by the crown. The *cortes* approved variations in the civil and penal codes and in taxation. The judicial provisions established unity in civil, penal, and mercantile codes, guaranteed the independence of judges and provided publicity in criminal procedure. Constitutional guarantees were provided for the rights of citizens, such as the inviolability of the home, personal security, and the abolition of torture. Equality in taxation was established and individual and corporate privileges were suppressed.[24]

This charter is primarily significant because it represented the effort of Napoleon to gain the confidence of the liberal element and of the Spanish people. He might have introduced even more radical reforms had they not been at variance with deeply rooted Spanish traditions. In any event, he succeeded only in arousing further opposition and ridicule for the Constitution of Bayonne. The people of Spain were too greatly aroused by French intervention to accept

[23] Zabala y Lera, I, 24-25.
[24] *Ibid.,* I, 26-28.

even a restoration, much less an extension of their liberties at the hands of the Emperor.[25]

Meanwhile, the insurgent *juntas* had refused to recognize Joseph and had begun to coöperate for unified resistance against the invaders. A central committee of twenty-four, later of thirty-five members, was created and functioned until January 1810. It then appointed a regency of five for the purpose of convoking a *cortes* representative of the nation and resigned. The question of calling such an assembly had been intensified by a conflict between the central committee and the Council of Castile over the legality of the powers of the former. The aims of the various factions diverged sharply. The *fernandistas* and adherents of the traditional monarchy desired that the duties of the *cortes* should be restricted to the defense of the national territory and the restoration of the *fueros* and customs of Spain. Jovellanos, who had first urged the convocation of an assembly, also desired to reëstablish the ancient political traditions. On the other hand, the extremists were not disposed to struggle for the independence of Spain and again place themselves at the mercy of a capricious court, the ambition of a favorite, or the variable will of a sovereign. They wished to establish a real constitutional régime, to guarantee and consecrate the rights of the citizens.[26]

This extraordinary *cortes* met at Cádiz in September 1810. The memory of the exact status and powers of the earlier *cortes* was vague, but that which assembled in 1810 was unlike any other that had ever been convoked. The 105 deputies from the towns, provincial *juntas,* and the American colonies united in a single chamber. On the whole, it did not reflect the real conservatism of Spain since most of the deputies were from the more radical coastal regions rather than the interior of the country. The first act of the assembly was the recognition of Ferdinand VII as the legitimate monarch, and the second was the declaration that the sover-

[25] *Ibid.,* I, 29-30.
[26] *Ibid.,* I, 75; Ballesteros, VII, 83.

eignty of the nation resided in the *cortes,* which exercised
the legislative power. The deputies then introduced various
reforms in which the lines between the two divergent parties
were sharply drawn. The law establishing the freedom of the
press was passed by a majority of 70 to 32.[27] The Constitution of 1812, however, was the most important accomplish-
ment of the Cortes of Cádiz, for it became the constitutional
precedent which survived until the twentieth century. A constitutional commission was appointed on March 2, 1811, and
the debate continued for a year. The project was signed on
March 18, 1812, and promulgated the following day. It consisted of 384 articles in ten titles.[28]

The Spaniards had refused from foreign hands many of
the provisions which were incorporated into the Constitution of 1812. It established an hereditary monarchy and the
sovereignty was vested in the nation. The legislative power
was assigned to the *cortes* and the king. The former was a
unicameral body, composed of deputies indirectly elected by
citizens over twenty-five years of age. It met annually for
three months and was endowed with extensive powers, such
as the initiation of laws, the ratification of treaties, and general control of finance. It was specifically provided that the
cortes should encourage education and stimulate industry.
In short, the *cortes* now assumed the rôle that the absolutism
of the preceding centuries had denied it. Despite the separation of powers, its domination was assured by the establishment of ministerial responsibility for infractions of the constitution and a permanent committee which should guard
the constitution and laws of the land against royal aggression
between sessions.[29]

The king was required to take an oath to protect the
Roman Catholic faith, support the constitution, and respect
private property and individual liberty. His ordinances had

[27] Zabala y Lera, I, 85, 87.
[28] *Ibid.,* I, 87.
[29] *Constitución de la monarquía española.* Cádiz, 1812. Zabala y Lera, I,
87-88; Ballesteros, VII, 594-596.

to be countersigned by responsible ministers. He was advised by a Council of State of forty persons, including four members of the clergy, four grandees, and at least twelve representatives of the colonies. It was named by the king from lists presented by the *cortes*. Although the person of the king was declared "sacred and inviolable" and he could do no wrong, his powers were carefully restricted. He controlled foreign relations, civil and military appointments, and the royal patronage, but was prohibited from dissolving or suspending the *cortes*. He could not make a treaty, alienate any national territory, levy taxes, leave the kingdom, or contract marriage without the consent of that body. His exercise of the royal sanction, however, was of the nature of a veto, since his refusal to sanction a law might postpone its consideration from year to year.[30]

In the administration of justice, unity of the civil, criminal, and commercial codes was established and a hierarchy of courts under the Supreme Tribunal was erected. Citizens were guaranteed protection against arbitrary arrest and search. The use of torture and the confiscation of the estates of criminals were prohibited. The ancient system of local administration was abandoned and Spain was divided into artificial and merely administrative divisions. This represented an effort to unify the nation for the Peninsular War. Taxation was placed in the hands of the *cortes,* which confirmed or established all taxes annually, while it was specifically provided that taxes should be assessed on all Spaniards in proportion to their ability without exemption or privilege. An entire chapter was devoted to the army, which was also subjected to the *cortes*. The process for the amendment of the constitution was a complicated one, designed to prevent rash changes in the fundamental law of the land.[31]

A principal aim of this constitution appears to have been the limitation of the power of the Bourbons and the establishment of the principle of national sovereignty. It was more

[30] *Constitución de la monarquía española* [1812].
[31] *Ibid.*

liberal, however, than the majority of the people at that time could accept. The Cortes of Cádiz held its last session on September 14, 1813, and following the close of the Peninsular War Ferdinand was restored to the Spanish throne. He immediately fell under the influence of the conservatives and a period of reaction ensued. The Constitution of 1812, therefore, enjoyed a transitory existence. It was abolished in 1814, and a severe persecution of the liberals was begun, impelled by the king's desire to restore his absolute prerogatives, the attitude of the other European monarchs, and the feeling of the majority of the nobility, clergy, and people.[32]

The ferocity of the repression of the liberals not only discredited Ferdinand VII at home and abroad but failed to crush liberalism in Spain. Spasmodic insurrections occurred and, in 1820, the revolt of Rafael Riego forced Ferdinand to restore the Constitution of 1812. The extreme reactionaries, however, took advantage of the factional dissension that developed among the liberals, and the crisis was resolved by foreign intervention. Louis XVIII was given a mandate to restore the prerogatives of his Spanish cousin, and the French army quickly suppressed the constitutionalists and restored Ferdinand VII to his position as an absolute monarch.[33]

The reaction that followed did not appease the extreme supporters of Ferdinand VII. A party gathered around his brother with the hope of achieving the triumph of absolutism through the accession of Don Carlos to the throne. The childless king married María Cristina of Naples, and the opposition of the Carlists forced him to rely on the support of the liberals. The new queen bore a daughter, María Isabel, in 1830. Thereupon she persuaded Ferdinand to restore the law of 1789 by which Charles IV had abrogated the Salic Law. Don Carlos was barred from the succession. Three years later Ferdinand VII died and his infant daughter ascended the throne with her mother as regent.[34]

[32] Zabala y Lera, I, 100-102.
[33] *Ibid.*, I, 106-111; 122-126; Ballesteros, VII, 148-212 *passim*.
[34] Zabala y Lera, I, 131-136.

A struggle with the Carlists began almost immediately. María Cristina was forced to depend upon the liberals and she was unable to pursue as absolute a policy as she desired because the moderates who returned from exile desired a representative régime. Hence Martínez de la Rosa tried to effect a compromise between the absolute monarchy and the Constitution of 1812. The Royal Statute of 1834 was little more than a translation of the French Charter of 1814 and gave the crown the powers necessary to make it the final authority.[35]

A *cortes* consisting of two *estamentos,* the *procéres* and the *procuradores,* was established. The former represented the privileged classes. Its membership was either hereditary or by royal appointment and was unlimited. The *procuradores* were elected but had to satisfy such extreme qualifications that this chamber was far from representative of the nation. The crown possessed the exclusive power of convocation, suspension, and dissolution of the *cortes,* and that body was not permitted to deliberate upon any matter which was not expressly submitted for examination by a royal decree. Although the two chambers met separately, one could not be convoked without the other and the only real privilege of the *cortes* was the right of petition.[36]

Such a compromise greatly disappointed the liberals, who had anticipated the restoration of the Constitution of 1812 or as advanced a document. The charter was also unsatisfactory to the Carlists who refused to grant any concessions to representative government. The dynastic and political civil war dragged on, and the supporters of Isabella II divided into two political factions, the Moderates and the Progressives. A mutiny at La Granja, in 1837, forced María Cristina to agree to the publication of the Constitution of 1812, pending the convocation of a *cortes* to express the will of the nation. The deputies, however, formulated a new constitution,

[35] *Ibid.,* I, 319-312; Ballesteros, VII, 580-598.
[36] Hilario Abad de Aparicio and Rafael Coronel y Ortiz, *Constituciones vigentes de los principales estados de Europa y America.* Madrid, 1863. I, 495-499.

which was approved by the regent. It was more conservative than the Constitution of 1812, but was likewise more liberal than the Royal Statute. In short, it reflected a moderate tendency and the desire to effect a peaceful compromise and restore the confidence of the nation.[37]

The Constitution of 1837 provided the usual guarantees for personal liberty and the protection of private property. A bicameral legislature consisting of a senate and a house of deputies was established. The senators were named by the king from lists prepared by the provinces and were renewed by one-third at each general election. The deputies were directly elected for three years on the basis of proportional representation. The *cortes* initiated financial legislation and the royal ministers were responsible to it. If the sovereign failed to convoke the *cortes* every year it met automatically. The powers of the crown were restricted. The constitution declared further that justice should be administered in the name of the king, but granted exclusive civil and criminal power to the courts. Public trials in criminal cases and the responsibility of judges were also provided. The organization of local government was still centralized, based on provincial deputations and municipal councils. Unauthorized taxes were declared illegal and an annual budget was required. Thus the Constitution of 1837 was, in reality, an extension of the Royal Statute toward the restoration of the more liberal provisions of the Constitution of 1812.[38]

The next constitutional product of the struggle between the two political factions was the work of the Moderates under the leadership of Narváez. Isabella II had just attained her majority, and the new government was hardly organized before it began to consider the question of constitutional reform. It was suggested that a royal charter should replace the Constitution of 1837, but the government finally convoked a constituent *cortes* to meet in October 1844. The Progressives refrained from participation in the elections

[37] Ballesteros, VII, 510-524, *passim;* Zabala y Lera, I. 345.
[38] Abad de Aparicio, I, 500-506.

and Narváez obtained an overwhelming majority in this reactionary body. The address of the queen stressed the importance of the suppression of the principle of national
sovereignty; the substitution of an aristocratic assembly
named by the crown for the elective assembly; the prolongation of the life of the ordinary *cortes* from three to five years;
the suppression of the national militia, which was imbued
with liberalism; and other suggestions tending to increase the
royal authority.[39]

These suggestions of the government were approved by
the *cortes* and promulgated in the Constitution of 1845. This
document modified the democratic tendency of 1837 and
established a dangerous precedent. The life of constitutions
was definitely linked to the vagaries of politics. All of the
customary individual guarantees were preserved, but the
declaration of the Catholicism of the nation was accentuated
and the state continued to sustain the Church and its ministers. The legislative power was vested in the *cortes* with the
king. The senators, whose number was unlimited, were
named by the crown, with property qualifications high
enough to maintain the aristocratic influence in that body.
The principle of proportional representation in the house
of deputies was retained, but they were elected for five years.
Both the crown and each chamber had the right to initiate
legislation.[40]

The executive power, including the authority necessary to
maintain public order and protect the security of the state,
was vested in the crown, and the royal sanction of legislation
was retained. The king named his ministers, but they might
be impeached by the deputies and tried in the senate. The
provisions for the administration of justice and the organization of local government were almost identical with those of
the Constitution of 1837. The provision for a national
militia was suppressed.[41]

[39] Zabala y Lera, I, 423-425.
[40] Abad de Aparicio, I, 506-514.
[41] *Ibid.*

In 1852, after a series of Moderate ministries, the reaction was accentuated by the example of the *coup d'état* of Louis Napoleon in France and the attempt on the life of Isabella II. Bravo Murillo took advantage of this opportunity to prepare a constitutional reform. The establishment of the Catholic Church was to be made even more exclusive and the crown was to be empowered to legislate by decree if the occasion warranted. The guarantees of individual liberty were to be continued, except freedom of the press which was to be suppressed. The number of the deputies was reduced and their officers were made dependent on the crown. The senate was to consist of two classes, those by right of birth or office and those by right of heredity. This effort was little more than an attempt to legalize actual practice, but it tended, in reality, toward the abrogation of parliamentary government. Both the Moderates and Progressives united to combat the reform, Bravo Murillo was forced to resign, and the act was not accepted.[42]

The political pendulum swung toward the Progressives in 1854, when Espartero and Leopoldo O'Donnell secured control of the government. They immediately convoked a constituent *cortes* consisting of a single chamber. In the ensuing elections, the Liberal Union, consisting of Moderates and Progressives and effected by the reconciliation of the two leaders, was triumphant.[43] The *cortes* began to consider constitutional reform in January 1855. The coalition was divided on the question of whether the Constitution of 1837 or that of 1845 should be the basic law of the land. Finally, however, it was decided to formulate a new constitution. The document which was reported in 1855 reiterated the declaration of the sovereignty of the nation. This was convenient as long as the politicians could control that sovereignty for their own ends. Catholicism was recognized as the national faith, but no person could be prosecuted for contrary opinions unless they were publicly manifested. A bicameral legislature was

[42] Zabala y Lera, I, 448-450.
[43] *Ibid.*, I, 460-461.

provided and the election of its officers was restored to the senate. The provision for life membership in that body was abolished and the senators were appointed for twelve years on the basis of a property qualification. The deputies were elected for three years by proportional representation and the *cortes* was to convene annually. The *cortes* controlled financial legislation and the size of the army. The permanent committee was reëstablished. On the whole, the proposed constitution was liberal in its provisions, restoring the freedom of the press and abolishing capital punishment for political offenses. It was approved in January 1856, but reaction overtook the Progressive majority during the long debates over its promulgation and it was never proclaimed.[44]

The coalition finally divided and O'Donnell seized power in 1856. The Constitution of 1845 was reëstablished with an additional act, promulgated without the approval of the *cortes*. O'Donnell, however, had some respect for constitutional principles, and the act was more liberal than the constitution it supplemented. It provided that a law of public order should be in vigor during the suspension of the guarantees of personal liberty, but that no Spaniard could be expelled or exiled from the kingdom. A senate, not to exceed 140 members, was created. The crown was permitted to name the senators only when the *cortes* was in session. The royal authority was further restricted by the provision that a special law was necessary for the grant of general pardons and amnesties. A Council of State was established. The king, however, was given the power to name *alcaldes* in cities of over forty thousand and could intervene in the internal affairs of other cities by law. This addition was soon suspended, when O'Donnell was forced to resign, shortly after its publication, and Narváez returned to power.[45]

His new ministry proceeded to abrogate the reforms effected during the last two years. The Constitution of 1845 was reëstablished with the innovations established by the law of

[44] *Ibid.*, I, 463-467.
[45] *Ibid.*, I, 470-471; Abad de Aparicio, I, 514-515.

July 17, 1857. This reform dealt primarily with the senate. It modified its composition by an increase in the property qualifications but strengthened its moral authority by adding persons who were senators in their own right to those named by the crown. In addition, the two chambers were to formulate their respective rules of procedure.[46]

During the next twelve years the liberals were restless and continued their agitation for a real constitutional monarchy. There were occasional insurrections, and Isabella II was the target of a great deal of personal criticism. A large proportion of the Spanish people joined the liberals in demanding a more liberal government. The ministry was unable to suppress the radical newspapers, which delighted in exposing every scandal involving the Queen. Meanwhile, Isabella II had lost two staunch advisers in the deaths of Narváez and O'Donnell. Finally, in 1868, González Bravo tried to banish the liberal military leaders, but they returned from exile to force the Queen to flee to France. The Revolution of 1868 was successful and General Juan Prim, who had won recognition in Morocco and the Mexican expedition, was the arbiter of the destiny of the Spanish nation.[47]

A provisional government was established with Prim as Minister of War. It began a series of liberal reforms. The freedom of the press and education were decreed, and the individual rights of pacific reunion and association were guaranteed. Finally, a constituent *cortes* was convoked for February 11, 1869. This body assembled as a single chamber, in which the Progressives, Unionists, and Democratic Monarchists had the largest representation. The opposition parties consisted of the Republicans, the Absolutists, and a few loyal supporters of the exiled Queen. The provisional government resigned its powers to the *cortes* and received a vote of confidence from the deputies. The commission appointed to draft a new constitution completed its task in twenty-five days. The *cortes* approved the Constitution of 1869 on June

---

[46] Zabala y Lera, I, 472-473; Abad de Aparicio, I, 516-517.
[47] Zabala y Lera, I, 474-514 *passim.*

1, by a vote of 214 to 55, and five days later it was promulgated.[48]

This constitution transformed Spain into a strictly limited monarchy. It recognized the sovereignty of the Spanish nation and strengthened the guarantees of individual rights. Private property could not be expropriated except for common utility and by due process of law. Spaniards in possession of full civil rights could not be deprived of their suffrage. Censorship was prohibited and military leaders were forbidden the power of imposing any penalty not previously prescribed by law. The Catholic Church was sustained in its privileged position, but a limited toleration was extended to persons professing other creeds, provided they did not transcend the universal rules of law and morality. This was a definite step toward religious liberty. A further liberal provision guaranteed the privilege of founding and maintaining educational institutions to every Spaniard, subject only to the inspection of the state in matters of hygiene and morality.[49]

The legislative power was declared to reside in the nation, which exercised that power through a bicameral *cortes*. The chambers were equal and their members represented the nation. Four senators were indirectly elected from each province, and the senate was renewed by one-fourth at each general election unless the *cortes* was dissolved. In that case, the entire senate was renewed. The deputies were chosen by proportional representation. The *cortes* met annually and shared the right of the initiation of legislation with the crown.[50]

The executive power resided in the king. Ministerial responsibility for offenses in office, however, was subject to impeachment by the deputies and trial by the senate. The judicial power was vested exclusively in the courts in civil and criminal cases. The judges were named by the king on

[48] *Ibid.*, II, 2-4
[49] *Constitución de la nacion española votada definitivamente por las cortes constituyentes en 1º de Junio de 1869.* Madrid, 1869.
[50] *Ibid.*

the proposal of the Council of State and were personally responsible for infractions of the law. Trial by jury was established. Local government was continued on a centralized basis, although the local organs were given greater independence. The constitution could be amended by the *cortes* or on the proposal of the crown through a process designed to protect the fundamental law against rash innovations.[51]

Following the promulgation of the Constitution of 1869, the government faced serious disorders, which were attributed to the Republicans and Socialists, and the difficult task of finding a new dynasty for the Spanish throne. Several princes were approached. Leopold of Hohenzollern accepted General Prim's offer, but his candidacy was not withdrawn quickly enough to prevent the diplomatic rupture that led to the Franco-Prussian War. Finally Amadeo of Savoy accepted the proffered crown of Spain, and his selection was approved by the *cortes* by a vote of 191 to 116. He was crowned in January 1871. Unfortunately, however, he had lost his principal adviser three days earlier when General Prim was assassinated. Various parties appeared in opposition to the new sovereign. The Alfonsists, led by Cánovas del Castillo, desired a limited monarchy under the son of Isabella II. The Republicans had mustered sixty votes to oppose the election of Amadeo I. The Carlists continued to demand an absolute government, and represented great strength as a result of the support of the clergy. Amadeo tried to conciliate the various parties and fulfil his constitutional obligations in good faith. The Carlists again resorted to rebellion and as a result of the ministerial instability there were six new governments and three general elections within two years. In 1873, Amadeo abdicated and left Spain.[52]

On February 11, 1873, the senators and deputies, in violation of the constitutional provision that there should be no joint deliberation, met in a single chamber and declared Spain a republic by 258 votes to 32. The occasion for such a

[51] *Ibid.*
[52] Zabala y Lera, II, 6-23.

declaration could hardly have been less propitious. The Democrats controlled the assembly and the Republicans were masters of the government under the presidency of Estanislao Figueras. A secessionist movement created anarchy in Catalonia, the Carlists were in armed resistance to the First Republic, and there were other insurrections. Three presidents, Pí y Margall, Salmerón, and Castelar, succeeded Figueras in less than a year. Finally General Pavía sent an armed force to the *cortes* and forcibly dissolved it. The Republicans had convened a constituent *cortes* but they had been unable to formulate a constitution.[53]

Alfonso, the exiled son of Isabella II, subscribed to the Manifesto of Sandhurst, eulogizing representative institutions. Then, through the efforts of Antonio Cánovas del Castillo and Primo de Rivera, Captain-General of Madrid, he was placed on the Spanish throne. The people of Spain desired peace above everything, and Alfonso XII gave them a hope of stability under a representative régime.[54]

The principal achievement of Cánovas del Castillo was the Constitution of 1876. He convoked a constituent *cortes* which was opened in February 1876. It was drafted by a commission of illustrious men, named by an assembly of six hundred ex-senators and ex-deputies. It was less liberal than the Constitution of 1869. It established religious toleration instead of religious liberty. The power of the crown was not so definitely restricted. Spain, however, was declared a constitutional monarchy and the power of legislation was vested in the *cortes* and the king. The senate was composed of 180 senators who held their dignity in their own right or were nominated by the crown, and 180 others who were elected by corporations. The deputies were indirectly elected by proportional representation. The *cortes* met annually, and the deputies controlled the initiation of financial legislation. The person of the king was "sacred and inviolable," but his ministers were responsible to the *cortes*. While the local govern-

[53] Zabala y Lera, II, 23-32.
[54] *Ibid.*, II, 34 ff.

ment was rendered more independent, the centralized organization into provinces was retained.[55]

The Constitution of 1876 guaranteed the traditional individual rights, with the exception of the jury system, which was abolished. The provision for their suspension, however, was also a tradition. The individual guarantees could be temporarily suspended by a law for the security of the state in extraordinary circumstances. When the *cortes* was not in session the government could suspend them. This clause was invoked by Primo de Rivera in 1923 and again rallied the liberals to the cause of constitutional revision.

[55] *Constitución de la monarquía española promulgada en 30 de Junio de 1876*. Madrid, 1876.

IV

THE FORCES OF LIBERALISM

THE PROMULGATION of the Constitution of 1876 definitely established the government of Spain as a limited monarchy with the customary observance and protection of individual rights and liberties. These had been consecrated in a century-old tradition of written constitutions. Various factors, however, soon effected a change in the Spanish nation of which the ruling bureaucracy was only barely conscious or strangely indifferent. By the dawn of the twentieth century the liberalism of the nineteenth century, with its emphasis on individual liberty and *laissez faire* was confronted with a new social and economic philosophy which had been widely accepted. Liberty, equality, and fraternity had undergone an ideological transition. Liberty too often meant licence, equality appeared impossible as a result of the increasing inequality of economic and social opportunity, and fraternity, in the real sense of the word, became the most important of the trinity. The conviction was growing in the Spanish nation that although individual liberty had to be guaranteed, it had also to be subordinated to the social and economic welfare of the nation as a whole.

Alfonso XIII was sixteen years old, in 1902, when he was declared competent to assume his position as king of Spain with its consequent responsibilities. He swore to defend and enforce the Constitution of 1876, the principal aim of which was to restrict the royal prerogative. He was ill fitted, both by education and temperament, for such a responsibility. He was trained in a school of thought that was contemporary with the reaction which followed the fiasco of the First Republic. His tutors were intellectuals who were intensely loyal to the monarchy. True to their environment and experience, they could not foresee or understand the new forces that were rising in Spain, even if they became aware of them. Repression was the only weapon they knew that could effectively combat agitation.[1]

The last of the Spanish Bourbons was a politician of the first order, a master at insinuating his personal charm and winning the good will of the people. His manner and personality gave him an appearance of democracy that was not real. He was not a statesman and was totally unprepared for the almost impossible task of adapting Spanish traditions and the Spanish temperament to a liberal and democratic régime. He did not evolve a political philosophy that might hasten the renaissance of his country. The majority of his advisers, moreover, had less foresight than he had, and they viewed the social movements in the nation from the point of view of personal politics. Alfonso XIII was unable to devise a program or control his ministers with the firm hand necessary to insure ministerial stability. Peasant revolts were countered by increasing the number and salaries of the Civil Guard, rather than by the solution of the social unrest that produced the disturbances. The king came to rely on the reactionary parties of the nation and recognized only the Church and the army in his policies and the distribution of royal favors.[2]

Gradually, the parliamentary system established in 1876 decayed. Politicians became hesitant and vacillating in the administration of the affairs of state. They were unable to rely upon either the King or the people. Cánovas del Castillo managed to consolidate the monarchy for a generation after the Restoration. He did not, however, protect it against the ravages of partisan politics. He and Sagasta inaugurated a political comedy. Elections were controlled from Madrid by manifold methods of corruption. Spain, therefore, displayed a pretense of parliamentary activity, but no real endeavor to educate an intelligent public opinion was made.

[1] Madariaga, 114-115, 260.
[2] *Ibid.*, 116-118, 262-263.

The people lost confidence in politics to the extent that the universal suffrage, which had been granted in 1889, became a paper suffrage.[3]

Periodic efforts were made to improve the situation. Canalejas, from 1909 to 1912, tried to subject the religious orders to the laws of the nation by enforcing the provisions of registration and taxation. The politicians, however, were too divided to carry out the effective reform of an institution which was supported by the King and accepted by the mass of the people. Canalejas was assassinated in 1912 and the liberals were leaderless and disorganized. Factional politics defeated the efforts at reform.[4]

Agitation for reform, however, was not dead. The Republicans had failed in 1873, when all of their oratory could not bridge the chasm between centralism and federalism and enable them to take advantage of the opportunity of putting their theories of democracy into practical political use. Plagued by factional division, they nevertheless succeeded in reconstituting the party in 1903. The various factions were united into the Republican Union under Nicolas Salmerón and Joaquín Costa. They were not yet able, however, to take advantage of their opportunities. In 1905 they succeeded in electing thirty deputies to the *cortes* but the divisive tendency reappeared.[5] Four years later, they formed a coalition with the Socialists and, in 1913, succeeded in gaining thirteen seats in the *cortes*.[6]

During the minority of Alfonso XIII republicanism had "receded from practical politics into professional polemics."[7] The real republican revival, therefore, was effected in the ranks of the intelligentsia. The educational renaissance had established the *Institución Libre de Enseñanza*, the *Junta para Ampliación de Estudios,* and the lay schools. These were

---

[3] Joseph A. Brandt, *Toward the New Spain*. Chicago, 1932. 361-362; Madariaga, 79.

[4] Madariaga, 274.

[5] Zabala y Lera, II, 340-341, 348; Ballesteros, VIII, 502.

[6] Ballesteros, VIII, 553.

[7] Young, 76.

not only academies of research but were associations for the propagation of liberal and republican doctrines.[8] In the course of time, thousands of potential republicans were recruited in these schools for the renaissance of Spain. Their influence extended to the universities and it is not surprising that the Spanish professor and student became the apostles of a new régime in Spain, one more consonant with the demands of the twentieth century.

In 1898 another group began to attempt the task of arousing the people of Spain. Galdós had worked to bring them to a purely national point of view rather than the prevailing indifference which was accentuated by partisan politics. A group of intellectuals, however, reacted from the defeat and mismanagement of the Spanish-American War and threw their efforts into the awakening of the spirit of Spain. Four men dominated the "Generation of '98": Joaquín Costa, Angel Ganivet, Miguel de Unamuno, and José Ortega y Gasset. Costa urged the necessity of an economic and cultural revolution in order that the Spanish people might develop a sane political life. Ganivet desired to cultivate and refine the positive qualities of his fellow countrymen. Unamuno sought to effect a Christian evolution by adapting the formula of religious unity to a liberal and modern atmosphere. José Ortega y Gasset, on the other hand, was more critical of purely Spanish values and became the proponent of Europeanization. These intellectuals, therefore, urged both the salvation and development of the innate qualities of the Spanish people and an evolution through the influence and example of Europe.[9]

Another factor which was active in bringing foreign ideas into Spain was the rapidly developing Spanish press. It had been liberated from official interference by the triumph of the individual liberties during the nineteenth century. The Spanish newspaper was generally limited in circulation as a result of the individualistic quality of the Spanish mind and

[8] *Ibid.*, 31.
[9] Madariaga, 100-107.

was usually dominated by one directing personality. It was more independent of business interests, however, than was the case in many other more progressive nations. It emphasized opinions and ideas rather than news. The great journalist of modern Spain was Ramiro de Maeztu, the interpreter of Anglo-Saxon ideas. The great liberal newspaper was *El Sol,* founded in 1918 by Nicolás María Urgoiti.[10] On the eve of the Revolution of 1931, the Republicans were far better supplied with periodicals and pamphlets than their opponents. Nicolás de Urgoiti also controlled *Voz.* The Catalans owned the anticlerical and radical *El Liberal* and the popular *Heraldo de Madrid.* The conservative organs, *ABC,* the clerical *El Debate,* and others had an even smaller circulation and were less effective in influencing the middle and lower classes to whom the republican propaganda was directed.[11]

Meanwhile, the Industrial Revolution had transformed many aspects of Spanish life, with its accompanying ferment of social problems. The disorder of the Peninsular War had nearly obliterated the industry that Spain, dependent as it was upon foreign manufactures, had developed during the eighteenth century. The application of machinery to manufacturing had occurred in Catalonia in 1805, when Samuel Crompton's spinning-mule was first used. In 1832, José Bonaplata, with the aid of the government, founded a factory in Barcelona for the construction of machinery which used steam power. Catalonia, therefore, continued to forge ahead of the other regions of Spain, and Barcelona became the first modern industrial center in that country.[12] From 1833 to the end of the century, Spain was distracted by continuous civil disturbances, yet her industry began to expand. The mining industry, with the assistance of foreign capital, had increased its production to more than 400 million *pesetas* by 1900 and employed some eighty thousand workers. The other

[10] *Ibid.,* 110, 288.
[11] Young, 113.
[12] Zabala y Lera, I, 209-212.

industries did not keep abreast of this development, but new factories were founded and railroads were built.[13]

This activity was emphasized after the restoration of the Bourbons in 1875, and was accelerated by the World War. Spain was a neutral state and enjoyed a great expansion in commerce, particularly with the American countries. Spanish capital increased to such an extent that a large proportion of the industrial and national debt was paid off and the Bank of Spain was able to report a reserve of 2,223 million *pesetas* in 1918, compared with 567 million in 1914. The industrial development was especially rapid in the Basque Provinces, Catalonia, Asturias, Seville, Valencia, and Zaragoza.[14]

The development of Spanish industry and the resultant concentration of great working masses in the focal points, where the cost of living was high, produced a social question by the middle of the nineteenth century. The first working organization, the *Sociedad de los Tejedores,* was founded by Munts in 1840. Fourteen years later there was a confederation of laboring organizations. Their aim was purely economic, coöperation in production and consumption. The ideology of the early French Socialists had penetrated into Spain. Fourier's doctrines were circulated. Fernando Garrido was active as a socialist propagandist, and Joaquín Abreu founded a socialist review in Madrid, in 1856.[15]

Meanwhile, the socialist movement had become an international one and had been given a definitely revolutionary and class concept by the Communist Manifesto. The International Union of Workers was founded in 1864 and Karl Marx succeeded in imbuing it with his revolutionary and international program. Four years later the Italian propagandist, José Farinelli, appeared in Madrid, in 1868, and organized the International Association of Workers.[16]

Two rival concepts, however, soon divided the Socialists

[13] *Ibid.,* II, 164-170.
[14] Madariaga, 293-295
[15] Zabala y Lera, II, 177; Ballesteros, VIII, 695.
[16] Zabala y Lera, II, 178; Ballesteros, VIII, 697.

into two factions. One party accepted the scientific and evolutionary ideas of Marx, while the Congress of Córdoba constituted a purely anarchist association. It was composed of the adherents of Bakunin, the mystic and individualist, who had been expelled from the Hague Conference in 1872. Bakunin's philosophy sought release for the oppressed masses in the destruction of the state, religion, and capital, as the trinity of iniquity, and appealed especially to the Spanish worker. The anarchist association grew rapidly.[17]

Barcelona and Madrid were the focal points of anarchist activity, but the field of experimentation was among the workers of Andalusia. The extreme individualism of the Andalusian peasant and the indigenous socialism produced by the policy of *desamortización,* which enriched some persons and left the masses in misery, gave the movement a special impetus. There had been a movement among the peasants for the division of the land as early as 1861. The Anarchists sought to take advantage of the disorder in 1873 and overthrow all existing institutions, reconstructing them on a communal basis. There were great revolts in southern Spain, and the Anarchists seized control in Barcelona, Seville, Cádiz, and Cartagena. The effort was suppressed and the repression which followed led the Anarchists to concentrate their activity in secret societies and resort to terrorism and assassination.[18]

Pablo Iglesias was the important influence and figure in the development of orthodox socialism in Spain. Born in Ferrol in 1850, he was the son of poor peasants. His father died and his mother took her family to Madrid when Pablo Iglesias was ten years old. He was placed in the *Hospicio de San Fernando.* He learned the printing trade and, in 1870, joined the International Association of Workers. Thenceforth his life was devoted to a tireless struggle for the improvement of working conditions. He coöperated with Paul Lafargue, the son-in-law of Marx, in publishing *La Emancipación.* La-

[17] *Ibid.*
[18] Ballesteros, VIII, 696-697, 700-701.

fargue had fled to Spain following the Paris Commune, and their publication became the organ of the orthodox Marxists in Spain. In 1871 a printer's union was founded in Madrid, and Iglesias became its president three years later.[19]

While anarchism was driven into secret channels, socialism continued to flourish. Article 13 of the Constitution of 1876 granted the right of peaceful reunion and association for the ends of human life, and labor unions began to assume a more definite organization. The pure Marxists decided on political action and founded a clandestine party in 1879.[20] Iglesias was a leader in this movement and became secretary of the central committee of the party two years later. The *Unión General de Trabajadores* was organized in 1887, and the Socialists decided to engage in direct action through strikes and labor agitation as well as to effect their program through political regulation. Their first efforts in politics failed but, in 1897, they elected three Socialists to the city council of Bilbao. Two years later the General Union of Workers moved to Madrid, and Iglesias, who had already won indisputable prestige in Spain, became its president. The Socialists intervened in every political or social event which occurred, campaigning for an eight-hour day and against the Moroccan War. Pablo Iglesias was offered the secretaryship of the Institute of Social Reforms by Antonio Maura in 1904, but he was never a partisan of collaboration with the other political parties and did not wish to accept it.[21]

The Socialists participated in the municipal elections in Madrid in 1905, and three socialist candidates were victorious, including Iglesias and Fernando Largo Caballero. When the General Union of Workers established the *Casa del Pueblo* in Madrid, in 1908, it had 39,668 members, and the party had seventy-one councilors in thirty *ayuntamientos*. The revolutionary strike in Barcelona in 1909, and the political execution of Francisco Ferrer produced the clamor which defeated

[19] *Ibid.*, VIII, 700-702.
[20] *Ibid.*
[21] *Ibid.*, VIII, 702-703.

the conservative government of Maura and the coalition of the Republicans and Socialists. Iglesias had at last accepted the idea of coöperation in order to defeat the monarchy. He was elected to the *cortes* in 1910. The central committee of the union and the party included Julián Besteiro, Largo Caballero, Daniel Anguiano, Andrés Saborit, Luís Araquistain, and Manuel Cordero, and boasted a membership of some eighty-five thousand.[22]

The severe repression which followed their second revolutionary outbreak, in 1892, had prostrated the Anarchists. At the close of the century, however, they began to revive in the guise of Syndicalism. This was a non-political movement of workers, consolidated in smaller units. The syndicalist program had been proclaimed in the Charter of Amiens in 1906, which declared that the general strike should be freely used for the complete emancipation of the workers. It aimed at the development of the syndicate as the base of social organization, production, and distribution. The immediate objective, however, was the coördination of the forces of the workers to effect such improvements as shorter hours and higher wages. The syndicates were to avoid all political contamination.[23]

At the beginning of the twentieth century the Syndicalists concentrated their efforts in the general strikes at Gijón, Seville, and Coruña. The agitation decreased from 1901 to 1904 and was replaced by attempts on the lives of politicians and employers. The most ardent partisans of the movement were concentrated in Valencia, Aragon, Asturias, Seville, and especially Catalonia. The regional federation in the latter region published a paper, *Solidaridad Obrera,* which was supported by the majority of the Anarchists.[24]

A most significant episode in the early history of radical agitation among the workers was the political assassination of Francisco Ferrer Guardia, in October 1909. Martial law had

[22] *Ibid.,* 703.
[23] *Ibid.,* 703-704.
[24] *Ibid.,* 704-705.

been proclaimed in Barcelona following a revolutionary strike. Several leaders of the movement were summarily executed and Ferrer, founder of the Modern School, was seized by the police. He was a Catalan intellectual who had devoted his means to the establishment of lay schools for workers. These numbered a hundred by the beginning of the century and had become an effective factor in the education of the workers. Their tenets were largely socialistic but Ferrer's cheap editions of manuals were often written by men of eminence. He was accused of anarchist and revolutionary activity and, in reality, his education of the workers had become a menace to clerical and conservative influence in Spain. The declaration of martial law presented an opportunity for effectively curtailing his activity, and he was summarily tried before a council of war and shot.[25]

Spanish radicals immediately got in touch with their other European centers and manifestations were organized in Paris, London, Brussels, Rome, Lisbon, and other capitals of Europe. The indignation aroused in Europe produced a reaction in Spain against the repressive policy of the conservative government. The Liberals joined the opposition, Antonio Maura was forced to resign, and the proscription and executions were ended. Nevertheless the working class believed that Ferrer was a martyr to their cause, and held the Church responsible. In the ensuing disorder convents and monasteries were burned and two monks were killed, one with a rifle in his hand.[26]

The Syndicalists held a congress at Barcelona in 1910, and created the *Confederación Nacional del Trabajo*. There were many strikes and outrages the following year. Canalejas, the liberal leader, resolutely followed the old policy of repression, and the National Confederation of Labor was suspended and its affiliated centers closed. The syndicalist union was not reorganized until 1915 and *Solidaridad Obrera* reappeared in the same year.[27]

An important period for both anarchism and socialism

[25] Young, 31-32; Zabala y Lera, II, 359-360; Ballesteros, VIII, 527-528.
[26] *Ibid.*
[27] Ballesteros, VIII, 705.

began in 1917. The two unions agreed upon joint action in an effort to force the government to give the people minimum living conditions. The syndicalist leaders, Salvador Seguí, known popularly as Noi del Sucre, and Angel Pestaña adhered to the agreement for the National Confederation of Labor. The government countered this action by suspending the constitutional guarantees and arresting those who had signed the manifesto. The reaction of the nation to this policy was evident the following year. Besteiro, Largo Caballero, Anguiano, Saborit, and Indalecio Prieto were elected to the *cortes*. All but Prieto were members of the strike committee.[28]

The success of the Communists in Russia stirred the Syndicalists to further activity. In May 1918 a congress at Seville organized a regional syndicalist federation. A month later, the Catalan Syndicalists met in Barcelona and created the *Sindicato Unico,* which was successful in several strikes against the employers. An assembly at Madrid, in December 1918, adhered provisionally to the Third International and threatened to blacklist all workers who did not enter the syndicalist National Confederation of Labor within three months.[29]

The government, which had adopted a more tolerant policy, now became more energetic in repressing the activity of the Syndicalists. The members of the *Sindicato Unico* in Barcelona replied with a free use of pistol and bomb to inaugurate a period of terrorism. The employers resorted to similar tactics and formed the *Sindicato Libre.* Eduardo Dato was assassinated in Madrid, and the crimes extended to Valencia, Bilbao, and Andalusia. The assassins of the *Sindicato Libre* murdered the Catalan deputy, Francisco Layret, the attorney of the Syndicalists, and attacked the republican leader, Guerra del Río. An attempt on the life of Pestaña in Manresa failed, but Noi del Sucre was killed in Barcelona (1923).[30]

[28] *Ibid.*
[29] *Ibid.,* VIII, 706.
[30] *Ibid.,* VIII, 707.

A second secession from the ranks of the Socialists occurred in 1921, when the majority at the congress remained loyal to the Vienna International and a few adhered to the Red Third International. The Communists devoted their agitation to gradual penetration and proselytism among the established unions. Communism, however, had little strength at the time of the Revolution of 1931. It had engaged in active propaganda in the provinces of Seville and Malaga and in the industrial zones of Vizcaya and the mining regions of the Asturias. Its principal organ was the *Mundo Obrero,* founded in November 1930. This newspaper was suspended by Berenguer, after the fall of Primo de Rivera, but it reappeared during the campaign for the municipal elections.[31]

A fourth type of socialism had arisen in the last quarter of the nineteenth century to counteract the influence of revolutionary socialism and to practise Christian principles. Bishop Ceferino González founded Catholic circles in Córdoba in 1876 and 1877. Toward the end of the century, a Jesuit, Father Vicent, and the Marquis of Comillas organized 114 Catholic workers' centers with some 21,000 members. They were federated into a central organization in 1910, the *Consejo Nacional de las Corporaciones Católicas Obreras* under the presidency of the Archbishop of Toledo. In this manner the Church tried to maintain its influence over the workers, counteract the increasing agitation, and conserve social discipline.[32]

The government had also manifested some interest in working conditions. A royal order of 1853 had recommended to the municipal councils of Madrid and Barcelona the construction of cheap and hygienic houses for workers. Twenty years later an attempt was made to regulate the labor of women and children. In 1883 a Commission of Social Reforms was established by Moret, while a royal decree of 1888 provided an asylum for injured laborers. The Labor Accident

[31] Enrique Matorras, *El comunismo en España.* Madrid, 1935. 16-20, 25, 27; Ballesteros, VIII, 597.
[32] Ballesteros, VIII, 707; Madariaga, 142-143; Zabala y Lera, II, 179.

Law and another law regulating the labor of women and chil-
dres were passed in 1900. Nevertheless, as the socialist and
syndicalist activity developed, the government tended more
and more to meet agitation with repression. The Socialists
coöperated with the dictator in an effort to secure further
reforms, and Largo Caballero was appointed to the Council
of State. Such legislation as was enacted, however, was only
effected slowly and against the opposition of the industrial
employers. Many of the acts that were passed remained unen-
forced and in the realm of good desires.[33]

[33] Ballesteros, VIII, 707; Zabala y Lera, II, 179.

V

THE REVOLUTION OF 1931

THE ADVENT of Miguel Primo de Rivera and a military dictatorship through the *coup d'état* of 1923 was an important event in the development of the struggle between reaction and reform in Spain. It consolidated and aimed to perpetuate the economic and political power of the Church, the vested interests of the landed aristocracy, and the intervention of the army in the civil life of the nation. Yet the period of internal peace and comparative calm which it inaugurated served only to make the situation more acute. The forces of liberalism and reform were driven into coöperation and given more substantial reasons for agitation and propaganda than they had had heretofore.

Primo de Rivera was a simple and direct soldier whose *coup d'état* was undoubtedly stimulated by other reasons than the desire to protect the honor of the army and the responsibility of the King following the Annual disaster. One motive arose from his disgust with the routine of Spanish politics, in which ambitious politicians manipulated their factions for personal rather than national ends and which had twice procured his dismissal for forthright speech. Alfonso XIII had demonstrated his preference for coalition ministries and had hastened the decomposition of the old party system. At the same time, the activity of the republican and socialist groups and the development of a more intelligent public opinion through educational reform gradually emancipated the electorate from royal and ministerial control. The management of elections from Madrid became more uncertain, and the criticism of the royal government became more open and defiant. Ministry had succeeded ministry in a dizzy fashion. Party discipline had become more difficult. There was not a *cortes* after 1914 in which the government had a real numerical majority. From October 1917 to September 1923 there were no less than twelve governments and three parliaments, each as ineffective as the preceding one.[1]

Another factor that motivated the dictator was undoubtedly derived from his experience as captain-general at Barcelona. He held that position during the period of terrorism between the rival labor and capitalist syndicates and had dealt severely with the perpetrators of the outrages. Likewise, he was deeply concerned over the movement for separatism. As a member of the military bureaucracy and a servant of a unified Spain he was alarmed at the agitation which threatened the unity of the nation. He sought a remedy in repression which could not cure the malady he sought to exterminate.[2]

The establishment of the dictatorship, however, served to alienate the very forces which Primo de Rivera sought to curb, and further to weaken the royal government. The substitution of an effective military government for an ineffective civil one did not reëstablish the contact with the will of the electorate and public opinion. The civil cabinets had been too weak to formulate any consistent program, but the generals sought to counteract the increasing discontent in the nation with the suspension of individual liberties. Martial law was proclaimed throughout Spain in an effort to reëstablish order and security. The *cortes* was dissolved, freedom of speech was restricted, trial by jury was abolished, and a rigid censorship of the press was imposed. The king was further removed from the will of the nation, surrounded by a military and civil bureaucracy which aimed to stimulate a fear of republican institutions rather than to reconvert the people to the cause of monarchy. The liberal propaganda was still ignored and the government appeared indifferent to the reality of its problems.[3]

[1] Madariaga, 282-285; Salvador Canals, *La caída de la monarquía. Problemas de la república. Instalación de un régimen.* Madrid, 1931. 12, 28.
[2] *The Times*, March 20, 1930.
[3] *El Sol*, May 21, 1931.

The Republicans were incited to greater activity by the suspension of the constitutional guarantees. They rallied their scattered forces to demand a constituent *cortes* that would reëstablish the individual guarantees and amend the constitution to prevent a recurrence of military rule. The dictatorial efforts at reform were vain. A civilian ministry was inaugurated in December 1925, and martial law was abolished. In 1926 a National Assembly was convoked in an effort to reëstablish the form of representative government and quiet the opposition with the elaboration of a new constitution.[4] Every effort was made to restore the material prosperity of the country and modernize Spain. Highways, dispensaries, and hospitals were constructed. Projects for electrification, irrigation, and sanitation were undertaken. Production was stimulated to such an extent that it became necessary to control it in the national interest. The Madrid University City was founded, more than four thousand new schools were opened, and many new public buildings were erected.[5]

The financing of the nationalist program was accomplished by exploiting the economic resources of the state through monopolies, by pressure against tax evasion, by raising tariffs and taxation, and by borrowing from foreign banks. In the end, however, the financial question was an important factor in weakening the monarchy, and the fall of the *peseta* was a cause of the Revolution of 1931. The damage to the essential Spanish credit abroad which was attributed to foreign interests antagonized by the oil monopoly; the accumulation of a heavy debt to carry the burden of the public works program; the continued deficit in the balance of trade; and the declining confidence in the dictatorial policy in regard to monopolies and corporations undermined the *peseta*. It was weak in 1926 and fell to thirty-nine to the pound sterling, the lowest point it had reached since the Spanish-American War. The financial crisis led some of Primo de Rivera's advisers, including Calvo Sotelo, Minister of Finance, to urge the dictator

[4] Young, 95-96.
[5] *Ibid.*, 97-99.

to convoke a *cortes*. When the latter refused, Calvo Sotelo resigned.[6]

Probably the fundamental cause of the failure of Primo de Rivera lay in his inability to build a strong personal party in Spain. He used the military forces in his *coup d'état*. Then, he sought to emulate his Italian model and created the Patriotic Union. This effort, however, was made after his *coup d'état* rather than before it. The Patriotic Union never became an effective political party, Although it supplied the representatives for the Consultative Assembly and enjoyed the fruits of the dictatorial patronage, this procedure only aroused antagonism by substituting a new form of partisanship for the old corruption. His attempt to silence opposition by the proclamation of martial law had already arrayed many intellectuals and liberals against him. His clerical policy alienated others who had hitherto supported the monarchy. He closed the military colleges and came into conflict with many of the younger officers. The attempt to grant the Augustinians and the Jesuits the right of bestowing degrees equivalent to those of the universities aroused the students of the University of Madrid, and the agitation spread throughout Spain.[7]

At last Primo de Rivera lost the confidence of Alfonso XIII. The king refused to permit the new constitution which the National Assembly had formulated to be imposed on the nation. The dictator, therefore, resorted to an appeal to the army through its commanding officers for a vote of confidence. There was no reply. Alfonso called for Primo de Rivera's resignation.[8] The principal contribution of the Directory in undermining the monarchy was that it aroused resentment against the person of the King.[9] The latter had sworn to uphold the Constitution of 1876, and when he permitted Primo de Rivera to rule Spain without the constitution, the continuity was broken. The Republicans placed the

[6] *Ibid.*, 99, 105.
[7] *Ibid.*, 102-103.
[8] *Ibid.*, 106.
[9] *El Sol*, July 3, 1931.

responsibility upon the King, who was no longer able to protect himself behind a ministerial camouflage.

General Berenguer and Admiral Aznar, the successors of the dictator, faced the difficulty of restoring the constitutional guarantees and liquidating the dictatorship. In the face of the clamor for constitutional revision and radical propaganda they were unable to find a solution for their problem and were forced into an unfortunate inconsistency. They continued the suspension of the civil liberties while they relaxed those measures of vigilance which would curb the activity of the Republicans and Socialists. In the summer of 1930, the latter were able to organize their plan for concerted action in the establishment of a republic without hindrance from the government. Its half-hearted efforts to handle the situation merely contributed to the stimulation of greater republican activity.

The continuation of the economic crisis heightened the discontent. The *peseta* continued to fall in the international exchange and the government was unable to stabilize it. The middle class became dissatisfied, and proletarian agitation became more intense as a result of the increased cost of living. The cost for an equivalent standard of living rose from four *pesetas* a day in 1920 to 7.20 *pesetas* in 1931.[10] The Socialists had been accused of collaboration with the dictator because they had accepted the unemployment legislation. Their leaders had traveled incessantly through the country, ostensibly to educate the working class to the advantages of the *comités paritarios,* but in reality to organize the workers and incite them to revolutionary sentiment against the monarchy.[11] The greater part of the working class was converted to republicanism and socialism with the assistance of Primo de Rivera and his successors.

An eventful union of all of the republican elements was effected in the Hotel de Londrés, in San Sebastian, on August 17, 1930, and the coöperation of the parties opposing the

[10] *Ibid.,* April 11, July 31, 1931.
[11] Canals, 33; *El Sol,* July 21, 1931.

monarchy was guaranteed. The Pact of San Sebastian included three fundamental points. The Republicans agreed to compromise their differences and establish the republic, by revolution if necessary. Religious liberty and civil rights were to be guaranteed. The right of the regions to frame political and administrative statutes and submit them to the representatives of the nation was recognized. The government was aware of the preliminary meeting but did nothing to prevent the reunion in the afternoon. All of the principal republican leaders were there: Alcalá Zamora, Alejandro Lerroux, Alvaro Albornoz, Miguel Maura, Marcelino Domingo, Sánchez Román, three representatives of the Catalan Republicans, and the Socialist, Indalecio Prieto. The various forces which had been striving to establish the republic were reconciled and, however ambigous the understanding appeared in the light of later interpretations, simultaneous and disciplined action in the whole country was assured.[12]

The immediate result of the Pact of San Sebastian was the organization of the revolutionary committee by the Republicans. Committees of action were established throughout the country in order to enlist the forces of civil and military discontent. Negotiations were opened with the Socialists almost immediately and they agreed to enter into a coalition which should endure until the convocation of a constituent *cortes*. It was further agreed that three Socialists should represent their party in the Provisional Government which would be established, namely, Fernando de los Ríos, Indalecio Prieto, and Largo Caballero. The campaign of organization and propaganda which had begun at a conference in the *Ateneo* at Madrid, May 30, 1930, was gradually assuming large proportions.[13]

Four months after the meeting at San Sebastian, two revolutionary attempts with the aid of the radical element in the army were undertaken. It was proposed that the revolu-

[12] Brandt, 372; Canals, 69, 71, 142-143; *El Sol,* October 6, 1931, contains an account of the meeting by one of the participants, Jaime Ayguáder y Miró.

[13] Brandt, 372; *El Sol,* May 3, 1931.

tionary officers in the garrison at Jaca and the air field at Cuatro Vientos should coöperate with the Socialists, who would incite a general strike at Madrid, thereby forcing the acceptance of the republic. The plans miscarried. The revolt at Jaca, December 12, was immediately localized and extinguished by the loyal part of the garrison and the civil elements which hastened from Madrid and Zaragoza. It was premature and poorly synchronized with the other elements in the revolutionary movement, but it was important because it created two martyrs for the republican cause, Captains Fermin Galán and Angel Garciá Hernández. They had led the rebels at Jaca and were tried by a military tribunal and shot. Their execution canonized their heroism in the hearts of the Republicans and aroused sympathy in liberal circles. The revolt of the air force at Cuatro Vientos was suppressed on December 15. The aeroplanes of the rebels soared over Madrid, scattering republican manifestoes, but the indifference of the people and the failure of the general strike to materialize revealed that the revolution by force was as yet premature. The leaders of Cuatro Vientos, however, were more fortunate than those of Jaca. Both General Queipo de Llano and Major Ramón Franco escaped to Portugal.[14]

The Republicans now conducted their revolutionary propaganda with greater intensity, particularly after the arrest of the revolutionary committee for the clandestine circulation of a bitter manifesto attacking the monarchy.[15] The Reformist leader, Melquiades Alvarez, who had been clamoring for constitutional reform, was joined by the liberal Count of Romanones in urging the King to convoke a constituent *cortes*. The Berenguer government had ordered the elections for such a body to be held early in January 1931, but they were postponed because of the necessity of revision of the electoral census following the constitutional hiatus during the seven-year period of the dictatorship. On Febru-

---

[14] Brandt, 374; Canals, 144-146; *New York Times*, December 13, 15, 16, 1930; *El Sol*, October 6, 1931.

[15] *New York Times*, December 18, 1930; Brandt, 374.

ary 7 the elections were arranged, the municipal and provincial elections on March 1, and the selection of the *cortes* on May 15.[16] The constitutional guarantees were also reestablished in an effort to provide a free and impartial election without governmental interference.[17]

Ten days later the Berenguer government resigned. It had continued the dictatorial policies in a vacillating fashion that had really contributed to the political ferment. Vain attempts had been made to silence the revolutionary agitation, and the universities had been suspended to maintain order during the elections. During the latter part of January the university students had declared a strike and incited riots.[18]

José Sánchez Guerra was asked to form a cabinet. He was a former Conservative whose declaration for the republican cause had been given wide publicity. He failed to form a government, however, because the Socialists and Republicans refused to coöperate. A coalition ministry was then formed by Admiral Aznar. He immediately assured the country that a constituent *cortes* would be convoked before summer. On February 23 it was decided to celebrate the municipal elections on April 12.[19] The die was cast. The convocation of the elections and the *cortes* was a belated gesture by the monarchy which did not realize how deeply the revolutionary and antimonarchist sentiment was rooted in the country. The Republicans, however, were given an opportunity to capitalize their activity in a peaceful manner, in elections that were held to be equivalent to a national referendum on the question of monarchy or republic.

A feverish campaign ensued. The Socialists declared that they would not participate in the general elections for the *cortes* but would vote in the municipal elections. This represented the triumph of Prieto, De los Ríos, and Largo Cabal-

[16] *New York Times,* October 17, November 11, December 30, 1930, February 5, 6, 1931; Brandt, 374.

[17] José Gutiérrez-Ravé, *España en 1931. Anuario.* Madrid, 1932. 28-31.

[18] *New York Times,* January 30, February 5, 15, 1931.

[19] Brandt, 375; Gutiérrez-Ravé, 43-44.

lero. Besteiro, Saborit, and Ovejero resigned from the national committee because they favored an opposed policy.[20] The monarchists urged the electorate to support the King, religion, and country, playing on the middle class fear of radicalism, possible disorder, and revolution. They relied mainly upon the support of the conservative forces that were so deeply entrenched in the country. They also directed appeals to the women of Spain as a conservative force of considerable influence.[21] The Republicans refuted the charges of the Monarchists and focused their attack on the King, emphasizing the necessity of a change of régime. The day before the elections Alcalá Zamora declared:

We are going to establish the republic, through the elections or through force, by the legal way or, if that way is closed, by revolution. The revolution which is affected must not retain social injustices but correct them slowly, with serenity. . . .[22]

The Reformists, as the moderate element, insisted on the convocation of the constituent *cortes* in order to decide through an impartial election the régime that should prevail in Spain.[23]

The campaign was complicated by the trial of the revolutionary leaders in the latter part of March and the demand for the pardon of political prisoners. The trial of the members of the revolutionary committee excited great interest. Despite their defense by such eminent jurists as Victoria Kent, Angel Ossorio y Gallardo, Bergamín, Sánchez Román, and Jiménez de Asúa, they were convicted of inciting military rebellion and were sentenced to six months and a day in prison. On the following day, however, the sentence was suspended for three years and the prisoners left the Model Jail amid the plaudits of their enthusiastic partisans.[24]

The result of the municipal elections was a great surprise to the Monarchists. Although they had assigned them a

[20] Gutiérrez-Ravé, 44-45.
[21] *ABC*, April 1, 4, 7, 1931; *New York Times,* March 25, 1931.
[22] *El Sol,* April 11, 1931.
[23] *Ibid.,* April 10, 1931.
[24] Gutiérrez-Ravé, 63-73.

plebiscitary value they were unacquainted with the real intensity of public feeling. There were 150,000 candidates for the 80,280 seats on the 8,943 municipal councils. The official returns on April 14 gave the Monarchists 22,150 seats and the Republican-Socialist Coalition 5,875. The latter, however, had concentrated their energy in the larger cities, where their propaganda had revealed its effectiveness in a surprising victory. In Madrid, thirty Republicans were elected and only twenty Monarchists. Alcalá Zamora, the ex-Liberal, received the largest vote in that city, 12,275 to 6,299 for the leading monarchist candidate. In Barcelona, the *Lliga Regionalista* was defeated by Colonel Maciá's Catalan Left party.[25] The returns from Santander, the summer home of the King, gave the Republicans twenty-six seats to thirteen for the Monarchists. The latter amassed their greater number of seats in the less populous and more conservative rural sections where *caciquismo* played an important rôle in any election.

The Republicans had won a greater victory than even they had anticipated. *ABC* declared that the anti-monarchist victory in Madrid was not surprising. Their triumph, however, had been more overwhelming than expected because many electors who had not figured in the official party organizations had voted against the King.[26] Many people, ordinarily inclined toward the monarchy, voted against those who swore that a republican victory would be followed by assaults on the banks and the disappearance of the family. This was a reaction to the ill-conceived campaign of fear employed by the Monarchists. The deciding factor in the election was the neutral element which voted against the existing régime rather than for the republic. The most impressive result was the intense interest of the electorate in the issue placed before it. Eighty-five per cent of the voters of Spain went to the polls on April 12.[27]

[25] Brandt, 376; *El Sol*, April 14, 1931; *ABC*, April 14, 1931; Gutiérrez-Ravé, 97-99.

[26] *ABC*, April 14, 1931.

[27] *El Sol*, April 14, May 27, 1931.

The Count of Romanones, an intimate adviser of the King and a member of the Aznar government, declared in an interview:

The result of the election could not be more deplorable for us, the Monarchists. . . . They have at this very moment lost thirty-five provincial capitals. The defeat has been so general that it can be credited neither to the experience of the governors nor to the lack of organization of the loyal forces nor to fortuitous and external circumstances. Eight years have finally exploded.[28]

El Sol was jubilant over the decisive victory of the Republicans. Its expression was prophetic of the policy immediately adopted by the victors.

The will of the nation has manifested itself at the polls. This is the fact which is revealed and made evident to the governors. Not even Admiral Aznar has dared deprecate the incontrovertible strength of the figures.[29]

The Republicans and Socialists issued an official note as soon as the returns were sufficiently conclusive.

The vote of the Spanish capitals and principal urban centers has had the value of a plebiscite unfavorable to the monarchy, favorable to the republic. It has achieved the dimensions of a verdict of guilt against the royal government. All of the social classes of the country have collaborated in the formation of this adverse judgment.[30]

It was necessary, therefore, for Spaniards to submit to the national will, which could not be interpreted by silence or by the rural vote.

The afternoon of April 13 was filled with rumors. The cabinet assembled and was unable to agree on the best course of action to be followed, although the ministers denied that Alfonso would abdicate. The Basque city of Eibar, small but industrial, proclaimed the Republic on the morning of April 14. By noon of that day it had been proclaimed in Zaragoza, Asturias, Seville, Valencia, and Barcelona. Alfonso continued

[28] *ABC*, April 14, 1931; Gutiérrez-Ravé, 99.
[29] *El Sol*, April 14, 1931.
[30] *ABC*, April 14, 1931; Gutiérrez-Ravé, 101.

to confer with representatives of all parties. In the afternoon coaches with red and republican banners passed through the streets of Madrid, while placards alluding to the victory and pictures of Galán and García Hernández, the martyrs of Jaca, were carried through the capital.[31]

While the republican crowds were demontsrating in the streets, the decisive interview between the Count of Romanones and Alcalá Zamora was held to decide the fate of the monarchy. They met in the home of Dr. Gregorio Marañón, who acted as the intermediary. The object of the interview was to arrange the transmission of power from the monarchy to the republic. Both parties wished to avoid violence and bloodshed. Romanones had declared in a cabinet meeting that force of arms was useless against the moral force of the vote. Romanones did all that he could to conciliate the Republicans and save the monarchy. He had already advised Alfonso, who was hesitant and indecisive in the crisis, that he should leave Spain. The King had asked him to ascertain the true situation and the plans of the Republicans.[32]

Alcalá Zamora declared that the salvation of Spain required the immediate departure of Alfonso because the republic would be proclaimed before sunset. It might be difficult to restrain the people if they were not advised of the course to be followed. Romanones asked for an extension of time in order to effect the transmission of powers, but Alcalá Zamora insisted. Finally the Count of Romanones realized that further discussion was useless and promised to give a true account of all he had heard to the King and the cabinet.[33]

Romanones then returned to the palace to report to Alfonso, who desired to abdicate in favor of the *infante,* Don Carlos. It was too late for this. A year earlier such a gesture might have been possible if it had been accompanied by constitutional reform.

[31] *El Sol,* April 14, May 17, 1931; *ABC,* April 15, 1931.
[32] The events of this interview are related by the three participants: Marañón, *El Sol,* May 23, 1931; Alcalá Zamora, *El Sol,* May 17, 1931; Romanones, *El Sol,* June 4, 1931.
[33] *Ibid.*

Meanwhile the *concejales,* accompanied by their enthusiastic friends, had taken over the Madrid *ayuntamiento.* Alfonso's picture had been removed from the salon and replaced by a picture of Alcalá Zamora. Crowds gathered in the streets, advanced on the *Plaza de Oriente,* and invaded the *Puerta del Sol.* A red banner was raised on the Palace of Communications. A vain attempt was now made to reach Alcalá Zamora and get him to control the anxiety of the crowd. The ministers discussed the idea of declaring martial law and thereby gaining time for the departure of the royal family. It was abandoned only when it was found that it could not be executed.[34]

Eight members of the revolutionary directory had gathered in the home of Miguel Maura and decided to take possession of the government. The transmission of power had been agreed upon five hours before. They now proceeded to the Ministry of Government in two cars. It took them a half an hour to pass through the enthusiastic masses of people. The closed doors of the ministry were finally opened to them and the Provisional Government of the Republic established itself. Orders were issued to the provinces, notifying their authorities of the constitution of the new government, and a decree was directed to the people.

The Provisional Government of the Spanish Republic has the absolute security that the social and political forces which have cooperated in the establishment of the new régime will maintain themselves in the most absolute discipline. On that depends the prestige and fortune of the republic.[35]

A decree of full amnesty for all political crimes was also issued, a step necessary to enable the political exiles to return to Spain. Maura then addressed the crowds in the *Puerta del Sol* and Alcalá Zamora addressed the nation over the radio, announcing the advent of the republican régime and asking for the confidence of the people and the maintenance of order. At eleven o'clock the members of the new government

[34] *El Sol,* June 5, 1931; *ABC,* April 15, 1931.
[35] *El Sol,* May 17, 1931; *ABC,* April 15, 1931. Gutiérrez-Ravé, 106.

withdrew. The republic had been established without blood-shed.[36]

Alfonso XIII, meanwhile, had bowed to the inevitable. Resistance would have produced a civil war. He wrote his last manifesto, the publication of which was withheld until the royal family had safely left Spain. Alfonso chose Cartagena as the place of embarcation and all arrangements were con-cluded. He departed immediately, leaving his family to fol-low the next morning. It was an historic moment. The antechamber was crowded with courtiers who had been used to daily contact with their sovereign and favors from him. They were disappointed because the government had not resorted to force to save their King. At the same time the clamor of the people cheering the placards, the pictures of Galán and Hernández, and the banners of the republic re-sounded outside in the streets. Not until then did Alfonso come to a full realization of the real sentiment of the people. He sadly declared, "Many did not vote for the republic, they voted against me." At eight-thirty on the evening of April 14, Alfonso left the palace with his companions and drove to Cartagena, passing into exile.[37]

The royal manifesto to the people was published in *ABC* on April 17.

The elections celebrated on Sunday reveal clearly to me that I no longer have the affection of my people. My conscience tells me that that indifference will not be enduring, because I have always tried to serve Spain. My only solicitude has been the public inter-est, even in the most serious crises.

A king can be mistaken and undoubtedly I have erred at times, but I well know that our country has always been generous toward my unintentional misdemeanors.

I am the King of all Spaniards. I am also a Spaniard. I could find sufficient means to maintain my prerogatives in effective struggle with those who oppose me. Resolutely, however, it is my desire to desist from anything that may involve compatriots against

[36] *El Sol,* June 5 ,1931; *ABC,* April 15, 1931.
[37] *ABC,* April 15, 1931; *El Sol,* June 15, 1931.

each other in fratricidal civil war. I do not renounce any of my rights because they are not my own but a trust historically acquired, for the custody of which I must give a rigorous account some day.

I expect to know the authentic and complete expression of the national conscience. Until the nation speaks I deliberately suspend the exercise of the royal power and leave Spain, recognizing her as the only mistress of my destinies.

I believe that I fulfil the duty which my love for my country dictates to me. I pray that the rest of the Spaniards may feel it and heed it as deeply as I do.[38]

This was the last document of Alfonso as King of Spain. It was a magnificent gesture, but the destiny of Spain had passed into other hands, whose ideal was constitutional and democratic government. The last of the Bourbons had fled.

[38] *ABC*, April 17, 1931; Gutiérrez-Ravé, 117-118.

VI

THE PROVISIONAL GOVERNMENT
Leaders and Policies

THE PROVISIONAL Government of the Second Spanish Republic was formally organized on April 14, immediately after the republican and socialist leaders had taken possession of the Ministry of Government. In reality, it had been constituted since the Pact of San Sebastian and the adhesion of the Socialists to the republican cause had created the revolutionary directory. The leaders had conducted the campaign for the municipal elections from the Model Prison or exile and emerged to become the rulers of Spain.

As soon as the revolutionary committee had taken over the government it issued a decree nominating Alcalá Zamora as its provisional president.

Interpreting the unequivocal desire of the nation, the committee of the allied political forces for the establishment of the new régime designates Don Niceto Alcalá Zamora y Torres for the office of President of the Provisional Government of the republic.[1]

Alcalá Zamora was an experienced politician who had declared himself a Republican on April 14, 1930, in Valencia. Born in Priego, a small village in Córdoba, in 1877, he had studied law in Granada and Madrid. At the age of twenty-two he entered the *Consejo de Estado* and in 1905 became a deputy, distinguishing himself in the *cortes* as an orator of great eloquence. He was a member of the Liberal Party and became a subsecretary of Government, but withdrew from the party of Romanones and joined the Liberal Democratic faction of García Prieto. His reputation for skill in oratory

---

[1] Marcelo Martínez-Alcubilla, *Boletín jurídico-administrativo. Anuario de legislacion y jurisprudencia. Apendice de 1931.* Madrid, 1931. 260.

and profundity in debate won him portfolios in the governments of 1917 and December 1922. He became a resolute opponent of the dictatorship and was one of the leaders of the revolutionary directory. His enthusiasm and energy were important factors in making the establishment of the new régime possible.[2]

The provisional president declared the Aznar government at an end and appointed his cabinet, which included the following:

Minister of State	Alejandro Lerroux y García
Minister of Justice	Fernando de los Ríos Urruiti
Minister of War	Manuel Azaña Díaz
Minister of Marine	Santiago Casares Quiroga
Minister of Government	Miguel Maura y Gamazo
Minister of Public Works	Alvaro Albornoz y Liminiana
Minister of Public Instruction and Fine Arts	Marcelino Domingo Sanjuán
Minister of Finance	Indalecio Prieto Tuero
Minister of Economy	Luis Nicoláu D'Olwer
Minister of Labor	Francisco Largo Caballero[3]

Other decrees created and organized the Ministry of Communications, and Diego Martínez Barrios was chosen to fill the new portfolio.

Most of these men were successful politicians before the advent of the dictatorship. Lerroux was probably the most experienced of them all. He was born in La Rambla, Córdoba, in 1864, and was the oldest man in the new cabinet. Instead of entering the army, as his father desired, he had become a Republican and moved to Madrid. He had a varied career as a journalist and had moved to Barcelona, where he had opposed the resurgence of Catalan nationalism. He had been elected to the *cortes* in 1901, and was the founder of the Radical Party in 1906, after his break with Salmerón's Re-

---

[2] Carlos Primelles, José L. Barberán, and B. de Montenegro, *Los hombres que trajeron la república. De la carcel a la presidencia. Como acabó un reinado.* Madrid, n.d. 29-33.

[3] Martínez-Alcubilla, 260-261.

publican Union. Although forced at one time to seek exile in Argentina, he had returned to become a deputy for Barcelona. During the dictatorship he engaged actively in an anti-dynastic campaign and, as a result, had been arrested and prosecuted until the Second Republic was established.[4]

Other members of the Provisional Government had also been active in various professions and were experienced politicians and propagandists. They were all at the height of their powers. Their ages varied from forty-seven to fifty-two. Domingo, Prieto, Albornoz, De los Ríos, Largo Caballero, and Maura had served as deputies. All were Republicans except the three socialist representatives, Prieto, De los Ríos, and Largo Caballero. Miguel Maura was the son of Antonio Maura, the leader of the Conservatives, but had become a Republican in 1925, and had been a sharp critic of the dictator.

The group included some of the ablest propagandists in Spain, and Casares Quiroga, De los Ríos, Maura, and Albornoz had achieved some reputation as lawyers. The others were either men of letters or journalists. Marcelino Domingo was a dramatist and Azaña had won the National Prize for Literature in 1926. Their approach toward politics was, in some respects, more intellectual in its idealism than purely practical, although their skill in oratory and ability to sway the electorate indicated that they were well acquainted with the methods necessary to gain the votes and support of the Spanish people. Most of them were university graduates and heirs of the liberal educational activity that had followed the Restoration. Casares Quiroga was a member of the Republican Union founded by Salmerón. Fernando de los Ríos was a professor of law. A nephew of Francisco Giner de Los Ríos, he had taught for a time in the *Institución Libre de Enseñanza*. He had traveled extensively in Europe while a student in Germany, pensioned by the *Junta para Ampliación de Estudios*. In 1920 he had gone to Russia to study the Bolshevik régime and returned to write a book on his reactions.

[4] Primelles *et al.*, 34-37.

He was opposed to the union of Spanish socialism with international communism. Azaña had also been sent abroad as a student by the *Junta para Ampliación de Estudios*.[5]

It is evident that the members of the Provisional Government were men of maturity and experience. They had risen from the ranks of their various parties by their own merit. Now, as successful revolutionists, they faced the difficult task of solving the problems which had created unrest in Spain and which the monarchy had ignored. They had to reconstruct the Spanish political system after the period of the dictatorship. Their problem was that of consolidating the republic. They had to rebuild the political system of Spain on a tentative basis while awaiting the expression of the will of the people through their representatives in a constituent *cortes*. They had to maintain discipline in the ranks of their own parties and continue the victorious coalition. They had to defend their position against the attack of the conservative forces, which had dominated Spain for the last century, and the extremists of the Left. The latter employed the anarchistic methods of direct action in their impatience to obtain their demands and disrupt the ranks of their rivals. The *de facto* position of the new government rendered it vulnerable to attacks from both extremes, but it had to maintain that position until the *cortes* had framed a republican constitution. It was necessary to solve the problem of modernizing a medieval state. The conservative opposition was disorganized as a result of the elections, but it was deeply rooted in tradition. In the use of their methods of direct action the Anarchists placed themselves without the law. They had to be restrained in the interest of order. These considerations must be kept in mind in any evaluation of the work of the new government or any attempt to understand the vicissitudes of the republican régime in Spain.

On April 15, the ministers issued the Juridical Statute of the Provisional Government in an effort to justify their position and explain their aims to the Spanish people.

[5] *Ibid., passim.*

The Provisional Government of the Republic, on receiving its powers from the national will, fulfils an imperious political duty in assuring Spain that the coalition represented by this government does not respond to the mere negative coincidence of liberating our country from the old oppressive structure of the monarchical régime, but to the positive convergence of affirming the necessity of establishing as the base of the organization of the state, a network of norms of justice necessary and desired by the country.[6]

They declared that although they regarded their position as transitory they would exercise the sovereign powers of the state, and accepted the high and delicate mission of establishing themselves as a government of full powers. The basis of this statute indicated the judicial norms conditioning their activity and the principles which inspired their decrees.

They would submit their collective and individual work to a constituent *cortes* for its approval. Their first task in the defense of the public interest was the investigation of the responsibility of the monarchy, especially in the period of the dictatorship and in regard to the dissolution of the *cortes* in 1923. The work of the old régime in official, civil, and military affairs had to be revised, lest prevarication and arbitrary action, which had become habitual, should be consecrated. Complete liberty of conscience was guaranteed and the state would at no time demand that a citizen reveal his religious convictions. Personal liberty was recognized and the new government promised to protect the rights of citizens which were inherent in a constitutional régime. In addition, recognition was granted to both syndical and corporate personality. Private property was also guaranteed by law, and no expropriation would be undertaken except for public utility and with indemnization.

But this government, sensible to the absolute abandonment in which the immense Spanish peasant mass has lived, to the lack of interest of which the agrarian economy of the country has been the object, and to the incongruity of the law which orders it with the principles which inspire and must inspire the actual legislation,

[6] Martínez-Alcubilla, 261-262.

adopts as a norm of its activity the recognition that agrarian law must respond to the social function of the land.[7]

The Provisional Government would be guilty of a real crime if it abandoned the nascent republic to those who from their strong secular position and using their names, might render its consolidation difficult. Therefore, personal liberty and the rights of citizens would be submitted temporarily to governmental discretion, for the use of which it would give a circumstantial account to the Constituent Cortes.[8]

By this statute the Provisional Government invested itself with the authority to govern Spain for the next three months. It was demonstrated on April 12 that the republic had the support of the people of Spain. Twelve days later, it had been officially recognized by every power in the world except Japan and the Vatican.[9] It had already set about its task.

The first urgent need was the reorganization of various branches of the government. On April 15 the permanent part of the senate, provided in the Constitution of 1876, was dissolved and the ex-senators were deprived of their special rights. The Council of State was also dissolved and a councilor of state was assigned to each department. Later, the *Cuerpo de Seguridad* was reorganized and a body of local police was provided for the maintenance of order.[10]

Meanwhile the ministers had agreed on the method of revising the legislative work of the dictatorship. It was to be effected by the various departments. Some decrees were annulled without prejudice to the legal or judicial situations already created; some were totally annulled and their consequences invalidated; while others were modified or continued in their original form.[11] The *somatenes*, modeled after the Catalan institution, had been extended to all Spain by the dictator. They consisted of civilian volunteers organized for

[7] *Ibid.*, 262.
[8] *Ibid.*
[9] *New York Times*, April 24, 1931.
[10] Martínez-Alcubilla, 260-261.
[11] *Ibid.*, 374; *ABC*, April 17, 1931; *El Sol*, June 16, 1931.

the "defense of the fundamental interests of society." These were now dissolved because the Provisional Government sought to establish a new order of society. They were continued only in Catalonia, out of respect for the traditions of that region.[12] All services, contracts, and monopolies were subjected to a thorough examination to ascertain whether they were contrary to the interests of the state. The Code of 1928 and the penal laws of the dictatorship were annulled, while the Common Penal Code of 1870 was reformed and all passages referring to the king and the royal government or defining the crime of rebellion were struck out. On April 27 a decree provided for the reëstablishment of juries.[13]

The assessment of responsibility for the Annual disaster and the arbitrary measures of the dictatorship was another important task. This included not only the responsibility for the summary judgment which led to the execution of Galán and Hernández, but also the policies and conduct of those who served the dictator. The revision of the trials of Jaca and Huesca was begun, the mother of Galán and the widow and daughter of Hernández were awarded pensions, and legal processes were instituted to determine the extent of responsibility. Final decisions were reserved for the Constituent Cortes, but an attempt was made to keep those suspected of being responsible from seeking a haven in a foreign land.[14]

An effort was made to obliterate every vestige of the monarchist régime. The names of three warships were changed, and it was proposed to rename many of the streets of Madrid. Thus, the *Plaza de Oriente* was to be replaced by the *Plaza de la República* and the *Plaza del Rey* by the *Plaza de García Hernández*.[15] The Ministry of Grace and Justice became the Ministry of Justice, and the names of all organizations reflecting dependence or subordination to the monarchy were changed. The Provisional Government took over all property

[12] *ABC*, March 18, 1930; Martínez-Alcubilla, **263-264**.
[13] Martínez-Alcubilla, 264-269, 885.
[14] *Ibid.*, 263; *ABC*, April 30, 1931.
[15] *ABC*, April 28, 1931.

belonging to the crown, and commissions were constituted to effect the change in ownership. The rents were reserved to the public treasury. The *Casa de Campo* and *Casa de Moro* were given to the *ayuntamiento* of Madrid, destined as parks or for recreation and instruction, while the Alcázar was turned over to Seville and the Royal Palace of Pedralbes to Barcelona. These properties were all exempt from taxation. Likewise the concession and succession of titles of nobility were suppressed and various decrees to prevent the destruction of the artistic and cultural patrimony or its expatriation were issued.[16]

The tricolor of red, yellow, and dark violet was chosen as the national banner of the republic on April 27, and measures were adopted which would serve to stir enthusiastic fervor for the new régime and start traditions which would develop a cult of patriotism. April 15 was declared a national holiday for 1931, but in succeeding years the celebration was ordered held on the anniversary of the accession of the Provisional Government to power. May 1 was also declared a national holiday and the new government discouraged homage from its enthusiastic supporters. The *ayuntamientos* of Jaca and Eibar were each granted the title of *"Muy Ejemplar Ciudad"* as a reward for their patriotism in being the first to heed the verdict of the people on April 12 and proclaim the new form of government. Finally, the Hymn of Riego was substituted for the Royal March.[17]

The republican government immediately launched an attack on the principal supports of the old régime, the army, the Church, and the landed aristocracy. The measures approved were sweeping and, although subject to the approval or modification by the *cortes* when it assembled, were definite steps toward the consolidation of the republic and the constitution that was to be drafted. The men who promulgated these decrees were the leaders of the parties which were to dominate the Constituent Cortes.

[16] Martínez-Alcubilla, 301, 279-281, 361-363.
[17] *Ibid.*, 301, 263, 264, 266; *ABC*, April 28, 1931.

The personnel of the army was subjected to a drastic reorganization and restriction of its former power. The change
of the name of the Ministry of Army to the Ministry of War
was significant of the reforms that were to follow and indicate
the subordination of the power of the army to its primary
function in the state. According to Manuel Azaña, the reforms
had two aims, efficiency and rigid economy.[18] The old *ley de
jurisdicciones* was annulled and the military orders of Santiago, Calatrava, and Alcántara and Montesa, rich in ancient
tradition and landed wealth, were suppressed.[19] Some twenty-
two thousand officers were given the opportunity to retire on
full pay and the admission of new students to the military
academy of Zaragoza was suspended. Within two months some
225 colonels had asked for retirement under the first decree.
The rank and file of the army was drastically reduced when
the suppression of thirty-seven regiments of infantry, seventeen regiments of cavalry, and other regiments and battalions
was ordered.[20] By the middle of June, the power of the army
to intervene in the civil affairs of the state by a *golpe de
estado* was dealt a severe blow. The offices of captain-general
and lieutenant-general were abolished and the divisional
general became the ranking officer in the army of the republic.[21] The effect of the reduction in the official ranks of
the army was that the thirty-four divisional commands were
reduced to nine, the number of colonels was reduced by a
ratio of ten to one, and the number of majors from 3,104 to
387.[22] In addition, the Ministry of War was thoroughly reorganized by a decree of July 3.[23]

The navy had never gained the influence in the civil life
of the nation that the position of the army in the offices of
the military governors and as civil advisers in times of internal
distraction had given it. Now, however, the members of the

[18] Martínez-Alcubilla, 260; *El Sol,* April 23, 1931.
[19] Martínez-Alcubilla, 268, 271.
[20] *Ibid.,* 291-292; *El Sol,* May 26, 1931.
[21] Martínez-Alcubilla, 500-501; *El Sol,* June 17, 1931; *ABC,* June 17, 1931.
[22] *The Times,* June 27, 1931.
[23] Martínez-Alcubilla, 507.

navy were required to take a promise of loyalty to the Republic, to swear to obey its laws and defend it. All those who did not give this assurance were permitted to retire, for only those might "serve in places of confidence" who accepted the new régime. This did not prevent mutinies on several warships, but the outbreaks were suppressed.[24]

The cabinet had already tackled the religious issue. On April 17 it ordered the governors of the provinces to refrain from attending any religious services and provided for voluntary attendance on the part of the army.[25] The next day Maura declared that the separation of Church and state was a primary aim of the new régime and, on May 22, complete religious liberty was decreed in Spain.

> All the confessions are authorized for the public and private exercise of their cults, without other limitations than those imposed by the regulations and law of public order.[26]

The Catholics protested the separation of Church and state but the real issue in the matter was left to the decision of *cortes*.[27] The Provisional Government was primarily interested, for the moment, in the exclusion of the Church from political interference. The Church had been an ally of the monarchy and it was necessary to remove it from the sphere of politics in the approaching elections. This had to be done without arousing the Catholics to united action by any direct assault on the Church itself. Maura recognized this when he declared:

> . . . there exists an enormous Catholic conscience which thinks and feels Catholic and which lacks all comprehension for the two parts. Let us not disillusion ourselves. In Spain, for a long time, one will be able to govern without the Catholics, but one will not be able to govern by attacking the conscience of the Catholics.[28]

[24] *Ibid.*, 305; *ABC*, April 24, 1931; *New York Times*, May 9, 14, 1931.

[25] *New York Times*, April 18, 1931; Martínez-Alcubilla, 267.

[26] *El Sol*, May 23, 1931; Martínez-Alcubilla, 364; *New York Times*, April 19, 1931.

[27] *ABC*, June 13, 1931.

[28] *El Sol*, June 16, 1931.

A complicating factor in the religious controversy arose from the expulsion of Cardinal Segura y Saenz. Early in May he issued an appeal to the electorate, urging all good Catholics to elect deputies who would defend the Church. Aroused by the extremist attacks on convents in various Spanish cities, he had reported to the Vatican that the Provisional Government had not tried to protect the property of the Church. He also issued a statement censuring the government for its attitude in the riots and warned it against any attack on the Church or any act without an understanding with the Holy See. As a result, he was officially expelled from the country. Mgr. Tedeschini, the Papal Nuncio at Madrid, protested, and the cabinet issued a note explaining the matter, but refused to reconsider its decree of expulsion, declaring that it had acted in the interest of the public peace and of the Church.[29] The Catholics, however, were aroused by this act and began to organize in defense of their interests. Catholic Action appeared as a conservative party.

Clamor for educational reform had been continuous since the Republic of 1873, and the work of some of the pioneer liberal educators has already been noted. The Republicans now had the opportunity to reorganize the educational system of Spain according to their own theories. Accordingly, early in May the Council of Public Instruction was reorganized and obligatory religious instruction in the schools was abolished. Parents desiring religious instruction for their children, however, were granted the right to prescribe it. The local and provincial *juntas* of primary instruction were suppressed and replaced by councils.[30] Then a decree of June 23 created seven thousand new places for teachers in the national schools, each endowed with five thousand *pesetas*. Marcelino Domingo was interested in establishing equality in education by opening the universities to the rich and poor alike. He advocated a unified school system from the primary grades to

[29] *Ibid.*, June 17, 18, 1931; *New York Times*, May 7, 14, June 12, 16, 17, 18, 1931.

[30] Martínez-Alcubilla, 288, 319, 331, *ABC*, May 5, 9, 1931.

the universities, open to all classes and protected by the state. Then, however humble a student might be, he would find the aid necessary for his education, and entrance to the schools would be based upon the selection of quality.[31]

In the latter part of April the dictatorial law which had prohibited the use of Catalan in the primary schools of Catalonia was abrogated and Catalan was ordered taught in the normal schools within the region.[32] This was a clear recognition of the regional identity of Catalonia and its resurgent nationalism, in accord with the Pact of San Sebastian. Relations between the Provisional Government and the *Generalitat* were cordial. Official visits were exchanged and the Catalans had begun to draft their regional statute for submission to the people and presentation to the *cortes.*

Social problems involved in the question of agrarian reform and the demands of industrial labor were perhaps the most serious that confronted the new government. The rivalry of the socialist and syndicalist unions caused a great deal of disorder. The existence and stability of the new government depended upon the maintenance of order and the protection of property. Its revolutionary usurpation of authority and earlier attacks on the arbitrary measures of the dictatorship led it into obvious inconsistencies. It was forced to choose either a vacillating policy of conciliation or a strong one of repression, which savored of the methods of a dictator. It happened that Miguel Maura was a determined man and he chose the latter course. *ABC* and *El Debate,* the Catholic periodical, were suspended for their attacks on the new régime.[33] Maura also tried to restrain disorderly extremists and preserve as delicate a balance between the fears of the conservatives and the radical demands of the extremists and Anarchists as was possible. His position was a difficult one because his countrymen were impatient.

An alarming aspect of the agrarian problem was the exodus

[31] *El Sol,* June 16, 24, 1931; Martínez-Alcubilla, 455.
[32] Martínez-Alcubilla, 319, 519.
[33] *New York Times,* May 1, 1931.

of the rural laborers to the city. Largo Caballero declared:

It is necessary that the government tackle this question and it is clear that only with dispositions favoring rural labor it may be resolved. Unemployed workers arrive constantly in Madrid from neighboring villages and believe that they may have occupation immediately.[34]

Some of the laborers presented their demands for agrarian legislation to Alcalá Zamora on May 1. Accident indemnization should be extended to agricultural labor, and *comités paritarios* for agriculture should be established. They demanded that existing laws be modified in order to guarantee the minimum duration of twenty years for the lease of land. Renters should be indemnified for improvements, and the rent should not be higher than the legal interest on the value declared to the treasury. Sub-renting should be prohibited, and lands which were left uncultivated for four years should be municipalized and rented to societies of workers for exploitation in common under the technical direction of the state. Hunting and grazing lands should be designated, and national agricultural credit with long-term amortization should be created.[35]

The Minister of Government explained the agrarian ideals of the Provisional Ministry in a campaign speech at Zamora on June 15. The proposed project of law should

. . . end the great *latifundios,* that may end the régime of property that exists today in rural life and which may give to the workers of the country the absolute security that they are working for themselves, on lands on which, in the measure that they wet them with the sweat of their brow, they fertilize them for themselves. That is the first task of the Constituent Cortes.

The land should be placed in the hands of those who tilled it, and the social function and right of property had to be established in Spain.[36]

The agrarian situation was attacked immediately. On

[34] *ABC,* April 28, 1931.
[35] *El Sol,* May 2, 1931.
[36] *Ibid.,* June 16, 1931.

April 28, the employers of agricultural labor were required to give preference to the day laborers of their neighborhoods, and early in May an attempt was made to increase the employment of labor and the production of the land. The municipal police were ordered to investigate uncultivated lands and dictate the norms for their use. Accident indemnization was extended to agricultural workers, a belated expansion of the law of 1900, based on information supplied by the Institute of Social Reforms. On May 21 a commission on agrarian reform was appointed by Largo Cabellero. It was to draft bases for reform which were to be presented to the Constituent Cortes and included two representatives of the National Federation of Workers of the Land and the professor of agriculture at the institute of Córdoba. The commission was divided into four divisions to facilitate its work: *latifundios,* credit and fiscal reform, the redemption of communal properties, and taxes.[37]

The demands of the industrial laborers were ~~also included~~ presented on Ma in the petition to Alcalá Zamora. The right of suffrage should be granted to all citizens over twenty-one, and an eight-hour day should be guaranteed by the appointment of laborers as inspectors. They demanded that the government make some attempt to solve the problems of unemployment and the high cost of living, recommending that cheap houses should be provided and social guarantees should be extended to workers of both sexes. The promotion of the development of cooperatives should be considered and necessary schools should be created. Finally, a law providing for the syndical control of industry should be promulgated. The provisional president promised the petitioners social justice.[38]

A more radical program was adopted by the Syndicalists of Barcelona:

1. The admission of fifteen per cent more workers into the factories in order to remedy the unemployment situation.

[37] Martínez-Alcubilla, 114, 293, 308, 348.
[38] *El Sol,* May 2, 1931.

2. The annulment of all work under contract for religious orders.

3. The confiscation of the capital of the clergy for hydraulic works.

4. The occupation and cession to workers of all lands used for pleasure resorts.

5. The abolition of monopolies.

6. A forty per cent reduction of rents under a hundred *pesetas*.

7. The liberation of political and social prisoners.[39]

The Provisional Government immediately fulfilled most of the moderate demands. The eight-hour day for industrial establishments was adopted on May 1, by the ratification of the Convention of Washington of 1919. Nine days later regulations for the inspection of labor were issued. A national board was created to stimulate employment and prevent involuntary unemployment. It set to work immediately to try to resolve the labor crisis. Provisions were made for the legal conditions for the organization and control of coöperative societies. In addition, mixed juries for the regulation of relations between employers and laborers and intervention to settle disputes by arbitration were provided.[40]

While the other members of the cabinet were engaged in this reconstruction, Prieto, the Minister of Finance, was confronted with the difficult task of stabilizing Spanish finances. The problem was inherited from the old régime and the world economic depression. The *peseta* had begun to drop in the international exchange long before the advent of the Republic. Vain efforts at stabilization were made and then the anxiety which followed the bloodless revolution resulted in a sharp decline. By the end of April it had reached the lowest point since 1898. The attempts of various members of the Spanish aristocracy to emigrate with their fortunes contributed to the uncertainty. The Duchess of Alba tried to cross the French border with 750,000 *pesetas*. Prieto ordered all

[39] *ABC*, May 2, 1931.
[40] Martínez-Alcubilla, 58, 66, 146, 424, 440, 467-472.

funds that had been withdrawn for export redeposited within four weeks, and forty per cent of these funds were returned. The rumor of the threatened resignation of Prieto as a result of a division in the republican ranks caused the *peseta* to drop again until it was valued at 58 to the pound sterling.[41] Then, when it was beginning to recover slightly the cabinet authorized the issuance of new banknotes. Conditions slightly improved with the conclusion of the negotiations for a loan of 300 million *pesetas* with the Bank of France.[42] This uncertain state of the finances, during the elections for the *cortes* and the period of the consolidation of the republic, produced unrest and anxiety among the business interests, contributed to the stimulation of strikes throughout the country, and caused grave concern in the cabinet.

The work of the Provisional Government during its three months of existence as a *de facto* authority indicated clearly the tendency that would be followed in the Constituent Cortes if the government was victorious in the elections and the *cortes* approved its policies. The electoral campaign was in progress and the cabinet was not only trying to reconstruct Spain in such a way as to appease the appetites of the Left, but also had to reassure the Right and protect the government against the counter-attack of the conservatives.

[41] The *peseta* was worth about 25 to the pound sterling in 1926 and declined steadily until 1931.

[42] *New York Times*, April 18, 21, 24, May 30, 31, 1931.

VII

THE ELECTION OF THE
CONSTITUENT CORTES

THE PRINCIPAL aim of the Provisional Government of the
Second Spanish Republic was the reconstruction of Spain
on a constitutional basis. Primo de Rivera had suspended the
constitutional guarantees in 1923, and the clamor for constitutional reform and the procrastination of the dictatorship
in calling a constituent *cortes* formed one of the most important factors in the overthrow of the monarchy. The
municipal elections, the first step in a return to constitutional
government, had resulted in the bloodless revolution and the
establishment of the republic.

Now the first duty of the *de facto* Provisional Government
was the creation of a properly organized government in accord
with its campaign demands and for the consolidation of the
republic on a *de jure* basis. Preparations for the convocation
of elections for the Constituent Cortes were immediately
made. The government began to consider this matter on
April 22, eight days after its assumption of authority. June
21 was considered as a tentative date, provided the Minister
of Labor could revise the electoral roll by that time. It was
proposed to reduce the voting age from twenty-five to twenty-
three as a reward for the youth of Spain who had helped to
establish the republic.[1] This principle was embodied in the
decree of April 25, which officially set the minimum age for
electors at twenty-three and authorized the revision of the
electoral census on that basis.[2]

The Monarchists, recognizing the political tendency of the
Spanish youth, protested this reform. *ABC* declared that it

[1] *The Times,* April 24, 1931; *ABC,* April 24, 1931.
[2] Martínez-Alcubilla, 299.

was illicit for any government to change the suffrage in any way, because anything that affected the suffrage had to be achieved through a law expressive of the national sovereignty. This could only be done by the *cortes* and it was doubly illegal for a *de facto* government to manipulate the electoral balance in its favor and alter the juridical and legal disposition of the suffrage. This newspaper further declared: "The government excuses this and other initiatives alleging that it is the power of a revolution and is restrained by no law."[3]

The government, however, did not restrict its reforming activity. The basic principles of the electoral laws needed to be revised. *El Sol* was an active protagonist for revision and said:

Now that the old organizations of governmental and directing base are in decomposition, it would be an error not to take advantage of them on the impulse of the great doctrinal winds which can be unchained in the great circumscriptions.

The French example was cited as a warning to the Spaniards and those who advised delay in reform. France was struggling to change her electoral system, for in the district it was easy for deputies to keep their seats if they had them, and to gain them if they had money, property, and influence, even though they had no brains.[4]

The government, then, considered the elections as an opportunity for the consolidation of its power and tried in every way to take advantage of it. A decree of May 5 permitted those exercising public functions to be considered citizens and included in the revised census, although they had not lived in their localities for two years.[5] On May 8 the electoral principles were thoroughly revised by a decree reforming the law of August 8, 1907. The electoral age was reduced to twenty-three and the suffrage was extended to women and priests. The election was to be based on provincial circum-

[3] *ABC*, April 28, 1931.
[4] *El Sol*, April 29, 1931.
[5] Martínez-Alcubilla, 286.

scriptions instead of artificial districts. One deputy was assigned to fifty thousand electors in each of the fifty provinces which was to form an electoral district, while Barcelona and Madrid were to form separate districts. The voting was to be by lists, eighty per cent of the vote being cast for majority and twenty per cent for minority representation. In order to be elected, a candidate had to obtain not only a plurality but at least twenty per cent of the total vote in the constituency. Severe punishment was threatened for those who tried to purchase votes, and the provision that an unopposed candidate should be forthwith declared elected was abolished. In addition, the intervention of the Supreme Tribunal in the examination of protested acts was forbidden because of the greater rapidity possible in the normal activity of the constituent assembly.[6] The election of the *cortes* was thus provided on a much more liberal basis. The influence of the local "bosses" was thwarted and the youth of Spain, notorious for its liberal tendencies, was enfranchised.

A date for the elections was definitely fixed for June 28 in a cabinet meeting on May 20, and two weeks later the decree convoking the *cortes* and setting the date of the election was issued. The preliminary assembly of the deputies was announced for July 13, and the Constituent Cortes was to be formally opened the following day. It was to consist of a single chamber, elected by direct popular suffrage and was invested with the most ample constituent and legislative power. The Provisional Government promised to resign its authority before the *cortes* and to give an account of its acts, whatever might be its accord. The *cortes* was also vested with the power of nominating and removing the person who was to act as President and provisional head of the state until the constitution was promulgated.[7] The electoral census was rectified by June 5 and the elections, which had to be held twenty days after the completion of this task, were set for June 28. The

---

[6] *Ibid.*, 298; *ABC*, May 5, 1931; *The Times*, May 6, 1931; *New York Times*, May 5, 1931.

[7] Martínez-Alcubilla, 741; *El Sol*, May 21, June 4, 1931.

second election, required for those candidates who failed to secure twenty per cent of the total vote cast, was set for July 5.[8]

The campaign for the elections was already well under way and the issues had been drawn. The primary issue was the consolidation of the republic and the reconstruction of Spain on liberal and socialist lines. The work of the Provisional Government had given an indication of the direction in which the reconstruction would tend. The various parties immediately divided themselves into three main groups.

On the Right were the conservative parties which desired to protect traditional institutions and the vested interests of the Church and landlords. Their forces had been completely disorganized by their defeat in the municipal elections and their leaders began frantically to try to rally the conservative forces and arouse the indifferent to the menace of the reconstructive tendencies to Spanish traditions. Their hope lay in a strong reaction against the preliminary work of the Provisional Government and the violence that had been incited by the impatient radicals. Early in May, National Action was organized in Madrid to unify all those who agreed on the fundamental traditions, "Religion, Country, Order, Family, Work, and Property." Conservative groups with similar aims were organized throughout the country, and Catholic or National Action began to expand its organization. The principal leaders of the new conservative party were the Marquis of Lema and Angel Herrera, editor of *El Debate,* both of whom were candidates for the *cortes.*[9] They demanded the maintenance of order; the defense of the Catholic religion, which they wanted to inculcate in the new generations; the unity of the country, strengthened "by a generous and prudent system of administrative autonomy"; and the defense of the home and the authority of parents. They professed allegiance to the new régime and tried to gain the adherence of the proletariat by demanding social justice and the protection

[8] Martínez-Alcubilla, 298-741; *El Sol,* May 21, 1931.
[9] *ABC,* May 2, 1931; *The Times,* June 21, 31, 1931.

of labor, in order to make the lives of the people pleasant and easy. They further declared: "We desire that society should be renewed by the rise to property holders of the greatest possible number of laborers."[10]

The clergy also rallied to the defense of their interests within the new régime. Cardinal Segura y Saenz, the Catholic Primate in Spain and Archbishop of Toledo, issued a pastoral letter on May 1, urging Spanish Catholics to participate in the elections. They should adopt a policy of respect and obedience as their duty to the Provisional Government and for the maintenance of order and the common good. The Church, however, would defend its rights and those of its members if they were attacked. Catholics were urged to unite in order that candidates might be elected to the *cortes* who offered full guarantees that they would defend the rights of the Church and the social order, whether they were monarchist or republican.[11] The Spanish episcopate issued a collective declaration a month later, after the government had fully indicated its attitude toward the Church in various decrees and in the expulsion of the Cardinal-Archbishop. The bishops declared that they had been silent in order to avoid creating difficulties for the Provisional Government and in the hope that the rights of the Church would be respected. But their silence could not be interpreted as acquiesence to measures and deeds which had produced a very painful impression on the Catholics.[12]

Alfonso issued his instructions to the Monarchists in the electoral campaign but they displayed little energy, disorganized and discouraged by the success of the new régime and the suspension of *ABC* and *El Debate,* the chief organs of the conservatives, during the month of May. The Monarchist Club announced that it would abstain from voting in the elections, discouraged by the activity of the republican authorities in preventing successful monarchist candidates

[10] *ABC,* June 25, 1931.
[11] *Ibid.,* May 7, 1931.
[12] *El Sol,* June 12, 1931; *ABC,* June 12, 1931.

from taking possession of their offices in the rural *ayuntamientos*. The Marquis of Alhucemas withdrew his candidacy in León because of "the arbitrary annulment of a great number of municipal elections in which we had obtained an overwhelming majority without the least protest formulated before April 14."[13] The staunch old Liberal, the Count of Romanones, remained as one of the few Monarchists in the campaign.

A small group of conservative Republicans which entered candidates in the campaign was the *Agrupación para Ayudo a la República*. It included such politicians of the old régime as José Sánchez Guerra, Angel Ossorio y Gallardo, and Melquiades Alvarez, leader of the Reformists in the last days of the monarchy.

The Republican-Socialist Coalition, which had been prolonged until the convocation of the *cortes*, was the strongest group in the electoral contest. It included the Right Republican Party headed by Alcalá Zamora, the Radical Pary still led by its founder, Alejandro Lerroux, and smaller groups of varying differences of opinion. The Socialists led by Julián Besteiro, and the Radical Socialists led by José Salmerón and Eduardo Ortega y Gasset, coöperated in the coalition. It was a difficult alliance to maintain in view of the individualistic tendencies of the Spaniards and the differences which threatened to disrupt it. The Radical Socialists attacked Alcalá Zamora and Miguel Maura in their Congress, late in May, and Indalecio Prieto threatened to resign. In addition, the allegiance of the Republican Right wing to Alcalá Zamora and Maura was somewhat weakened by the admission of Chapaprieta, a professional politician, who had been appointed director of the June elections. He had been Santiago Alba's right-hand man until the dissolution of the Liberal Monarchist Party.[14]

Prieto's resignation was thwarted, however, and the Pro-

[13] *ABC,* June 20, 1931; *New York Times,* May 6, June 7, 1931; *The Times,* May 18, 1931.
[14] *The Times,* June 1, 1931; *New York Times,* May 19, 24, 1931.

visional Government maintained its solidarity and decided to concentrate all of its energy on the campaign. Maura declared: "The Government will go united to the parliament and the impatient ones who do not believe it waste their time."[15] The various members of the Cabinet took an active part in the campaign but none of them was more active than the Minister of State, Lerroux, who had already earned a reputation for statesmanship. As the elections drew near he spoke tirelessly in the interest of order, tolerance, and moderation. He exhorted the Monarchists and Catholics at Burgos, trying to reassure them, to induce them to coöperate with the republican government, and to be tolerant toward their opponents. He declared that the republic had come to serve not only Republicans but all Spaniards. Its reforms would be introduced without violence. The republic felt no hatred for religion but could not tolerate fanaticism.

Both God and Caesar must receive their due. Knowing that the country desires to live in peace with the Church, so does the republican government, on the condition that the Church respects democracy and the republic.[16]

On June 22 Lerroux spoke in Barcelona, where he pled with the federalists and regionalists to support the cause of a united Spain.

I want to continue being a Catalan within Spain and a Spaniard within Catalonia. We must all recognize a superior and spiritual ideal which unites us all, and it is Spain. There is an indestructible thing: the union of Catalonia with all its personality to the rest of Spain.

He continued:

Those who put the most faith in the republic be they of the right or of the left, they will be those who best serve the republic.

And he concluded with a plea for order:

Opposed to oppression, violence is a right, before liberty violence is fratricide.[17]

[15] *El Sol*, May 30, 1931.
[16] *The Times*, June 22, 1931.
[17] *El Sol*, June 23, 1931.

The third group consisted of the extremists who sought to effect the reconstruction of Spain by revolution rather than evolution and who produced most of the disorder and violence in the campaign because of their desire for immediate achievement of their aims through direct action. A study of this group naturally involves the rivalry of the socialist and syndicalist labor organizations, which were competing for the support of the laborers. The *Unión General de Trabajadores* was the socialist union which aimed at the reconstruction of Spanish society in the interest of social justice by political evolution. The Socialists had supported the republican coalition because they could attain their ideals more easily in the democratic régime than in the monarchy which they had helped to overthrow. They did not desire an immediate acquisition of power, if we may believe the statement of Besteiro.

Immediately, in a democratic republic, socialism will know how to gain nobly, by means of universal suffrage, a representation each time more numerous and more effective in the public corporations, principally in the towns and in the chambers. For my part I do not attribute as much importance to the number of representatives as to the effectiveness of their activity. It is more: a too rapid numerical increase does not seem to me desirable. Socialism would lose in moral force what it would gain in material extension, and that, which would certainly not be suitable for socialism, nor for the organization of workers animated by its spirit, would be prejudicial for the republic.

It is besides of common interest to the republic and to socialism that the access of the laborer representation to all the organisms of an economic or social character which may exist or can be created be opened. I do not claim with this any privilege, but simply the right of conquering by our own force the positions which in reality belong to us, penetrating each time more into the internal organization of the nation, mixing gradually more of socialism into Spanish life and acquiring a stability in our own positions and a dominion of the administrative and political technique which may permit us one day to assume the principal responsibilities of the government. A premature occupation of power, partial or total, I consider prejudicial for socialism and for the republic.[18]

That explains, perhaps, the motive of the Socialists in subordinating their exercise of power in the coalition with the Republicans. They hoped to obtain gradual control of Spain with their party discipline and organization, and then gradually evolve a reconstruction of the country on a socialist basis. They held that the

. . . highest national organization must be the organization of labor, and the only legitimate title of citizenship must be that of the laborer. To the worker is due respect in the work, and respect in fatigue, and respect in the enjoyment of the most noble benefactions accessible to man, which are the possessions of culture.[19]

Manual Muiño, one of the leaders of the *Unión General de Trabajadores,* pointed out the difference between his union and the *Confederación Nacional de Trabajo:* "We work with ideas, they with pistols." The union would never be associated with any government, but pursued the "socialization of the country." It was not possible to implant socialism by decree, but by making citizens. No one should believe that "the republic, by the sole act of being proclaimed, was going to solve all the problems." The program of the Socialist Party would include the expulsion of the religious orders and the solution of the land problem.[20]

The Communists were also active in the electoral campaign, conducting meetings and spreading subversive literature. Andrés Nin and Joaquín Maurín were their leaders. Maurín was a Catalan who favored separation, while Nin, a severe-looking, slight young man, with a shock of dark hair, was an internationalist. Both were forceful speakers, and their audiences in the Ateneo responded enthusiastically when they declared that the Revolution of April 14 should

[18] *Ibid.,* June 3, 1931.
[19] *Ibid.*
[20] *El Sol,* June 24, 1931.

be followed by a socialist revolution. In their opinion the immediate enemy was the Provisional Government and the useless Constituent Cortes. Nin said: "It should surprise no communist that the Provisional Government may be a reactionary government, and we must show the workers its true characteristic." The King had fled but the bourgeois revolution had solved nothing. The typical problems: the separation of Church and state, the expropriation of the *latifundios,* the bureaucracy, and the rights of women, could not be solved by the bourgeoise. The only possible revolution could be achieved by the establishment of the dictatorship of the proletariat.[21]

The Communists, however, were not as active in their propaganda as the syndicalist organizations, particularly the *Confederación Nacional de Trabajo.* The Syndicalists were much stronger than the Communists and differed from them in that they abstained from participation in the electoral campaign, preferring rather their methods of direct action, through strikes and violence, in an effort to paralyze the country and force the acceptance of their program. The rivalry of the Socialists and Syndicalists became more intense as the campaign progressed and they tried to convert the laboring classes to their respective unions. The Syndicalists were strong in Barcelona, the Socialists in Madrid, and the former were conducting an intensive propaganda in Andalusia.

The leader of the syndicalist organizations in Barcelona was Angel Pestaña, a watchmaker by trade, who had emerged after the murder of Noi del Sucre (Salvador Seguí), the idol of the party. Pestaña was a reserved and impressively simple man, less than forty years old.[22] He expressed the sentiment of the Syndicalists when he declared they had no intention of acting as a political party.

We are completely removed from what in Spain was understood and continues to be understood as politics. We will enter

[21] *Ibid.,* June 10, 25, 1931.
[22] *The Times,* June 23, 1931.

no candidates for the *constituyentes*. That interests us from outside. We are acting on the same plan as always, neither pact with any party, nor presentation of candidates. In this respect we restrict ourselves to observing.[23]

The Syndicalists had no sympathy with the Communists. In the words of Pestaña:

State communism, at least such as has been planted in Moscow, does not appear to us to be a solution. We are far from the Muscovite dogma, from the dogma of the Third International. It is necessary to educate the laborers for liberty and not for tyranny. People on the road to liberty will never erect despots, and, inversely, people educated for despotism cannot serve the ideals of liberty.

He believed that the social revolution was inevitable, but not in as short a time as many believed. It would arrive as a logical phenomenon, because the evolution of the Spanish people should determine profound transformations of an economic character.

Bourgeois democracy has already given us all it could give. I do not see any more prospects in it. It has fulfilled its mission and has to give way to other organizations.[24]

But he boasted at the Madrid debating club, the Ateneo, that if the Spanish Revolution neglected the claims of the workers and denied them their right to participate in the wealth of the nation, as the French Revolution had done, the Syndicalists could and would destroy the new régime.[25]

Dr. Pedro Vallina was the leader of the peasantry in the province of Seville. He lived among them, gave them his professional services free, and denounced those whom he considered their oppressors. He was known as "the lone tiger," the San Juan of the Andalusian peasants, and his creed consisted simply in a demand for land.

The peasant has reached his majority in age. He wants the lands because they are his. And either they give them to him or he

[23] *El Sol*, May 31, 1931.
[24] *Ibid.*
[25] *The Times*, June 23, 1931.

takes them. Today he still trusts the republic, and therefore has restrained the revolution.[26]

But if the peasants were not given land by October, they would take it or Andalusia and Extremadura would go up in flames from end to end. The land would be useless to them as individuals for they had no means of working it, but they could work it collectively through syndicalist organizations.[27]

In contrast to this realistic and active propaganda was the idealism of the intellectual Republicans and Socialists. José Ortega y Gasset, who had become the oracle of the republic after the publication of his article "Delenda est Monarchia" early in the year, wrote:

The magnificent and momentous hour has come when fate imposes upon Spaniards the duty of thinking grandly. It is the great moment that will not return for centuries.[28]

The members of the Provisional Government were thinking grandly, burying party differences in an effort to consolidate the republic. But they were opposed by the more realistic methods of the radicals who were willing to use any means to achieve their ends. This clash of idealism and realism explains, in part, the violence and disorder that accompanied the electoral campaign. It also contributes to the explanation of the gradual tendency of the politicians of the republican government to shift more and more to the Left in an effort to placate the clamor of the radical propagandists.

There was a great deal of violence during the campaign, but not as much as might have been expected from the threats of the radicals. The desire of Alfonso to save himself and flee rather than plunge Spain into a bloody, fratricidal conflict had made the revolution a bloodless one. The campaign, moreover, was a comparatively bloodless one when considered in contrast to similar attempts at revolutionary consolidation in other countries, and in view of the fiery individualism of the Spanish temperament.

[26] *El Sol,* June 9, 1931.
[27] *Ibid.; The Times,* June 23, 1931.
[28] *The Times,* June 23, 1931.

The Provisional Government was intent on maintaining perfect freedom of action in the elections, and on June 8 Maura issued instructions to the fifty civil governors, impressing upon them the duty of remaining strictly neutral during the election. They were forbidden to appoint delegates to the *ayuntamientos* during the electoral period and were not permitted to suspend the councils. Electoral propaganda was to be allowed complete freedom, but the authorities were to maintain order and note carefully all dangerous manifestations, to repress disturbers and turn them over to the courts. The liberty of the press, both in criticizing the work of the government and advancing political ideas, was to be respected, but all papers advising violence or preaching rebellion, whatever their tendency, were to be closed. The governors were further threatened with condign punishment for failing in their duties.[29]

Maura explained his attitude toward the campaign disturbances just before the elections.

Elements of the extreme left, as others of the extreme right, have the intent of disturbing the public order before the elections. The government, informed, is ready to prevent every misfortune, and the same design animates the republican parties. Thus if anything should be attempted it will be immediately suppressed. There is no one who may succeed in avoiding the advent of a sovereign *cortes* with all the strength which it must represent. Those who hope that it will not be constituted know that they are playing their last card, because the function of that *cortes* implies the annulment of their plans and ambitions.[30]

Before the republic was a month old its record for order had been marred by the burning of convents in Madrid, Murcia, Cádiz, Málaga, and other cities, and martial law had been declared in many parts of Spain. Alcalá Zamora charged that the Monarchists and radicals had collaborated against the credit and peace of the republic, and *ABC* and *El Debate* were suspended to end their opposition to the consolidation

[29] *ABC*, June 9, 1931; *The Times*, June 9, 1931.
[30] *El Sol*, June 25, 1931.

of the republic.[31] The rivalry of the Socialists and Syndicalists resulted in clashes and fatalities in various parts of the country, especially in Barcelona. On June 19 there was a riot at Oviedo, and Melquiades Alvarez, the orator, was threatened and the offices of his party sacked. His party charged that the dominant feature of the campaign was violence, "absolutely at variance with our political traditions and because of the evident absence of authority for the defense of the rights of citizens." The governor of Oviedo had been electioneering in Alicante on his own behalf, his substitute was absent at the time of the riot, and the Civil Guard had arrived too late. In indignation, Alvarez withdrew from the campaign.[32]

As the elections drew near, the Syndicalists planned a general strike of the telephone workers, in an effort to bring pressure to bear upon the government. The company accepted all of the demands and refused to recognize the syndicate. But the strike was finally postponed until July. General strikes also accompanied the elections in Granada and Málaga and the latter was placed under martial law.[33]

The issue appeared to be order against disorder, and the conservative press, which had formerly preached abstention, now advocated the support of those candidates whose program called for law and order, irrespective of party.[34] In many places electoral meetings were broken up by the opposition. At Ciudad Real the Undersecretary of Government was forced to stop, in the middle of his speech, and retire under police protection. In Madrid the police were more cautious. The clerical National Action Party scheduled a meeting in the Alcázar Theatre, in support of its four minority candidates. An hour before the meeting, the police intimated that the obstruction to traffic of persons going in and out of the theatre might lead to trouble and the meeting was called off.

---

[31] *El Sol*, May 13, 15, 1931.

[32] *Ibid.*, June 20, 21, 1931; *ABC*, June 20, 21, 1931; *The Times*, June 22, 1931.

[33] *El Sol*, June 25, 30, 1931.

[34] *The Times*, June 29, 1931.

The true reason for the official action was the information that some of the unruly element were planning a riot, which would be favored by the crowded streets as the theatre emptied.[35] A great deal of the disorder may be attributed to the natural rise of the mob spirit in a period of intense excitement and electoral agitation, but the attitude of the radicals undoubtedly encouraged it.

A feature of the campaign was the political propaganda of some of the army officers, a tradition that the reforms of Azaña had not abolished. General López Ochoa, divisional commander in Catalonia, was forbidden to present himself as a candidate, but Major Ramón Franco, head of the air service and a hero among the masses because of his sensational flights, was diligent in the service of the radicals. He formed a Revolutionary Republican Party which held that the republic had yet to make the revolution. When a platform at Lara del Río collapsed, he suffered a broken leg, but continued to direct the campaign by telephone from his bed in the hospital.[36]

Miguel Maura charged Franco with a plot to prevent the elections by a rising in Andalusia. Franco had a store of arms at the air base at Tablada, five miles from Seville, and had ordered military airmen from all over Spain to report there. According to Maura, he planned to arm the peasants under Dr. Vallina, seize Seville, proclaim an independent state in Andalusia, and then march on Madrid. But the police had checked his daily movements and reported that he was co-operating with the Syndicalists of Barcelona. At the last moment, having waited to permit him to show his hand and prevent his posing as a martyr and increase his popularity, the government acted. On June 26 General Sanjurjo, head of the Civil Guard, was sent to Seville. On the following day he took possession of Tablada with a military force. Few were implicated in the plot and the conspirators offered no resistance. The air base was placed under the protection of the

[35] *Ibid.*, June 24, 25, 1931.
[36] *El Sol*, June 24, 25, 1931; *ABC*, June 25, 26, 1931; *The Times*, June 25, 26, 1931.

Civil Guard and Franco was arrested and deprived of his post as chief of the air force.[37]

These scattered outbursts of violence undoubtedly tended to drive some of the conservatives to the support of the Provisional Government. Staunch conservatives like José Sánchez Guerra and the well-known lawyer, Angel Ossorio y Gallardo, rallied to its support. The latter declared that his whole family had become republican. Others were intimidated by the threats of violence. Feeling ran so high in the republican stronghold of Valencia that the Catholic candidates were forced to withdraw, after watching their automobiles burn and being threatened to be roasted alive if they continued their electoral propaganda.[38] The elections were characterized by clashes between the members of various parties. In Madrid an attempt was made to lynch a priest who was charged with purchasing votes. He was arrested in order to protect him from the young Republicans.

On June 21 the official list of the candidates for the 470 seats in the *cortes* was published. There were over a thousand candidates, representing more than twenty-five parties, the greatest number yet known in Spain. The Right Republicans had 124 candidates, the Republican-Socialist Alliance 115, and the Socialists 105. Of the other candidates, there were seventy-three Radical Socialists, fifty-eight members of National Action, twenty-two Communists, and six Monarchists. There were republican parties of all shades.[39]

The election returns revealed a decisive victory for the Republican-Socialist Alliance and the defeat of the extremists. *El Sol* declared: "The triumph of the candidacy of the coalition is equivalent to the consolidation of the republic."[40] The Socialists won the greatest number of soats, 130. Lerroux's Radical Republicans followed with 100, while the Right Republicans elected seventy-five deputies. The Cata-

[37] *The Times,* June 29, 1931; *El Sol,* June 27, 28, 1931; *ABC,* June 27, 28, 1931.
[38] *The Times,* June 27, 1931.
[39] *El Sol,* June 23, 1931; *ABC,* June 23, 1931; *The Times,* June 22, 1931.
[40] *El Sol,* June 30, 1931.

lans returned forty, the Catholics, Carlists, and Monarchists ninety, and the remainder of the seats were scattered among the radical groups of the Left. It is significant that not a single Communist was elected.[41]

Alcalá Zamora was elected on a minority list from Jaén and Alejandro Lerroux, who piled up 133,000 votes in Madrid, was victorious in seven districts: Madrid, Cáceres, Huesca, Valencia, Coruña, and the provinces of Barcelona and Tenerife. Marcelino Domingo was elected from Tarragona, Alvaro Albornoz from Zaragoza, and the province of Madrid returned two women, Victoria Kent and Clara Campoamor. Salvador de Madariaga and José Ortega y Gasset were among the new deputies and Franco was returned from Barcelona, although his revolutionary activity influenced his candidacy in Seville unfavorably. The old politicians won a few scattered seats and were represented by Santiago Alba, the Count of Romanones, Melquiades Alvarez, and Angel Ossorio y Gallardo. Maciá and his followers were triumphant in Catalonia and the Nationalists were successful in the north of Spain, especially in Guipuzcoa, where eighty per cent of the electorate went to the polls. In Salamanca, however, the coalition, which obtained only two places, protested the irregularities committed and charged the landlords with exercising undue influence over their tenants. Angel Herrera and Gil Robles were among the successful candidates of the National Action and Agrarian parties in Madrid and Salamanca respectively.[42]

It was an overwhelming victory for the republic. The country had endorsed the usurpation of power by the Provisional Government, and it remained for the *cortes* to approve its preliminary work for the evolutionary progress of Spain. The Socialists would be the strongest single party in the *cortes*, yet they were not willing to assume the responsibility of government. The success of the *cortes* appeared to

[41] *The Times,* July 1, 1931.

[42] *El Sol,* June 30, 1931; *ABC,* June 30, 1931; *The Times,* June 30, July 1, 1931; *New York Times,* June 28, 29, 1931.

be dependent upon the consistency of their coöperation with the Republicans. But their position was not impregnable. On the Left, the Syndicalists and other extremists demanded a continuation of the revolution and, on the Right, the new National Action Party was ready to rally the conservatives to reactionary policies if the Catholic and agrarian positions and the traditions of Spain were attacked too boldly.

VIII

THE CONSTITUTIONAL PROJECT

THE SECOND Spanish Republic was barely three weeks old when the cabinet began its preparations for the formulation of the new constitution. On May 6 the *Comisión General de Codificación* was dissolved and a *Comisión Jurídica Asesora* was established. The old commission, created in 1875, was held unfit to fulfil the demands of reconstruction, because it had served the dictatorship. Its structure, ends, and traditions did not meet the exigencies of the moment nor accord with the new legal approach. The aim of the *Comisión Jurídica Asesora* was to draft laws and supply information, thereby assisting the Provisional Government in the reconstruction of the political and social system of Spain.[1]

The new commission was divided into various subcommittees, the most important of which was the commission on the constitution. Its chairman was Angel Ossorio y Gallardo, who was also head of the commission as a whole. He was an eminent lawyer who had opposed the monarchy and had urged the abdication of Alfonso XIII. Although somewhat conservative in character, he was the logical person, both for legal knowledge and political experience, to be placed in charge of the important task of framing the document that was to be carried to the Constituent Cortes as the basis for the establishment of the political and juridical norms of the republic. He was assisted by an eminent and scholarly group of thirty men, including Luis Jiménez de Asúa and Adolfo Posada.[2]

[1] Martínez-Alcubilla, 194; Luis Jiménez de Asúa, *Proceso histórico de la constitución de la república española*. Madrid, 1932. 1.

[2] Jiménez de Asúa, 1-2; *El Sol*, June 23, 1931; *ABC*, June 27, 1931. The subcommission of the *Comisión Jurídica Asesora*, which framed the *anteproyecto*, consisted of Adolfo González Posada, Javier Elola, Valeriano Casa-

The subcommission spent eight sessions on the elaboration of the constitutional project and labored zealously to draft a sound foundation on which an enduring republic might be erected. Those held most responsible for the final project were Ossorio y Gallardo, Posada, Valdecasas, and Casanueva. Yet the task was not accomplished without compromise and differences of opinion. Many *votos particulares* (dissenting opinions) were offered to accompany the *anteproyecto* when it should be submitted to the *cortes*. In addition, there was no assurance that this body would approve the preliminary draft when it was presented to the deputies for their consideration.[3]

The principal differences of opinion grew out of the questions of the construction of the chamber of the representatives of the nation, the scope of the presidential powers, and the separation of Church and state. Some of the members desired two chambers: a senate, representative of the social and economic orders, and a chamber of deputies, representative of the people. Such a body would have followed the traditional bicameral structure, with its checks and balances, as well as the more modern idea that the economic orders of society should be consulted in the formulation of legislation. The majority of the Socialists took their cues from the leaders, Prieto and Besteiro, who wanted a single chamber. Prieto declared that to be the traditional socialist program, because two chambers were considered dangerous and the party had always demanded the suppression of the senate.[4]

There were three models for the establishment of the executive power: the strong executive, indirectly elected, as in the United States; the election of the president by universal suffrage, as in Germany; and the election of the president by the chambers, with its consequent responsibility, as in France. The discussions were particularly heated, but the

nueva, Manuel Pedroso, Nicolas Alcalá Espinosa, Agustin Viñuales, Antonio Rodríguez Pérez, Alfonso Valdecasas, Francisco Romero Otazo, Luis Lamana Lizarbe, Antonio de Luña, and Juan Lladó Sánchez-Calvo.

[3] *El Sol,* June 19, 1931; *ABC,* June 27 ,1931.

[4] *El Sol,* June 4, 19, 1931.

French type finally prevailed, as a reaction, perhaps, to the objection of the Republicans to a strong executive, who was not always amenable to the will of the people.

A third issue that divided the commission was that of religious liberty. Some of the conservatives opposed the separation of Church and state, while the Socialists had already adopted religious liberty as their principle. They held that every citizen had the right to refuse to contribute to the support of Catholicism for reasons of conscience.[5]

When the work of the subcommission was completed it was submitted to the plenary session of the *Comisión Jurídica Asesora*. There were two long and arduous sessions of the whole body on June 29 and June 30, when the *anteproyecto* was approved with few amendments. It was evident, however, that it was not supported by all the members of the commission. Individual opinions had been offered in the course of the development of the project. Many doubtless took the same position that Luis Jiménez de Asúa held when he declared:

I only attended one of the plenary sessions in order to register my disagreement with the basic principles of political orientation, although the technical part of the work appeared to me laudable.

He had just been elected a deputy to the *cortes* on June 28, and

I wanted to protect myself lest in the parliament I should have to follow principles opposed to those established in the constitutional *anteproyecto*.[6]

An analysis of the project was published in *El Sol* on July 1, but two days later that newspaper was forced to deny that the previous report was the one approved. Angel Ossorio y Gallardo, as chairman of the commission, was the person most responsible for the denial. He said:

. . . it interests the plenary session of the *Comisión Jurídica Asesora* to recall to public opinion that its work does not have the

[5] *Ibid.*
[6] Jiménez de Asúa, 2-3.

least importance in political transcendency. The commission limits itself to bring materials to the government which do not imply any political orientation, because the commission never received it from the government in any sense.

Therefore, it was erroneous to believe that the work of the commission prejudged "even remotely, what must be the solution of many of the political problems which Spain has planned." It was equally an error to attribute the work to definite members of the commission, "with the exclusion of others, the totality or nearly the totality of some of the work realized, being such that all have coöperated with equal zeal."[7]

The commission finished its work early in July, and *El Sol* published the *anteproyecto* on July 7. The day before Alcalá Zamora indicated that the government would introduce many modifications into the project. The disparity of the proposals of the ministers, however, led the cabinet to decide that the proposal would require so many modifications to please its various members that it would be impossible to reach a common understanding.

There was not only the intention on the part of many of the ministers of introducing substantial changes in the project, but that the disparity, in some cases complete, of the ministers of government became visible as soon as the question was discussed.[8]

Some of the ministers announced their intention of presenting *votos particulares* to the *cortes,* indicating their disagreement with the totality or essential aspects of the project. Therefore, the government gave up the idea of studying it, preferring to carry it to the *cortes* in a modified form as a ministerial proposal. It was decided that each minister should receive copies of the *votos particulares* presented by the different members of the commission, in order that each might study the project and the diverging opinions that had

[7] *El Sol,* July 3, 1931.
[8] *Ibid.,* July 7, 8, 1931.

arisen in its preparation. They could then carry to the *cortes* the personal policy that was considered opportune. Finally, in view of the impossibility of agreement among the various parties whose support was necessary for the adoption of the constitution, it was agreed that the Constituent Cortes should choose a parliamentary commission to draft the preliminary constitution, using the *anteproyecto* and the *votos particulares* as the basis for their discussion.[9]

It must be remembered that the constitutional project was not the only task undertaken by the *Comisión Jurídica Asesora,* for its function was to draw up various legislative proposals which the Provisional Government planned to present to the *cortes.* These included the reform of the judiciary: the *reglamento* or rules of procedure of the Constituent Cortes, the reform of the penal code, and the statute of the Church.[10] Therefore, the work of this commission should not be judged solely for its tentative constitutional effort, although that was the most important of its duties. Nevertheless the project is important in the evolution of the final constitution and it is important to analyze both it and the *votos particulares* that accompanied it. The best commentary on the project was the explanatory note written by the chairman of the commission, Ossorio y Gallardo, for the presentation of the draft to the Provisional Government.[11]

The question of the basic structure of the Spanish state was one of the first considered by the commission. Should a unitary régime be established, as the proponents of centralization desired, or should the nationalist aspirations of the various regions be recognized by the establishment of a federal régime? The commission tried to face realities rather than theorize upon a matter so grave and "to support itself on the undeniable reality of today and open the way to the possible

[9] *Ibid.,* July 8, 10, 1931.
[10] *Ibid.,* July 9, 1931.
[11] The *anteproyecto* and the explanatory analysis by Angel Ossorio y Gallardo can be found in *El Sol,* July 7 and July 9, respectively. The analysis and many of the pertinent articles of the project are included in Jiménez de Asúa.

reality of tomorrow." The recognition of the personality of
the provinces would not have satisfied the majority of the
people, but the autonomous personality of the regions was so
strong that only an unjust denial of the sense of liberty could
repress it. Therefore, the *anteproyecto* began by declaring
that Spain was a democratic republic, and organized the nation into cities, provinces, and autonomous regions. In accord
with a proposal of Ossorio y Gallardo, it adopted not a federal régime but a federable one.[12]

The commission preferred to facilitate the formation of
entities in order that to reach a greater or less autonomy they
might follow their own desires. In Article 2, it was provided
that local legislation should always have an autonomous
sense. The entities were to be not merely administrative
units, for they had to define their geographic and historic
characteristics. In addition, "the autonomous region, once
constituted, will fix for itself its interior régime in matters
within its competence." Ossorio y Gallardo continued:

No one who judges serenely will censure the establishment of
guarantees in order that the statute which the region must propose and the *cortes* vote, may assure that a great majority of the
interested country support it. A matter of as deep transcendency
as the autonomous life, with its advantages and dangers, must be
neither an academic theory, nor a party aspiration, nor the fruit
of a moment of exaltation, but so fully conceived and so explicitly
expressed that it may not be submitted to attacks in the future.

It was likewise necessary to insure that unity of thought and
action should constitute a pledge of the pacific coöperation of
all Spaniards. The commission tried to assign those inalienable attributes to the state which were established in the
federal constitutions of Europe and which the most studious
partisans of federalism in Spain had accepted.[13]

A *voto particular,* signed by Francisco Romero Otazo,
Manual Pedroso, Alfonso García Valdecasas, and Antonio de
Luña, was offered in opposition to the totality of the first

[12] Jiménez de Asúa, 5-6, 22.
[13] *El Sol,* July 7, 1931.

title. It consisted of fourteen articles, six more than the proposal of the commission, and postulated a more federable régime than that followed by the *anteproyecto*. The autonomous territories constituted a political nucleus within the Spanish state and, as integral entities of Spain, should not be the recipients of delegated powers from the state. The *cortes* should not have the power to withhold its approval of the regional statute, provided this was formulated according to the limitations imposed on it, that it should contain nothing contrary to the constitution. Nicolás Alcalá Espinosa and Javier Elola also offered propositions which dissented from the first title. They both aimed at a federal state, but differed slightly from the project in the means provided for arriving at that state. A *voto particular* of Fernández Clérigo expressed the desire of directly consecrating the supremacy of the civil power, and others were presented by Posada and Casanueva.[14]

The religious issue, which had already been the subject of various decrees by the Provisional Government, was attacked by the commission along lines similar to those embodied in the decrees. Church and state were separated and the liberty of conscience and sects was respected without any restrictions.

No one will be able to see in these declarations a persecuting spirit or a destructive sectarianism. Although every member of the commission would have wanted to see a Christian orientation in the moral activity of the state expressly safeguarded, it appeared preferable not to make a declaration on the matter and leave both powers independent, although agreed, as occurs today by general rule.

The Catholic Church, however, was considered as an institution of public law and religious teaching. The project, "ending the dangerous confusion," protected the spirituality of the citizen and recognized the social force and historical significance of the Church.[15]

[14] Jiménez de Asúa, 25-26.
[15] *El Sol*, July 7, 1931.

A *voto particular* was proposed by Ossorio, Pérez Rodríguez, and Puebla, which recognized the separation of Church and state but aimed at inspiring the activity and legislation of the state along the principles of Christian morality by proposing a new formula for Article 8. In contrast with this, Clérigo did not desire that this article should declare the Church a corporation of public law, and proposed that all of the religious confessions should be considered as associations submitted to a special law. Enrique Ramos suggested that a special law should govern the Church, while Adolfo Posada wished to reduce Article 8 to its first paragraph: "There is no State religion."[16]

Political and individual guarantees formed particularly important questions. The members of the commission had endured the dictatorial suspension of their cherished and hard-won liberties and did not wish to repeat the experience. Hence, those liberties which were appropriate among all civilized peoples and had been protected in previous Spanish constitutions were guaranteed. The dictatorship had also taught the Spaniards a lesson, and certain new guarantees were introduced in the project. Naturally, the extinction of all titles of nobility was a first consideration of the commission, to approve what the Provisional Government had already decreed. In addition, public action would be taken against illegal detentions, and both the authorities who ordered such detentions and the agents who carried out the orders would be held responsible. Syndical liberty was assured by the policy of considering the syndicates as organizations of public law in order that they might intervene in the social and economic policy of the state. The equality of the sexes in work was guaranteed and the right of associations of functionaries to seek recourse in the courts in defense of their members was recognized.

The suspension of the constitutional guarantees was regulated in terms which could harmonize both efficacy and responsibility.

[16] Jiménez de Asúa, 26-27.

It is attributed to the government, but it does not admit in times like these that the government should remain immobile and impotent awaiting the outcome of the parliamentary deliberations, while the security of the state is at stake.

The immediate convocation of the *cortes* was provided in that it should be assembled automatically if the government failed to call it within fifteen days.[17]

Pedroso, Casanueva, Viñuales, Valdecasas, and Luña offered a *voto particular,* requesting the inclusion of provisions for the protection of the national artistic treasure and the obligatory adjustment of various industries when the reasonableness of production and the interests of national economy required.[18]

It was a characteristic of contemporary constitutions to regulate social interests as carefully as individual rights had been protected. Hence a chapter entitled "Family, Economy, and Culture" was included in the *anteproyecto*. The traditional respect for matrimony as the basis of the state was maintained and placed under the special protection of the state. The equality of the rights of the sexes was provided, and protection for illegitimate children and the investigation of paternity were assured. Alcalá Zamora wanted Article 27 changed in order to give illegitimate children the same rights as those who were legitimate.[19]

The right of both individual and collective property was recognized, but with "an explicit declaration of its social function." The narrow concept of public utility in necessary expropriation was replaced by the more comprehensive one of social utility. Greater elasticity in the laws determining the form of indemnization was provided and it was declared that property could be socialized, while one *voto particular* requested an even more sweeping socialization than was included in the project.[20]

---

[17] *El Sol,* July 7, 1931.
[18] Jiménez de Asúa, 27.
[19] *Ibid.,* 28.
[20] *Ibid.*

Labor was placed under the special protection of the state "in order to assure every worker the minimum conditions of a worthy existence." New features were introduced in the regulation of professional institutions as organisms of public law and the participation of workers in the direction and profits of industries. The educational activity of Marcelino Domingo was approved in the provision which based access to primary and higher schools on aptitude and vocation rather than fortune. A student had the right to demand religious instruction but the teacher retained his liberty of refusing to offer that instruction if his convictions prevented it. The professor was assured complete independence, but the exclusive power of granting professional titles and establishing the requirements for obtaining them and the liberty of founding and sustaining educational institutions under state regulation and protection were assured. Four members of the commission signed a *voto particular* requesting the addition of another article establishing the *escuela única* in primary education and making labor incompatible with instruction for children under fourteen. Ramos opposed the inclusion of any religious instruction and suggested a final paragraph prohibiting private preparatory establishments.[21]

The prolonged debates over the structure of the parliament reflected the division of public opinion on this matter. Ossorio y Gallardo declared that three considerations led the commission to decide for the bicameral system: "The inconveniences of an unrestrained popular chamber, the necessity of greater support for the government and the example of the immense majority of the countries." The new senate, however, differed greatly from the old one. It had a corporative character and included representatives of employers, workers, and professional and cultural associations. It had no real political function but was established to act as a reflective and moderate element in legislation. It would exercise no political influence on the government but could never be dissolved and was renewable by half every four years.

[21] *Ibid.;* El Sol, July 7, 1931.

There was a respectable section of opinion which desired to substitute technical councils for the senate. The councils were created and their information was required for both laws and decrees, but the senate was retained. The *voto particular,* however, which accompanied this article had as much moral force as the report itself, since there was only a difference of two votes in the decision between the two. Ossorio y Gallardo declared there might have been another result if the attendance at the commission the day the article was adopted had been different.

Following foreign models, a permanent commission of sixteen deputies and eight senators was provided. The government was obliged to consult it in order to promulgate decrees that had the force of law, and it investigated the arrest and trial of members of the congress. The commission also undertook to solve the paralysis of legislative activity during the recess of the *cortes.* If the government had retained complete liberty of movement to legislate as it saw fit, it would have been a return to the evil of which Spain had had abundant and deplorable demonstrations. To solve both problems, the government was permitted to act in cases of urgent necessity by decree, but was obligated to consult the corresponding technical council and the permanent commission and obtain favorable opinions before publishing the decree as law. In any event, the government had to present the decree to the *cortes* as a project of law at the next assembly of that body.

A vote of censure was regulated so that a government might not be the victim of surprise, which would gravely injure the country, and which was motivated by small factional interests or personal grievances. A vote of censure had to be proposed by a fourth of the deputies, announced for discussion five days before, and approved by an absolute majority of the deputies constituting the *cortes.* In the face of an adverse vote the government was obliged to resign. Provisions were also included for the automatic assembly of the *cortes* on October 2 of each year, for a period of at least four consecutive months. The application of the theory of administrative silence in the trial of deputies and senators, in order to give the *cortes* greater efficiency and security, was provided. In addition, provisions were made for the ratification of international conventions that were considered to have the force of international law.[22]

The most important of the dissenting opinions on the fourth title was the one mentioned above. It was signed by twelve members of the commission and requested the suppression of the senate and the organization of the legislative power in a unicameral régime. Other *votos* referred to particular articles. One which was offered by three members, including Ossorio y Gallardo, desired to restrict the extension of the vote to women.

All Spaniards will have the right to vote, both women, spinsters or widows, as well as men. The law will regulate the other necessary circumstances for the exercise of the suffrage and the opportunity of conceding the vote to married women.

Alcalá Zamora desired to reduce the electoral age to twenty-one and two members wished to extend the privilege of electing senators to the religious sects. The fear of the return to a dictatorial régime was reflected in Adolfo Posada's petition to suppress Article 48, which gave the government the power to legislate by decree in the case of necessity.[23]

The separate treatment of the chief of state and the government was included in order to trace with greater exactitude their respective functions. The presidential powers were strictly representative and moderative. The president had the power to call extraordinary sessions of the *cortes*, direct international conventions and relations with the League of Nations, veto laws, and dissolve the *cortes*, although these powers were more restricted than those held by Alfonso XIII. In addition, the president would be held criminally responsible for the infraction of his constitutional duties and obligations.

[22] *El Sol*, July 7, 1931.
[23] Jiménez de Asúa, 29-30.

This extreme, new also in the constitution, is sketched with sufficient rigor, to avoid as far as possible events which in our country and others cause very serious disturbances and are accustomed to remain unpunished.

The president was to be elected by the *cortes*. The commission recognized the virtues of an election by universal suffrage, but its chairman declared:

The authors of this work believe that universal suffrage, an insuperable tool in order to elect representations of aspirations, ideas, and tendencies, is not adequate in order to discern capacities. . . .

These were conditioned by history, character, opportunity, and physical vigor, which the people could not sufficiently appraise.

Our impassioned temperament and our old electoral abuses would bring complications to direct election, which may compromise the life of the country and which it is difficult to rectify.[24]

One *voto particular* was offered to the fifth title, which aimed to strengthen the president of the republic, electing him

. . . by an assembly constituted by the Congress of Deputies and three representatives of the *ayuntamientos,* of each one of the actual provincial demarcations, chosen eight days before the presidential vote. . . .

Espinosa desired that the president should be indirectly elected, while Alcalá Zamora favored a direct election by universal suffrage. Posada offered the suggestion that the vice-president should preside over the senate, when not acting as president.[25]

It was important for the commission to consider the endowment of the ministry with the necessary authority and at the same time insure a strong parliamentary activity. While the government was protected against unpremeditated or im-

[24] *El Sol,* July 7, 1931.
[25] Jiménez de Asúa, 30-31.

passioned votes of censure, it was given the right to appoint
ministers without portfolio, in order to strengthen its moral
authority. The suspension of guarantees was also reserved to
the government, but it was held responsible, both civilly
and criminally, for the abuse of its power.[26]

The aim was to build a strong and autonomous judicial
power. All Spaniards agreed on its necessity, but it was difficult to obtain. Jurisdictions were unified; the election of the
president of the Supreme Tribunal was deferred to a competent technical assembly in order to secure his absolute
freedom from any influence; all judges and magistrates were
held to civil responsibility before the Supreme Tribunal, the
members of which were in turn criminally responsible to the
Court of Constitutional Guarantees; courts were permitted
to suspend their procedure before applying laws contrary to
the constitution; recourse against illegal administrative dispositions was provided; and trial by jury and publicity of
judicial procedure were guaranteed. These and other provisions aimed to secure a completely independent organism
which could function without external influence. All of these
principles were to be fully developed by an organic law.
Ossorio y Gallardo declared:

Any political construction of the present times would be useless
if it did not consider an administration of justice competent,
serene, responsible, and removed completely from political requirements.[27]

Various *votos particulares* were offered to particular articles of the section on justice. One, to Article 73, specified:
"The judges are independent in their function. They are only
subject to the law." Elola opposed the definition of the administration of justice as an autonomous power of the state.
Matilde Huici asked for the suppression of every class of
amnesty, while Alcalá Zamora wished to limit the exercise
of a general amnesty to exceptional cases.[28]

The provisions in regard to the treasury might be accused

[26] *El Sol,* July 7, 1931.
[27] *Ibid.*
[28] Jiménez de Asúa, 31-32.

of too great detail, but Ossorio y Gallardo declared the detail necessary,

. . . because parliaments, governments, and dictatorships have treated the financial order with such free confidence and have reached such extremes in mismanagement and favoritism, that it has come to be necessary to give the regulations and the guarantees a constitutional basis, in order that the contributor may be assisted and the governor more restrained and threatened.[29]

Posada desired to suppress the greater part of the articles specifying the details of the section on finance, holding that its content was not strictly constitutional.[30]

A new legal organism appeared for the first time in the *anteproyecto*, the Tribunal of Constitutional Justice. The commission desired that unconstitutional laws should not prevail; that conflicts between the state and the regions and between the regions should be easily settled; that criminal responsibility might be required of judges and magistrates, the ministers and the president; and that there should exist a jurisdictional function to examine the *actas* of deputies and senators. Various members of the Supreme Tribunal might have been called on to form the new institution,

But it has appeared, finally, that the temper of its functions would require something more than the strictly judicial aims, with the object that society should see the high judges freed from professional prejudices and spirit.[31]

Elola offered a long recommendation to expand the jurisdiction of the Tribunal of Constitutional Justice, while Posada tried to protect the power of the legal profession by providing that the majority of the magistrates in the new court should be selected from the Supreme Tribunal.[32]

Flexibility was also provided for the amendment of the constitution. A reform could be proposed by the government, the *cortes*, or twenty-five per cent of the electors. The proposal would then follow the ordinary legislative course and

[29] *El Sol*, July 7, 1931.
[30] Jiménez de Asúa, 32-33.
[31] *El Sol*, July 7, 1931.
[32] Jiménez de Asúa, 33.

would be approved if supported by four-fifths of the deputies. When the necessity of reform was agreed upon, the *cortes* would be automatically dissolved and a new election would be held within sixty days. It would meet as a constituent *cortes,* act on the proposed amendment, and then serve as an ordinary congress. Alcalá Zamora, however, wished to reduce the percentage necessary for the popular initiation of reform to fifteen or twenty per cent.[33]

Ossorio y Gallardo recognized the importance of nearly all of the *votos particulares.* They were born in disinterested and serene discussions, without precedent as examples of prudence and cordiality, responding to technical reasons or those of deep conviction. This ex-conservative who was trying loyally to change his monarchist traditions for the new ideals of the republic, concludes:

Although our labor is very deficient, we believe that it will require a long time and enthusiastic energy to fill with reality the molds which today we submit to the judgment of the government. Struggling always for a strong social advance, we have desired to avoid impossible illusions, servile copies, improvisations and routine, seeking the adaptation of Spain to the new times by roads of prudence and equanimity.

The commission sought "in the accommodation to the possibilities, that zone of national concord which we desire loyally and ardently for the consolidation and prosperity of the republic."[34]

The work of the *Comisión Jurídica Asesora* appeared to be discarded by the decision of the Provisional Government to recommend to the Constituent Cortes that it should appoint a parliamentary commission to draft the constitution. Nevertheless, this work was invaluable. It broke the ground for the constitution, accelerated the task of drafting the constitution in the *cortes,* and many of its provisions found their way finally into the constitution of the Second Spanish Republic.

[33] *Ibid.; El Sol* July 7, 1931.
[34] *El Sol,* July 9, 1931.

IX

THE OPENING OF THE CORTES

A s soon as the election returns were conclusive, preparations were begun for the formal opening of the *cortes*.
Early in June, Alcalá Zamora and Miguel Maura had in-
spected the *Escorial* in order to ascertain the feasibility of
transferring the sessions of the *cortes* there. It was held desirable to give the deputies the opportunity of performing their
task in a more temperate atmosphere than that afforded by
the midsummer heat of Madrid. The decision whether it
would sit in Madrid or transfer its activities to the *Escorial*
was left to the sovereign *cortes*.[1]

The *Congreso del Diputados*, however, was considered one
of the finest buildings in Madrid. It housed a rich collection
of works of art and historic mementoes. Its interior was
described as follows:

The Chamber of Ministers with its allegories—a symbolic mural
painting for each department—; the vestibule, spacious, with its
medallions, which are an homage to the figures of the parliament
of Spain—a vestibule which opens its doors only on the days of
the solemn opening of the *cortes,* and which, the rest of the time,
is the celebrated "buffet," the "Merendero del Cajo"—; its *salón
de conferencias,* with historic inscriptions, famous pictures, all
dominated by the bust of Castelar, with the appropriate citation,
admirable, of his work of the abolition of slavery; its presidential
offices, full of remembrances . . . its chamber of sessions, ample,
historic, decorative, with the golden homage for the men of past
parliamentary life; of the martyrs, like the Marquis of Duero,
Cánovas, Canalejas; the allegories of the Greek and Roman legis-
lators . . . all that, nothing less than all that, awaits the new
deputies of Spain.[2]

[1] *El Sol,* June 11, 1931.
[2] *Ibid.,* June 27, 1931.

Efforts were made to modernize the Congress of Deputies, to remove all reminders of the fallen régime and make it more comfortable for the deputies. A radio was installed in the chamber, with some twenty microphones scattered over the room. A cooling system was also installed.[3]

Meanwhile the deputies had been filing their credentials with the secretariat of the *cortes*. José Serrano Batanero, a representative from Guadalajara, was the first to present his *acta,* and became, therefore, the president of the preparatory session which was to be held on July 13. By July 4, some seventy-five *actas* had been received from prospective deputies, including Villanueva, Sánchez Guerra, Prieto, Besteiro, and Melquiades Alvarez. A week later, 345 *actas* had been presented.[4]

The preparatory session of the deputies was opened at 7:15 on the evening of July 13, by Serrano Batanero, 418 deputies having presented their credentials by that time. After the reading of the convocation decree by Gamoneda, Narciso Vásquez, as the oldest deputy, took the presidential chair, while the four youngest deputies acted as secretaries. A principal feature of the preparatory session was Maura's objection to the broadcasting of the debates lest they provoke public disturbances. It was decided to use the radio for the opening session and then remove it. Eduardo Ortega y Gasset attacked the *reglamento* which the Provisional Government had decreed and which the juridical commission had drafted. Maura defended the decree and declared the question out of order. The preliminary session then adjourned.[5]

On July 14, three months after the establishment of the Second Republic, the Constituent Cortes was formally convened. It was a festive occasion for the Spanish people. Early in the afternoon, for the first time since the municipal elections and the inauguration of the Provisional Government,

[3] *ABC,* July 4, 1931; *El Sol,* July 11, 1931.
[4] *ABC,* July 4, 5, 1931; *El Sol,* July 12, 1931.
[5] *Diario de sesiones de las Cortes Constituyentes de la república española,* No. 2, July 15, 1931, 9-18.

troops had marched through Madrid singing the Hymn of Riego, while the crowded streets had echoed with *vivas* for the army and the republic. The members of the cabinet assembled in the *Presidencia del Consejo,* while the representatives of the nation gathered in the chamber of the *Congreso del Diputados.* Troops lined the streets between the two buildings and there was great animation when, at 6:45 in the evening, the Provisional Government concluded its meeting and started for the *Congreso del Diputados* in automobiles. The ministers were received with cheers and waving handkerchiefs, the troops presented arms, and the band played the Hymn of Riego. The people climbed on the top of street cars and the pedestals of statues or sat perched in trees in an effort to get a better view of the procession.

The chamber, in which the deputies and guests had meanwhile been assembling, was decorated with the shield of the republic, and the smallest reminder of the old régime had been removed, even such a famous one as the statue of Isabella II. The tribunes were filled by six o'clock, and at seven o'clock Narciso Vásquez took the chair and called the chamber to order. The names of the eleven deputies who were to receive the Provisional Government were read and the session was suspended until the ministers arrived. Vásquez invited the deputies to go to the door and welcome the cabinet when it approached. It was a dramatic moment when these republicans passed through the gate to the plaza of the *cortes,* an entrance reserved for the sovereign during the old régime. They were received with great applause and the people in the streets broke into enthusiastic *vivas,* giving Alcalá Zamora and Lerroux an especially great ovation. The deputies gave way before the ministers, who passed up to the Blue Bench, reserved for the government.[6]

Alcalá Zamora then arose and began to speak in a clear, resonant voice. It was an effective address, gracious and persuasive as it should have been. After emphasizing the im-

[6] *El Sol,* July 15, 1931; *ABC,* July 15, 1931; Arturo Mori, ed., *Crónica de las Cortes Constituyentes de la regunda república española.* Madrid, 1932. I, 19-20. *Diario,* No. 1, July 14, 1931, 1-2.

portance of the historic occasion and paying a graceful tribute to the heroes of the long struggle for Spanish liberties,
he declared that, in his opinion, this was the last of the
Spanish revolutions, closing the cycle and marking the first
of the social revolutions which opened the way for justice.
The opportunity of coming to the *cortes* to address the deputies was the greatest thing of which he could dream, "after
which all the adventures of the earth seem to me the descent
from the greatest honor which providence has permitted me
to enjoy in this life."

The Provisional Government, which had no constitutional
basis except that of divine right of revolution, had now to
resign its supreme authority to the Constituent Cortes. Alcalá
Zamora begged the deputies to be severe in the examination
of the acts of the Provisional Government. It was their duty
to act as strict judges because of the sacred notion of responsibility,

without which laws are nothing and the past an audacity that
can return; you have to be judges or accusers of your enemies,
and in order to be inexorable, be severe with your own interests.

Here, then, was his threat that the old order should not
receive absolution from the new, that the ministers of Alfonso should stand before the bar of the *cortes* and bear the
responsibility for their unconstitutional acts.

Alcalá Zamora was confident that the revolution and the
acts of the Provisional Government would be vindicated. He
declared:

The government presents itself before you with hands clean of
blood and cupidity. In the revolution we were so self-denying,
so generous with our enemies, and in power we have been so
serene in the maintenance of order that the Spanish revolution
has no spot of blood to be imputed to the men who made it and
to the men who have governed it.

Although their hands were clean, they were not empty. The
Provisional Government brought two things to the *cortes,* an
intact republic and full sovereignty. It had suffered attacks

from both extremes, from the Right by sordid threats on the treasury in an effort to create a demoralizing panic, from the Left by the impatience of the extremists. The sovereignty was free from any vassalage to military leadership, an indispensable support but a threat to liberalism. Now the army was no longer to be feared.

In the army the republic has sure soldiers; if the hour arrives, loyal servants, undisputed heroes. Ah! but protectors, unnecessary; dominators, impossible; rebels, improbable.

The deputies arose and applauded at length. It was a moment of Latin enthusiasm. Then he pointed out that Spain was no longer to be governed by political oligarchies. This was the sovereignty and this the republic that the Provisional Government handed over to the *cortes*. The deputies had been chosen as the sculptors of the new constitution.

You have to repair with new forms the constitutional sculpture of Spain, the historic continuity lost, the thread of tradition broken. Do it, gentlemen. Do not forget that the difficulty of the effort consists in that in these sculptures one is not handling malleable sand nor clay which lends itself to the caprice of the sculptor: you carve upon rock which sinks deep into the earth, which rises above the tops of the trees and lives through the centuries.

The Provisional Government desired the fortune and the glory of the *cortes* more than its own. He concluded as follows:

We have, without lack of modesty, the tranquil conscience of duty fulfilled and of fortune attained, and we want you to obscure our work with another that is perpetual on top of it. And thus my last words are going to be without cajolery because you are our judges, without sorrow because you are going to be our successors, without pride and without low spirits because you are going to govern our conduct with your inspiration: be very successful, feel patriotism by impulse, have the certainty of your designs and, as the greatest recompense, be worthy of receiving the gratitude of the country and of enjoying the peace of conscience itself. . . .[7]

[7] Mori, I, 21-29; *Diario*, No. 1, 2-6.

The President of the Provisional Government returned to the Blue Bench amid great and prolonged applause. It was a splendid homage to the republic and the faith in the Provisional Government when the deputies rose in honor of Alcalá Zamora. It was accepted as a *fait accompli* that the *cortes* would approve the work accomplished by the cabinet, but it was necessary to keep the various factions together in order to complete the desired task. Alcalá Zamora's speech was an appeal to the whole of Spain to rally to the republic and support the *cortes* in its task.

Vásquez, the temporary president, then requested the deputies to attend the parade of the troops of Madrid, which was dedicated to the republic. The ministers and deputies went out on the portico and watched the procession which lasted an hour, during which the crowds continually raised their voices in *vivas* for the republic. The only untoward event was the hissing of the troops by some of the telephone strikers, but the hisses were drowned in the enthusiasm of the moment and ignored by the soldiers.

When the session was resumed at 8:40, the *cortes* turned to the question of its own organization. Julián Besteiro, the socialist leader and professor of logic, was elected temporary president, receiving 363 of the 371 votes cast. Ossorio y Gallardo received two votes and six were blanks. According to one chronicler, it would have been difficult to have found a temperament more exquisitely balanced than Besteiro's. He possessed great equanimity and was a slave of reason. Austere in manner, he possessed an inflexible spirit without losing his natural kindliness and an admirable tolerance. He had taught most of his life, first in the Institute of Orense, then in Madrid. Although a member of the Radical Republican Party, he had joined the Socialist Party in 1913 and eventually became its leader. He had participated in the revolutionary strike of 1917, had signed the strike manifesto, and was condemned by a military tribunal. Because of the fact that he was the leader of the largest representation in the *cortes,* his election as president of that body had long been conceded.[8]

The temporary *mesa* of the *cortes* was completed by the election of four vice-presidents and four secretaries, following a brief recess from 11:00 to 11:30. The vice-presidents were Manuel Marraco y Ramón, Francisco Barnés, Juan Castrillo, and Salvador de Madariaga. A teacher by profession, Bárnes had been a student of Francisco Giner de los Ríos and Manuel Bartolomé Cossío. He was a member of the Radical Socialist Party. Manuel Marraco received his position as a representative of the Radical Republican Party. He had been a deputy and had held many important positions in his native town, Zaragoza. Castrillo, a member of Alcalá Zamora's Right Liberal Republican group, was a lawyer by profession and the author of numerous juridical works, while Salvador de Madariaga was a student of international affairs. He had served as Professor of Spanish Studies in Oxford University and had been active in the League of Nations. He had gained great publicity from his writings and had been chosen ambassador to the United States.

The four secretaries had also been designated by the most important parliamentary groups, and their election was likewise a matter of course. Enrique Ramos Ramos was a lawyer and a member of Republican Action. Juan Simeón Vidarte had studied law in Madrid and had been active as a leader of the student opposition against Primo de Rivera. José Sánchez Covisa had organized his colleagues in the medical profession into a party and had not only opposed the dictatorship, but had also fought for the republic as a member of the Right Liberal Republican group. The fourth secretary, Ramón María de Aldasoro, was one of the youngest deputies in the *cortes*. He had served as civil governor of San Sebastian, however, and had been an active conspirator against the monarchy in the north of Spain.[9]

The temporary officers took their places immediately.

[8] *El Sol,* July 15, 1931; *ABC,* July 15, 1931; Mori, I, 35-37; *Diario,* No. 1, 6. For brief descriptions of the careers of the members of the definitive *mesa,* cf. *El Sol,* July 28, 1931.

[9] *El Sol,* July 28, 1931.

Julián Besteiro occupied the presidential chair and addressed the chamber, briefly but very much to the point. He thanked the chamber for the honor accorded him and spoke of the difficulties before the *cortes*. After proposing a vote of appreciation to the *mesa de edad,* he expressed his appreciation of the work of the Provisional Government; proposed that seven deputies be nominated for a commission on the *reglamento,* which should base its report on the provisional regulations and introduce the necessary modifications; and then suggested that the sessions should begin at five o'clock in the future. This was agreed and the session was suspended shortly before two o'clock in the morning.[10]

The *Comisión de Actas* was elected on July 15. It was composed of Manual Cordero, the chairman, and twenty others. In order to give it time to examine the credentials of the deputies and complete the task of fully constituting the assembly, it was agreed to suspend the *cortes* until July 18. There were twenty-five contested *actas,* and both the successful and the defeated candidates had to be heard. The majority of the contested seats, however, were for the last place on the list and were not very important. The commission undertook its task immediately and twenty *actas* had been approved by July 18.[11]

When the *cortes* reassembled it devoted most of its time to a study of the *reglamento,* which was quickly approved.[12] On July 20, the session lasted slightly over two hours and was devoted entirely to the *dictamen* of the *Comisión de Actas*. The report on the *actas* of Seville resulted in a sharp debate between Franco and Maura, in which the leader of the Revolutionary Republican Party charged that the elections in Seville had been accompanied by constant coercion on the part of the army and Civil Guard. The Seville report, however, was approved.[13]

[10] *El Sol,* July 15, 1931; *ABC,* July 15, 1931; Mori, I, 35-37. *Diario,* No. 1, 7-8.
[11] *El Sol,* July 16, 1931; *ABC,* July 16, 17, 18, 1931; *Diario* No. 2, 22; Nos. 3-5, appendices.
[12] *ABC,* July 19, 1931; *El Sol,* July 19, 1931; *Diario,* No. 3, July 18, 1931, 29-47.
[13] *ABC,* July 21, 1931; *El Sol,* July 21, 1931.

The two succeeding sessions were very brief and were devoted entirely to the contested elections. Various speakers in the session of July 22 expressed a desire for the immediate constitution of the chamber because of the urgent requirements of the country. A meeting of the leaders of the various factions was then called in order to ascertain whether the matter of the credentials could not be disposed of more rapidly.[14] Strikes were in progress in various sections and the situation in Seville was particularly grave. A revolutionary general strike was in progress there and truckloads of peasants, led by Dr. Vallina, had started for the city. The governor had received word that the movement was revolutionary in intent, and ordered the Civil Guard to stop the trucks. Many workers, including Vallina, were arrested and the others returned to work. Martial law was declared in Seville on July 21, and the government agreed on a decree for the defense of the republic, to be published if necessity required.[15] Angel Pestaña, the syndicalist leader, was also actively engaged in propaganda, taking advantage of the delay in the constitution of the *cortes* and in its attempt to settle the problems of the country, to appeal to the impatience of the laborers and to advance the cause of syndicalism.

The *Comisión de Actas* continued to work steadily but slowly. The session of the *cortes* on July 23 lasted only five minutes. Besteiro tried to excuse the delay by comparing the situation to the opening of the *cortes* in 1869 which took a day longer.[16] The next day the debates grew tense over the problem presented in the *actas* of Salamanca. The returns revealed that a hundred per cent of the electorate had voted. Galarza declared that this was impossible, since forty per cent of the workers were too busy to vote, and a bitter attack was launched against the agrarian landlords. Gil Robles rushed eloquently to the defense of the validity of the election and was supported by the agrarian and Catholic deputies. It was the first real clash with the conservatives and had

---

[14] *ABC*, July 23, 1931; *El Sol*, July 23, 1931.
[15] *El Sol*, July 22, 23, 1931.
[16] *ABC*, July 24, 1931; *Diario*, No. 7, July 23, 1931.

an ironic aspect since the report of the commission to annul the elections in Salamanca would have unseated Unamuno. Finally the commission accepted a motion asking for the total validity of the election and withdrew its nullifying report. Gil Robles had succeeded in gaining a brief triumph over the Republicans, his first parliamentary victory. The report on the credentials of the deputies from Lugo also involved charges of *caciquismo,* but that election was annulled by a vote of 83 to 52. This was the first real session of the *cortes* and lasted until 3:30 in the morning.[17]

As a result of the parliamentary action, Maura withdrew from the ranks of the Right Liberal Republican minority. Some of its members had voted against the *actas* of Lugo. Maura declared:

I have nothing to do with that minority and I have thus informed its chief, D. Carlos Blanco. It is not exactly because of the event of this night, but because this and other acts have separated me entirely from a group which is not bound by any political discipline. From this time, I am in the chamber only as a mushroom.[18]

This break marked a schism in the ranks of the Provisional Government, for Alcalá Zamora was the chief of the Right Liberal Republican Party and had only temporarily relinquished his position to Blanco while serving as the head of the Provisional Government. The news of the decision on the *actas* of Lugo produced great enthusiasm there.[19]

The *cortes* had now been assembled for nearly two weeks and the delay in its constitution gave rise to rumors. *El Sol* reported one to the effect that certain deputies proposed to set up a provisional constitution which would permit the rapid nomination of the president of the republic and give the opportunity for the formation of a nominal government. Then the *cortes* would be able to "discuss, study, and pro-

[17] *ABC,* July 25, 1931; *El Sol,* July 25, 1931; *Diario,* No. 8, July 24, 1931, 111.
[18] *El Sol,* July 25, 1931.
[19] *ABC,* July 26, 1931.

mulgate the definitive constitution of Spain with calm and serene meditation." *El Sol* pointed out, however, that there were two dangers in such a move. The first was that in Spain everything of a provisional nature tended automatically to become permanent. Thus Spain would have to live politically in perpetual provisionality. The second danger arose from the nature of the *cortes*. It would become less homogeneous and more divided in opinion with the passing of time and as the early enthusiasm for the republic gave way to party strife. Cohesion and discipline would be lost and the probability of a continuation of the Republican-Socialist Coalition under the strain of factional politics was indefinite. Neither political normality nor economic stability could exist under a provisional or transitory régime.[20]

On July 27, 1931, the *cortes* was finally constituted. The atmosphere in the chamber was heated by the excitement of the deputies and the high temperature which was only slightly alleviated by the air cooling system. The session was opened at 5:30 in the evening by Marraco and the first business was the election of the definitive *mesa*. The temporary officials were reëlected. Besteiro received 326 of the 332 votes cast. The deputies then filed past the president to take their oaths in answer to the question: "Do you promise to fulfil with loyalty the mandate with which the nation has entrusted you?" Alcalá Zamora led the members of the government to the presidency to congratulate Besteiro.[21]

Following an address by Besteiro, announcing the definitive constitution of the chamber, a debate developed over the proposal of the agrarian deputies to discuss the election of the president of the republic. Cordero, a Socialist, declared that the government was supported by general confidence and public opinion. Royo Villanova, an agrarian deputy replied: "In a parliament there are always deputies and others who aspire to govern. . . ."

[20] *El Sol*, July 26, 1931.
[21] *ABC*, July 28, 1931; *El Sol*, July 28, 1931; *Diario*, No. 9, July 27, 1931, 153-154.

Then a voice interrupted: "That which is not right is to be elected by the Patriotic Union."

The conservative then declared that Spain needed a constitution and a chief of state in order to enjoy normal political life. The failure in 1873 had arisen from the delay in the designation of a president. Alcalá Zamora was greeted with prolonged applause when he defended the necessity of continuing the provisional régime while the constitution was debated. Villanova was drowned out by the cries of the chamber, and Ossorio y Gallardo's demand for a vote on the proposal received only the support of the agrarian deputies. The session adjourned at 9:30.

The effort of the agrarians to force the election of a permanent president was incorporated in a proposition presented to the *mesa* before the session. It demanded that as soon as the *cortes* was constituted a president should be elected. His powers would be limited to the nomination and recall of ministers and the issuance of decrees necessary to the execution of the laws. Villanova was furious at his defeat. He declared after the session:

> They have not let me rectify, a thing never seen in a parliament. . . . I would have demonstrated to Señor Alcalá Zamora that I know political law and that his arguments lacked foundation. I would have demonstrated to him, besides, that I had planted a juridical theme without any political influence.[22]

On July 28 the chamber was packed. It was the day that the political debate was to begin. The Provisional Government was presented to the deputies in order to ask them to ratify the provisional decrees. It expected an ample margin of confidence, for it was logical that the people should support the republic. The session was opened at 5:25, and without any preliminary debate Alcalá Zamora rose to address the chamber. He plunged immediately into the task of rendering the account of the Provisional Government to the *cortes* which now possessed full sovereignty. Five realities, he

[22] *ABC*, July 28, 1931; *Diario*, No. 9, 160-166.

declared, had determined the action of the government: the reality of an accomplished revolution which could not be frustrated; the reality of its endowment with full powers by the people; the reality that it was a coalition government, which was its strength, although a threat of dissension would endanger the republic; the reality that it was a provisional government, preparing the way for the *cortes;* and, finally, the reality that it was a part of the Spanish revolution which had overthrown systematic and prolonged tyranny, a dictatorship which had broken the Spanish liberal and juridical tradition.

The first task of the government was the revision of the work of the dictatorship. He analyzed the acts, skilfully condemning the dictatorial régime and justifying the republic. The Provisional Government had to assume the responsibility which would have absorbed all of the time of the *cortes.* It was the duty of the government to prepare the indictments of responsibility, of the *cortes* to judge in its complete sovereignty. Alcalá Zamora delivered a clever defense of the measures undertaken to maintain the Provisional Government before the *cortes* had endowed the republic with constitutional authority, declaring: "We have taken all of the precautions in order that your work may be complete and ours, on the other hand, may be rectified."

The liquidation of the work of the dictatorship, however, was only a prologue to the task of the government.

It was necessary to establish the foundations that would mark the paths of the revolution, and one of the tasks which I believe attained is that desire of all democracies, that task of all the republics, which many times, even after installation, have delayed years and decades in affirming the constitution of a civil power. . . . And that civil power, dream of all democracies, the task of every republic, we believe that we have sketched, and we believe more: that we have defined it, in order that you may have the materials with which to trace the definitive work.

Alcalá Zamora then cited the administrative reforms of the Provisional Government, stressing the reforms in education and the cohesion and unanimity of the members of the government. He said: "We have arrived without any rupture of relations, without any sharp conflict, without any difficult hour, without any moment of inquietude." Military reform had served to make the civil power independent in fact. The army was a sumptuary fiction, not a defensive reality, and democratic reform of the army was at the same time a technical reform.

The problem of public order was more difficult to explain and defend, But Alcalá Zamora attacked it in a direct manner. The disorders were

. . . the inevitable complication, the fatal continuation of those inevitable violences in all revolutions, included in the most pacific, like the Spanish. They are, certainly, a strange but natural prolongation, which follows all revolutionary processes.

After the pacific days of April 12-14, the Spanish Revolution

. . . continued presenting itself before all similar commotions as the most orderly, as that in which life paid less tribute, fortune less contribution, and the principle of authority the least loss of prestige.

The greatest danger to the republic was the belief that a dictatorship was necessary to maintain order, for the government of the republic knew how to conserve it within the law.

And it is necessary to destroy that belief in the timid people, who hand over the authority to the dictator to preserve order, and in the apparently audacious people who endure with unworthy meekness the years of personal power to render difficult with criminal impatience the beginnings of a democracy.

The chamber broke into applause and Alcalá Zamora continued, declaring that it was necessary to teach timid and audicious people that "the power of the republic, being just, knows how to be strong, in order that the pusillanimity of some and the audacity of the others may disappear."

Then the provisional president explained that the government, by a show of good faith, had maintained good relations with the *Generalitat* of Catalonia and had paved the way for an effective constitutional solution. He praised the work of the Ministers of Labor and Economy in attacking the social problems, and, turning to the three socialist ministers, declared: "Come what may as a consequence of this debate, the part of the social program which is agreed and not executed has anew the guarantee of our signatures, renewed publicity. . . ." There was applause, and Alcalá Zamora turned to the right of the Chamber.

And to the people of order, to the people of the extreme Right, to those who represent the interest which possesses, to those who have solicited us that certain reforms, the most transcendental, should come to the *cortes,* if the urgency permitted it and our duty by it consented to it, we give this warning, the path to law is not procrastination. Ask the parliament as guarantee, then know that the guarantee denaturalizes and debases when it converts into fraud, and that we are not disposed to bring a reform to the *cortes* in order not to realize the ideal of justice to which we aspire.

In regard to foreign policy, he said that Spain was going to possess sufficient moral force to be a factor for peace in the concert of the world and would resist any desire to enter war. He stressed the Pan-Hispanic policy which the republic had already begun to cultivate with the Latin countries of the new world. He concluded amid prolonged applause.[23]

The debate on the approval of the work of the Provisional Government began at once. The agrarian deputy, Fanjul, was the first to oppose the government. He was continually interrupted by the Socialists. Then Barriobero took up the attack and outraged the Socialists when he told one of their deputies he "lacked honor, decency, and education." There was a demand for a parliamentary investigation of the events at Seville, and Cordero and Maura defended the policy of the government, while Companys accused it of acting in a reactionary manner and Samblancat shouted that it was a

---

[23] Mori, I, 59-69; *El Sol,* July 29, 1931; *ABC,* July 29, 1931; *Diario,* No 10, July 28, 1931, 168-175.

political and ministerial maneuver to cover up Maura's policy. After electing the constitutional commission the session adjourned.[24]

The debate continued through the next two days. Charges of dictatorial methods were brought against the government by the Catholic deputy, Estévanez, of Burgos. The government had dictated dispositions against the consciences of the Catholics of Spain, who were in the majority. Samblancat declared that he believed hunger, the landlords, and the Civil Guard ruled in Andalusia and that the banner of the republic, stained with blood, would be converted into a red banner. The debate revealed all the factions that were struggling for power in the country, the Syndicalist-Socialist struggle, Catalan separatism, and the differences within the Provisional Government.[25]

Finally, on July 30, 1931, the proposal for the ratification of the work of the government was made and Besteiro announced that such a step seemed to be the sentiment of the debate. The approval was voted by acclamation while the ministers were retiring from the chamber. They returned to their seats amid the applause of the deputies, who rose from their seats. The text of the vote of confidence was as follows:

> The *cortes* ratify their confidence in the government constituted April 14; approve the declarations of the president of the government, and trust that it will know how to continue defending the republic, inspired by the democratic principles of social justice proclaimed by the Spanish people, until the approbation of the constitution and designation of the chief of state.[26]

With the approval of the Provisional Government the way was cleared for the discussion of the constitution. The triumph of the government in receiving a vote by acclamation, despite the vociferous charges of the extremists of both

[24] *Diario*, No. 10, 175-189.
[25] *ABC*, July 28, 29, 1931; *Diario*, Nos. 11, 12, July 29, 30, 1931.
[26] *ABC*, July 31, 1931; *Diario*, No. 12, 247.

Right and Left, was sweeping. The constitutional commission had been designated and the ratification of the provisional decrees by the *cortes* indicated that the constitutional provisions would follow the lines laid down by the Republican-Socialist Coalition.

X

THE CONSTITUENT CORTES

Parties and Procedure

THERE were some twenty-five parties represented in the Constituent Cortes, but they soon began to organize themselves into *blocs*. It is, therefore, rather difficult to follow the shifting lines between the parties. Parties split, individuals withdrew from their nominal groups, and others followed a consistently independent course from the first.

The largest *bloc* in the *cortes* was the *Alianza Republicana,* formed through the coöperation of the deputies professing allegiance to the Radical, Republican Action, and Federal parties. Some of the Federals, however, including Soriano, Pí Arsuaga, and Barriobero, chose to follow their traditional lines of action and refused to coöperate in the alliance. It was managed by a directory, whose secretary was Honorato de Castro, and consisted of 145 deputies. Guerra del Río was the leader of the Radical group in the chamber because of the fact that Lerroux had to remain officially aloof from parliamentary political strife while he sat on the Blue Bench, José Franchy led the Federals and José Giral was the chief of the Republican Action deputies.[1]

The Socialists had the largest unified and disciplined representation in the *cortes,* with 114 deputies. They were directed by a commission consisting of Remigio Cabello as president, a vice-president, a secretary, and two other members. All party proposals had to be submitted to this commission for approval before being presented in the *cortes* and were subject to veto by the president. The commission designated the speakers to represent the Socialist Party in the parliamentary debates, and other members of the party

[1] *ABC,* July 15, 18, 26, 1931.

were to remain silent. The group united an hour before each session to adopt the appropriate procedure. The relations with other party groups and the president of the *cortes* were left entirely to Cabello.[2]

The Radical-Socialist Party was the next most important group, with fifty-six representatives, led by Emilio Baeza. The Right Liberal Republican group, which was represented in the government by Alcalá Zamora, consisted of twenty-eight deputies. It was somewhat weakened by the withdrawal of Miguel Maura. Carlos Blanco was chosen as director of its parliamentary activities.[3]

The regions were strongly represented in the *cortes*. The Catalan Left, headed by Luis Companys, had forty-two members. It named its representatives on the various permanent commissions and they intervened in all matters affecting the interests of Catalonia.[4] The *Federación Republicana Gallega,* representing the regional interests of Galicia, consisted of twenty-two members and was led by Antonio Villar Ponte. It had one member in the government, Casares Quiroga. The Vasconavarros numbered sixteen and were led by Joaquín Beunza.[5]

There were nineteen Agrarians in the *cortes,* representing the conservative interests, whose principal aim was the defense of the rights of property and the Church. They were directed by José Martiñez de Velasco and included such men as Antonio Royo Villanova, Casanueva, and Gil Robles. The other conservative forces included the two members of National Action, a Monarchist, the Count of Romanones, and a few independents.[6]

In addition there were fourteen deputies who were termed independents, three dissenting Federals, and two who termed themselves Liberals. Many conservative Republicans and a number of intellectuals were more or less removed from the

[2] *Ibid.,* July 17, 26, 1931; *El Sol,* July 18, 1931.
[3] *ABC,* July 17, 26, 1931; *El Sol,* July 18, 1931.
[4] *ABC,* July 17, 26, 1931; *El Sol,* July 18, 1931.
[5] *ABC,* July 16, 17, 26, 1931; *El Sol,* July 18, 1931.
[6] *ABC,* July 16, 17, 26, 1931; *El Sol,* July 18, 1931.

partisan strife within the chamber. José Sánchez Guerra and Angel Ossorio y Gallardo had been active under the old régime and, although they professed allegiance to the republic, were inclined to defend conservative traditions. Santiago Alba, Melquiades Alvarez, and Calvo Sotelo also maintained their independence of action. The intellectuals had organized themselves into a minority called *Al Servicio de la República*. Its membership included such men as José Ortega y Gasset and Dr. Gregorio Marañón.[7]

On July 16 the chiefs of the minorities met with Julián Besteiro, to arrange the location of their respective groups within the semicircle and avoid any anomalous grouping of the deputies. It was agreed that they should occupy their benches according to the numerical order of the minorities. Thus, the Socialist Party would have been placed on the extreme left of the presidency, then the Radical Party, next the Radical Socialist Party, and so on. The three parties which had formed the Republican Alliance, however, wanted to sit together. The Radical-Socialists refused to give the two smaller groups precedence in the seating arrangement, and the Radical group was forced at last to give in and be seated with the members of Republican Action and the Federals, on the extreme right of the chamber, behind the Blue Bench. The special composition of the chamber and the scarcity of seats prevented the deputies from being seated in the traditional European manner of Right and Left.[8]

Julián Besteiro declared:

Today we have begun this exchange of impressions with a puerility. Each party wanted to be more to the left than the others and to choose a place in the Chamber of Sessions similar to that of the members of the convention in the French Revolution. . . .[9]

As a result, the section on the extreme right of the chamber was occupied by the Republican Alliance, the Radicals, Republican Action, and the Federals. The Right Liberal Re-

[7] *ABC*, July 14, 17, 22, 26, 1931.
[8] *ABC*, July 17, 1931.
[9] *Ibid.*

publicans were placed in the center, for they desired to orient themselves toward the left in order to be the center party as in Germany. Then came the Agrarians, National Action, the independent members of the Federal Party, the autonomous groups of Galicia and the Basque provinces, and the independents and undefined deputies. The section on the left of the presidency was occupied by the Left Republicans, the Radical Socialists, and the Socialists.[10]

It is also important to understand the professional interests of the deputies. *El Sol* declared:

Our Constituent Cortes is composed principally of persons of the middle class, more or less wealthy. The liberal professions abound. There are many doctors, and many lawyers. There is an important representation of the priestly class. There are some intellectuals and enough laborers. The compound could not be more uniformly democratic.[11]

Its rival, *ABC,* was also pleased by the composition of the *cortes.* "The Constituent Cortes is qualified by the intellectuality of the great mass of its components."[12]

An incomplete report reveals that 123 of the deputies professed to be lawyers, including such persons as Eduardo Ortega y Gasset, Clara Campoamor, Serrano Batanero, Romanones, Carrasco, Ossorio y Gallardo, Victoria Kent, and Luis Companys. There were forty-one physicians, including Pí Arsuaga and Gregorio Marañón, and fifty university professors. Among the latter were Royo Villanova, José Ortega y Gasset, Gil Robles, Unamuno, and Salvador de Madariaga. In addition, there were thirteen other *maestros.* Thirty deputies indicated that they were editors, three that they were architects, sixteen that they were engineers, and fifteen, including Araquistain, Marcelino Domingo, and Samblancat, that they were publicists. There were eight priests and eight military men, including Sanjurjo and Fanjul. Juan March was the most notable of the eighteen industrialists or

[10] *Ibid.; El Sol,* July 17, 1931.
[11] *El Sol,* July 16, 1931.
[12] *ABC,* July 19, 1931.

merchants. The remaining members of the *cortes* were scattered among the various professions and trades of the middle class. There were four notaries, two registrars, two seamen, six public officials, six pharmacists, four landlords, two veternarians, one jeweler, a tailor, a chauffeur, and a baker. Finally, there were twenty-seven laborers, three miners, and six printers.[13]

Thus, it is evident that the *cortes* was representative of all classes in Spain and that it was dominated by the intellectual classes whose idealism had been instrumental in the revolutionary movement, checked the radicalism of the extremists, and made the revolution a political evolution. Such a body of men could frame a constitution representing the interests of all classes, provided they could bring their interests into harmony. If they were guided by idealism they would frame a constitution incorporating the most advanced ideas, and by realism, a workable one. And the dominance of the chamber by the coalition of the Republicans and the Socialists indicated that idealism would predominate, while the necessity of a certain amount of compromise to placate all groups was a promise of the balance that would give that idealism a sound foundation. *El Sol,* in its enthusiasm for the body that was to make the new Spain, reported that no parliament "exists in the world which concentrates such a volume of ideas and of sensibility."[14]

The rules of procedure governing the *cortes* had been entrusted by the Provisional Government to the *Comisión Jurídica Asesora.* The commission was asked to draw up a provisional *reglamento* for the consideration of the *cortes,* which would examine and approve the definite rules. The council examined the report of the commission on July 10 and approved various modifications. The provision for the nomination of a temporary president of the republic was suppressed. The project had provided for a president *ad interim,* but the *cortes* had not yet agreed upon the powers

---

[13] *Ibid.,* This information was reprinted in *El Sol,* July 21, 1931.
[14] *El Sol,* July 16, 1931.

that were to be given to the chief of state and it was decided that the nomination should not be made. Therefore the Spanish Republic would have no permanent executive until the constitution was approved. The report of the commission had omitted a provision for a parliamentary committee to draft the constitutional project. The government, however, deemed it advisable to simplify the debates by means of a commission. Hence, it was decided to appoint such a body as should include representatives of all the political groups in the *cortes*. It was also agreed that a commission should be appointed by the *cortes* for each ministerial department, the aim of which would be the study of the various projects presented to the *cortes*.[15]

In the preparatory session of July 13, the question of the right of the Provisional Government to dictate the rules of the *cortes* was raised. Maura, who as Minister of Government had been active in the final revision and modification of the provisional rules of procedure, rushed to the defense of the project and declared that it was nearly a literal copy of that of 1873. He questioned the right of the preparatory session to raise the issue of the *reglamento* and declared that, since the project was only provisional, the chamber retained full liberty to accept or reject it. Ortega y Gasset cried in his stentorian voice, "The *reglamento* is coercive and will strangle the discussions."[16]

Two days later the parliamentary commission on the rules of procedure was chosen. It began to study the project of the *Comisión Jurídica Asesora* and made the modifications necessary to reconcile the respect due the sovereignty of the *cortes* with the desire to lay down norms that would make that body active and sober. The parliamentary committee maintained the division of the chamber into political groups rather than in sections, and regulated the deputy's intervention in the debates, although the chamber or its president might give greater elasticity to the discussion. The

[15] *Ibid.*, July 11, 1931; *ABC*, July 11, 1931.
[16] *ABC*, July 14, 1931.

questions directed to the ministers and the interpellations were to be verbal rather than written, and in general the aim was to protect the liberty and rights of the deputy. A Commission of Responsibilities, which was not provided in the *anteproyecto,* was now specified.[17] The parliamentary commission completed its work on July 17, and the draft was introduced into the *cortes* the next day. Various amendments were offered. A few were accepted, some, like Franco's proposal to broadcast the debates, were defeated, and the *reglamento* was quickly approved.[18]

The presiding officer at the preliminary session, which had met on July 13, was the deputy who first presented his credentials. Then the oldest deputy and the four youngest were to be president and secretaries respectively. These deputies enjoyed only a brief tenure and the interim *mesa* or board of officials was elected. These nine officers, a president, four vice-presidents, and four secretaries, were elected by separate ballots, cast in three urns. To be elected the president had to have an absolute majority of the votes. Each deputy voted for three men for the four vice-presidencies and two for the four secretaryships. The four of each class elected were those receiving the greatest number of votes.

As soon as the *mesa* was constituted, each deputy was to present a signed declaration indicating the political party in the chamber with which he wished to be identified. Those deputies who did not belong to any party could unite among themselves or indicate the group which they preferred to join in order to effect the political régime of the chamber. The independent deputies should be identified as a single group. Each of the groups had to have at least ten deputies and could be represented on the various commissions in proportion to its numerical strength. It should have a president and a secretary to direct its internal organization.

A commission of *actas* was provided to render a decision in contested elections, or in case any doubt was cast on the

[17] *ABC,* July 17, 1931; *El Sol,* July 17, 1931.
[18] *ABC,* July 18, 19, 1931; *El Sol,* July 19, 1931.

credentials, aptitude, or legal capacity of any deputy. Its judgment had to be approved by the *cortes*. It consisted of twenty-one deputies elected by list in the chamber. The deputies were given fifteen days to qualify and those elected from more than one district had to choose a single constituency within the same period. All vacancies were to be filled by new elections. No civil governor could serve as a deputy except the civil governor of Madrid, who did not have to absent himself from his capital to attend the *cortes*.

The *cortes* would have a quorum for definitive constitution as soon as 236 deputies were admitted. The permanent officials were then to be elected, although the eligibility of the interim *mesa* for reëlection was provided. When the deputies had taken their oath to fulfil loyally the mandate conferred upon them by the nation, the *cortes* would be officially constituted and ready to receive the message of the president of the Provisional Government.

This procedure outlined above had already been fulfilled. The remainder of the *reglamento* dealt with the constituted chamber. It was to name a special commission to present a constitutional project as soon as possible. This commission was to consist of twenty-one members also, each deputy casting his vote for fourteen. As soon as the project was presented the debate would begin, dealing first with the totality of the project. In this discussion the debate was definitely restricted to three speeches for the project and three against it, although any group not represented in the six speeches might indicate its attitude. The constitution would then be debated, article by article. Again the discussion was restricted, both in the number and length of the speeches. A deputy might consume ten minutes in explaining or rectifying his concept, and he could explain his vote in five minutes. No one would be granted the floor, however, to make a personal allusion. Only the government and the members of the commission could intervene without consuming a turn. Finally, when the absolute majority of the chamber, on the proposal of fifteen deputies, the president of the *cortes,* or the government, considered that an article had been fully discussed and the turns in the debate had been consumed, the discussion would be suspended and the vote taken. The commission could then take the results of the discussion and modify its text in accordance with the principles agreed upon in the debate. The project would then be submitted for definitive approval and would be sanctioned on obtaining an absolute majority.

The deputies had the right and duty of attending the sessions of the *cortes*. They enjoyed inviolability for their opinions expressed in the chamber and for their votes. They were subject to disciplinary action by the *cortes* only in case of an infraction of the rules governing that body. No deputy could be arrested without the consent of the *cortes* unless he had committed a serious crime. Notice of such an arrest had to be given to the *cortes* immediately, and no court could act against a deputy without the consent of the chamber. When it was notified of the arrest the *cortes* would appoint a commission of nine deputies, representing the various groups, to render a judgment. This would be read in the chamber within twenty days, and after a debate, restricted to two speeches for and two against the deputy, the chamber rendered its decision in regard to the prosecution of the case against the deputy concerned. Each deputy received a thousand *pesetas* a month and was given free passage on all railroads, airlines, and steamships.

The power of the president of the *cortes* consisted primarily in the maintenance of order in the discussions and the direction of the debate with impartiality and the respect due to the chamber. He determined the questions which were going to be discussed and voted, granted the floor in the order in which it was requested, arranged the order of the day for the following session at the end of each session, and maintained communications with the government and other authorities. He could interpret the *reglamento* and supply any omissions or complete any doubtful clauses. He called the deputies to order when they used disrespectful language, offensive to the decorum of the chamber, individuals, the government, or foreigners, and when they tried to break the order of the debate. When a deputy was called to order three times in a single session, the president was to consult the *cortes* in regard to denying him a hearing for the rest of the session, and if a deputy insisted on being disorderly the president might require that he abandon the chamber. If he refused to leave, the session would be adjourned and reassembled without him, adopting measures for his exclusion during the remainder of the session. Any recalcitrant person might be expelled from the public galleries and handed over to the competent authorities. The president of the *cortes* also controlled the police and all employees in the *Congreso del Diputados*. He might take part in the debate but had to relinquish his authority to a vice-president and leave the chair, returning only when the matter under discussion was voted upon.

One of the duties of the secretaries was to keep the minutes, using a separate book for the secret sessions. They also edited the minutes, had charge of all communications sent to the *cortes,* signed resolutions, declared and published the results of the votes, and directed the secretariat and editorship of the *Diario de Sesiones*.

The *cortes* named permanent commissions for interior government, the reform of the rules of procedure, the examination of accounts and pensions, and for each ministry. The first three consisted of nine members each, while the ministerial commissions were composed of twenty-one deputies, elected proportionally from the various party groups. Two other commissions were named also, the commission on the budget of thirty-five members, and a Commission of Responsibilities, charged with the investigation of the guilt for the dissolution of the Cortes of 1923 and the dictatorship. The latter consisted of twenty-one members.

Two types of sessions were provided, the ordinary and the extraordinary. The former was held four days each week and the latter when the circumstances required and the *cortes* ordered it. The procedure within each session was rigidly prescribed. No other measure could be introduced until the *cortes* approved the constitution, unless the government or a hundred deputies proposed it. In that event, it was to be accepted as a case of extreme urgency and the debate would proceed along with that on the constitution. An hour of each session was devoted to questions and interpellations which the deputies desired to explain or have explained by the government. The *mesa* or government had to answer questions on matters of national interest. It was specified that the interpellations should be addressed to the *mesa,* indicating the ministry affected and the matter involved. The *mesa,* in accord with the proper minister, then set the date for the interpellation, within a period of eight days. The sessions were generally public, but secret ones were held when matters affecting the decorum of the *cortes* or that of its members arose, or when, in the judgment of the *mesa,* the matter to be debated required it. Each session was opened and closed by a prescribed formula, i.e., *abrése la sesión,* to open it, and *se levanta la sesión,* to close it.

The presence of one hundred deputies was necessary for a vote, although the *cortes* might be opened with fewer deputies present if there was no need for an agreement. In the consideration of any project, the matter was first given to the proper commission for its opinion and the *mesa* then fixed the date for the debate. Any amendments had to be signed by from seven to fourteen deputies, and no amendment involving an increased expenditure or a decrease in income could be considered unless signed by at least fifteen deputies.

In order to harmonize the brevity of the debates with their efficacy and the respect for the rights of the deputies, the following restrictions were established. No deputy could speak on an unimportant matter for more than fifteen minutes, or on an important one for more than thirty minutes. In the debates on the totality of the constitution each turn lasted an hour, in the debate on chapters forty-five

minutes, and in the discussion of articles the time was limited
to thirty minutes. These restrictions, however, might be submitted to the *cortes,* which, on the proposal of the president
and in its soverign wisdom, might extend the time conceded
if the importance of the debate made it advisable.

No deputy could speak without having requested and obtained the floor. The ministers could obtain the floor whenever they asked for it, and a deputy might interrupt at any
time to request the observance of the rules of order, citing
the article, the enforcement of which he requested. Any deputy alluded to in person or in action might have the floor
if the president judged the allusion genuine, and if he was
not in the chamber the day the allusion was made, he might
request the floor at the next session.

For agreement on the articles and amendments to the constitutional project a quorum of one hundred deputies was
required, the majority of those voting being sufficient for
their approval. Five forms of voting were provided. The first
was mere assent to the presidential proposal. In ordinary
voting the deputies who approved of the proposal rose and
those disapproving remained seated. A secretary announced
the result, and if there was any doubt as to the outcome of
the vote, the president named two deputies from those who
rose and two from those who remained seated. One of each
group counted those who approved and the other two
counted those who disapproved. To prevent confusion no
deputy was permitted to enter or leave the chamber while
the votes were being counted, and every ordinary vote had
to be repeated when the deputies counting the votes were
not in agreement after two counts. When fifteen deputies
requested it, the vote might be nominal. This consisted of
a roll call in which the deputies remained seated and answered yes or no according to their attitude toward the proposal. Every election of persons was by ballot, unless the
chamber agreed to make it by acclamation. The vote by
balls was used whenever any vote in which the act or conduct of any person was censured or when the *cortes* agreed

by a majority of the deputies present. In this method of voting, each deputy approached the *mesa* and received a black and a white ball from the president. He deposited one of them in the urn, the white if he approved, the black if he disapproved, putting the remaining ball in a separate urn. The secretaries, meanwhile, kept an exact list of those voting and the president and secretaries counted the balls and announced the result. All of the deputies could adhere to the resolutions of the chamber, even though they were not present at the time the resolutions were taken, but their adhesion could not modify the agreement reached.

The internal organization of the *cortes* was in the hands of the Commission of Interior Government. It directed the *Extracto Oficial* and the *Diario de Sesiones de las Cortes Constituyentes,* in which it was to insert and print, wholly, faithfully, and impartially all of the acts which occurred and all of the discourses which were pronounced in the public sessions, organizing their editing and printing in such a manner that these publications should appear regularly. This commission also had oversight of the vacant positions in the *cortes,* but it could not increase them, diminish them, or abolish them without the approbation of the chamber. It controlled the budget of the expenses of the *cortes,* receiving and administering the funds from the public treasury, directing the various services, and presenting a monthly report to the chamber which was to be approved in a secret session and read publicly in the first session of each month.

The various projects of law which the government presented to the *cortes* were passed immediately to the respective permanent committees unless, on the proposal of the president, the chamber decided by a nominal vote to send the law to a special commission of seven members. Legislative proposals initiated by deputies had to be signed by their authors and handed to the president. No project could' be initiated by less than seven deputies. The proposals were passed to the proper commissions which authorized their reading in a public session. Immediately after the reading one of the authors was called upon to explain the motives and bases of the project. The chamber was then asked whether it would consider the project. No debate was permitted on this resolution. The same regulations governed the debate on legislative projects which regulated that on the constitution. Petitions were received by the *cortes* and placed on a list in numerical order, indicating only the name of the petitioner and the object of the petition. A commission of nine deputies was provided to judge the petitions received each month and determine whether they should be entertained or rejected, or whether they should be sent to the competent minister for consideration at an opportune moment.[19]

[19] Mori, I, 38-52; *Diario*, No. 3, Appendices 1, 3.

XI

THE PARLIAMENTARY COMMISSION

THE *reglamento* had provided that the Constituent Cortes should elect a special commission to present a constitutional project.[1] This became all the more important after the discrepancies among the members of the Council of Ministers had prevented the government from presenting the *anteproyecto* of the *Comisión Jurídica Asesora* to the chamber. The tardy constitution of the *cortes* in its full sovereignty delayed the election of the commission, and it was not until July 28, two weeks after the opening of the *cortes,* that it was chosen.[2]

The constitutional commission of the *cortes* consisted of twenty-one members. The parliamentary minorities were represented in proportion to their numerical strength. Two of the original members were later replaced, but in its definitive membership it consisted of five Socialists, four Radicals, three Radical Socialists, and two Catalans. The remaining seven members represented Republican Action, the Galician Republicans, the Federals, the Right Liberal Republicans or Progressives, the *Agrupación al Servicio de la República,* the *vasconavarra* group, and the Agrarians.[3] Three of these

---

[1] *Diario,* No. 3, July 18, 1931, Appendix 1, Art. 21.

[2] *Ibid.,* No. 10, July 28, 1931, 190.

[3] Jiménez de Asúa, 33-35; *Diario,* No. 3, Ap. 1. The original commission consisted of the following:

Socialists: Luis Jiménez de Asúa, Luis Araquistain, Trifón Gómez San José, Jerónimo Bugeda, Enrique de Francisco.

Radicals: Emiliano Iglesias Ambrosio, Ricardo Samper Ibañez, Clara Campoamor, Justo Villanueva.

Radical-Socialists: Leopoldo Alas, Juan Botella Asensi, Fernando Valera.

Catalans: Gabriel Alomar Villalonga, Antonio Xiráu Paláu.

Republican Action: Mariano Ruiz Funes García.

Galician Republican: Antonio Rodríguez Pérez.

men, Jiménez de Asúa, Valdecasas, and Rodríguez Pérez, had served on the *Comisión Jurídica Asesora,* while the latter two had been members of the subcommission which had formulated the *anteproyecto.*

This commission constituted itself immediately and notified the *cortes,* on July 29, that it had begun to function. Luis Jiménez de Asúa was chosen president and José Franchy Roca became vice-president. The latter was replaced by Emiliano Iglesias when he resigned to accept the office of *Fiscal General* of the Republic. The *mesa* of the commission was completed by the election of two secretaries, Fernando Valera and Alfonso García Valdecasas.[4]

Jiménez de Asúa has described the contributions of some of his colleagues as follows:

Araquistain was the culture and sensibility of the international man; Bugeda, the generous impetuosity; De Francisco, the serene equilibrium, and Trifón Gómez, the revelation. . . . Trifón Gómez listened in the midst of the commission with all of his assimilating power active, and when the moment was most difficult, when the debate became complicated, he asked for the floor and was nearly always certain to propose solutions.[5]

According to another contemporary, Luis Jiménez de Asúa was one of the outstanding men in the *cortes.* He was an ardent Socialist. Gabriel Alomar had won a literary reputation. Born in Majorca, he was a Catalan in temperament, although he always wrote and spoke Castilian. Valera was a young man of thirty who had become one of the popular

---

Federal: José Franchy Roca.
Progressive: Juan Castrillo Santos.
Agrupación al Servicio de la República: Alfonso García Valdecasas.
Vasconavarra: José Horn.
Agrarian: José María Gil Robles.
José Maria Leizaola replaced José Horn, *Diario,* No. 13, July 13, 1931, 257. Bernardino Valle Garca replaced José Franchy Roca, *Diario,* No. 16, August 6, 1931, 298. Emilianio Iglesias Ambrosio was expelled from the chamber as a result of the March Affair.

[4] Jiménez de Asúa, 35. The author cites August 29 as the date of the first report of the commission to the *cortes,* but corrects himself on page 39.

[5] *Ibid.,* 38.

leaders in Valencia. The extreme Right was represented on the commission by Gil Robles, a Catholic and journalist. Clara Campoamor, one of the two women in the *cortes,* warmly defended the rights of women and was a facile and able speaker. Emiliano Iglesias was an old comrade-in-arms of Lerroux and a traditional Republican. One of the secretaries, Valdecasas, was a studious representative of the intellectual liberals who had organized the *Agrupación al Servicio de la República.* Juan Botella y Asensi was a Radical-Socialist from Alicante. He was a journalist and a man of experience and enthusiasm. Ricardo Samper, *alcalde* of Valencia, was an audacious propagandist. Juan Castrillo, the representative of Alcalá Zamora's Progressive Republican Party in the formulation of the parliamentary project, was another important member. He regarded the draft approved by the commission as too revolutionary, and formulated a *voto particular* of eighty-nine articles, many of which were incorporated in the definitive constitution.[6]

The attitude of the ministers toward the *anteproyecto* of the *Comisión Jurídica Asesora* made it questionable whether the constitutional commission should draft a new project or take the *anteproyecto* as a base. This was discussed in the first meeting, on July 28, and it was agreed that the report of the juridical commission and the various *votos particulares* of the dissenting members were worth considering. Technically the work was regarded as fine, but the more radical members of the commission desired to give their *dictamen* or project a more democratic content. The *Comisión Jurídica Asesora* represented the liberalism of the nineteenth century. The commission of the *cortes,* elected after the triumph of the Republican-Socialist Coalition in April, was more cognizant of the social implications of the economic developments of the twentieth century. The five Socialists formed the radical wing of the commission and met to study the work of the juridical commission before

---

[6] Mori, I, 160-161; *cf.* the description by Luis Araquistain in *El Sol* December 8, 1931.

they assembled with their parliamentary colleagues. They carried a more advanced formula, in the form of an amendment to the articles of the *anteproyecto,* to the debates of the commission.[7] The Radical-Socialists also drafted a report which was very similar to the political program of the Socialists in its emphasis on economic and social matters.[8]

The constitutional commission undertook its work in the same leisurely fashion in which the *cortes* had opened. It met only four times the first week, following the example of the parliamentary recess. Under the stimulation of the government and the press the weekly recesses were soon abandoned and the commission worked morning and afternoon. The government and many deputies still urged greater activity on the part of the commission, and the newspapers continued to censure it. Jiménez de Asúa believed that the latter were badly informed concerning the manner in which the commission worked. Finally the project was completed and presented to the *cortes* on August 18. The discussions had been concluded four days earlier, but the intervening time had been spent in rearranging the articles and giving them a definitive draft.[9]

The commission had thus completed its work in twenty days. Its chairman boasted that no such group had acted with greater haste, and criticized those who had obliged it to work in this manner.

I maintained the entirely opposed opinion, and I warned the ministers who urged us, that the more laborious our task was, the more brief the discussion in the chamber would be.[10]

Early in August, he had declared that the commission had to have tranquillity, sustained attention, and meditation to elaborate its project.[11] It had been his intention to arrange with the representatives of all parties to avoid *votos particu-*

---

[7] Jiménez de Asúa, 36-37.
[8] *El Sol,* August 1, 1931; *ABC,* August 5, 1931.
[9] Jiménez de Asúa, 39-40.
[10] *Ibid.,* 40.
[11] *ABC,* August 8, 1931.

lares. The haste which had been forced upon the commission made it impossible to prevent or even to reduce the number of dissenting *votos.*

If more time had been conceded to the commission, the project, more finished and smoother in its sharp tones, would not have necessitated such an extensive and impassioned debate. Reality has proved we were right. My aim was to reverse the extremes; a couple of months of tranquil work in the commission and a month of public exhibition before the *cortes.* Unfortunately, my opinion was disdained, and the chamber wasted three long months in parliamentary polemics and in sterile discourses.[12]

The impatience of the government and the liberal press was natural. The Constitution of 1876 had been held in abeyance for nine years. The Provisional Government was in as vulnerable a position in this respect as the governments of Berenguer and Aznar, unless the constitution was quickly approved and promulgated. It was anxious to consolidate its position as soon as possible, and that could be achieved only through the establishment of a constitutional government sanctioned by the representatives of the nation. Theoretically it would have been more ideal to have given the commission as much leisure as its chairman desired, but Spain was far from calm. The decline of the *peseta* and the social and economic disturbances within the country made governmental stability urgent. However desirable the tranquil evolution of a document that could have been easily approved through compromise may have been, it was more important that the evolution should take place in the open forum of parliamentary debate rather than behind the closed doors of a parliamentary commission. The enthusiasm of the electorate had been keyed to a feverish pitch by the convocation of the Constituent Cortes. The disorders of the extremists and the growing anxiety and organization of the conservative agrarian and Catholic forces could be appeased only by permitting the public to view the progressive evolution of the constitution. Such a course, on the other hand,

[12] Jiménez de Asúa, 40.

gave publicity to the factional divisions within the governing coalition and made its work a more obvious target for the criticism of both extremes of party opinion. The task was undoubtedly retarded by this publicity, but the consequences of a more protracted study by the commission, particularly since the work of the juridical commission had not been approved, might have been productive of more serious results. The difficulties of the government and the impatience of the public made haste inevitable, with all of its attendant waste of time in parliamentary exhibitionism.

Meanwhile the Constituent Cortes had been engaged in electing the various permanent commissions and in attacks on the government through economic interpellations. A group of deputies, including Ossorio y Gallardo, Marañón, and Gil Robles, proposed that until the constitution was promulgated the individual rights and liberties of the Spaniards should be respected in the terms prescribed by the Constitution of 1876 and its complementary legislation. This led to an extended debate and the proposal was finally withdrawn. Ossorio y Gallardo, who defended it, declared that there was no intent of denying the confidence granted to the government.[13] The debate on the *dictamen* for the Commission of Responsibilities and the report of the commission charged with the investigation of the revolutionary incident at Seville was continued through several sessions.

The chamber was so occupied with these matters that when the constitutional project was read on August 18, it was laid upon the table.[14] It was not until August 27 that the discussion of the constitution was begun. Jiménez de Asúa presented the *dictamen* of the constitutional commission to the chamber. Just before he delivered his explanatory address, Ayuso, a member of the historic Federal minority, recalled the agreement of various elements to frame a federal republic. He raised one of the most delicate points that had to be con-

[13] *Diario*, No. 18, August 11, 1931, 340-361.
[14] *Ibid.*, No. 22, August 18, 1931, 468.

sidered in the framing of the Constitution of 1931, for he inquired whether Lerroux, Azaña, and Marcelino Domingo retained their faith. Besteiro exercised his authority to cut the intrusion short and the chairman of the constitutional commission addressed the chamber.[15]

Jiménez de Asúa began by paying a tribute to the *Comisión Jurídica Asesora*. The *anteproyecto* and its *votos particulares* had not only served as indispensable guides, but had saved much time in the accelerated task which the commission had undertaken. The project which he presented was the work of all, but its very heterogeneity had necessitated many *votos particulares*. Some of these might have been eliminated if the commission had been allowed more time. The proposed constitution was not extremely long. It had only 121 articles. The Constitution of Cádiz, 1812, had 384, while the contemporary German and Austrian constitutions had 165 and 150 articles respectively. Experience had taught that charters granted by sovereigns were always short and that popular constitutions were always long. Their aim had been to make a popular constitution.

In his reference to that part of the project dedicated to the rights and duties of Spaniards he alluded to the transformation that had occurred in the dogmatic sections of recent constitutions. Their aim had been to include all of the rights, aspirations and desires of the people, "placing them in the constitutional charter in order to give them thereby, not the current legality, which is at the mercy of the inconstancy of a parliament, but the superlegality of a constitution."[16] Popular desires were included in the new constitutions of Mexico (1917), Russia (1918), and Germany (1919). Each of them had a series of precepts and principles which had previously been excluded in pure constitutional theory. He continued:

It is necessary to recognize that there is a struggle between the technical concept and the popular concept, and therefore who-

[15] *Ibid.*, No. 28, August 27, 1931, 642; Mori, I, 186.
[16] *Diario*, No. 28, 643; Mori, I, 189.

ever compares the *anteproyecto* drafted by the *Comisión Jurídica Asesora* and the one which this commission brings in its *dictamen*, will see that many of those technical principles have been respected, but that, in addition, they have been filled with the living political blood which has been transfused from democratic veins.[17]

Jiménez de Asúa then compared the draft to contemporary European constitutions, specifying articles in them and revealing a comprehensive grasp of recent constitutional developments. Articles 128ff. of the constitution of Czechoslovakia respected the rights of religious and linguistic minorities. Article 152 of the German charter prohibited usury, while the fundamental laws of Roumania and Mexico considered mining and petroleum rights. Therefore it was not possible to argue that it was unconstitutional to include some of the precepts which figured in the fundamental law designed for Spain. The prohibition of corporal punishment and the establishment of divorce were included lest an inconstant parliament, "against the principles and rights which the public claims, override all those popular desires which are latent and the chamber must protect."[18] A résumé and explanation of the import of various articles followed. In the chapter on national organization the commission had deliberately wished to avoid a declaration that Spain was a federal republic. Both the unitary and federal concepts were in a theoretical and practical crisis. It was their aim to establish an integral state, "in which the great Spain may be compatible with the regions, and making possible, in that integral system, that each of the regions may receive the autonomy which it merits by its grade of culture and progress."[19] The Socialists had succeeded in incorporating this concept into the *dictamen* because they were not a political party but a civilization. They desired the integral state rather than the federal state, and since they were a civilization they

[17] *Diario*, No. 28, 643; Mori, I, 189.
[18] *Diario*, No. 28, 644; Mori, I, 190.
[19] *Diario*, No. 28, 645; Mori, I, 191.

could not fail to recognize that the regions had a right to live autonomously when they desired it.

The majority of constitutions left the problem of nationality to law. It was the tradition in Spain, however, to consider these problems in the constitution. The commission had not merely translated a German or French constitution, although these and the Mexican constitution had had an influence in the discussions. They had considered double nationality because of the cordial sentiment of the former Spanish colonies across the Atlantic. It had not been established with a general character because that would have given rise to insoluble legal problems. Instead a policy of reciprocity in regard to double nationality for individuals of Spanish and Portuguese speech was adopted, in the interest of *Hispanoamericanismo*.[20]

It had been necessary to include collective entities as well as individuals in the extension of the rights of man. The evolution was not limited to the rights of family and economic life. It was necessary to avoid a declaration of the rights of man that would be merely a declamation. That accusation had been brought against the Constitution of Weimar.

What we intend is that they may not be declamations, but true declarations, and for this it does not suffice to extend the rights, but that we give them secure guarantees: on one hand the concrete and guiding regulation; on the other, the recourses of aid and the proper jurisdictions necessary to make them effective.[21]

The citizens were guaranteed against attacks from the executive power in the project presented by the commission.

The great parliamentary problem was the choice between the bicameral and the unicameral systems. Few constitutions declared for unicamerality. Jiménez de Asúa declared that the secondary chambers were decadent, a memory of the past. People desiring to realize great popular desires framed a single chamber. The commission had chosen the unicameral

---

[20] *Diario*, No. 28, 645; Mori, I, 193.
[21] *Diario*, No. 28, 646; Mori, I, 193-194.

system because the other impeded progressive legislation, and the parliament was so weak when there was a legislative deadlock that it became an easy prey to an aggressive executive power.

A permanent parliamentary commission had been introduced as a novelty in the legislative power. It had a glorious antecedent in Spain in the permanent deputation created by the Cortes of Cádiz, in 1812. Similar bodies were also provided in the constitutions of Germany, Austria, Mexico, and Czechoslovakia.

The executive power presented another point of contention in constitutional law and theory. The post-war constitutions had not established the presidential system, and the commission had been inclined toward the parliamentary type. Germany had adopted the strong presidency. There the president was elected by the people, empowered to legislate by decree and to dissolve the chamber in certain cases. The weak president had been established in France. He was elected by a joint session of the two chambers and had no power to dissolve them. The aim of the commission had been to synthesize the two. The president was elected by the people and could legislate by decree, as in Germany, but he could dissolve the *cortes* only through a referendum. The ministry had been fashioned in such a manner as to strengthen it against possible votes of fortuitous and capricious censure.

Jiménez de Asúa considered that the theory of separation of powers was in a critical situation:

Today the power resides in the people, is incarnated in the state and is exercised through its organs. There is no necessity of making that division, but of affirming instead the security and the permanence of the labor of each.[22]

Another novelty had been introduced in the technical councils. In this respect the *dictamen* had precedents in the economic councils of Germany, Ireland, and Jugoslavia. The proposal was not as advanced as the German model. The

[22] *Diario*, No. 28, 647; Mori, I, 195.

latter provided that a member of the council could present himself in the chamber to defend a measure which the government had not wished to initiate. The *dictamen* had provided that the technical councils should act in an advisory capacity.

Contemporary tendencies had been to make the judicial power very strong. In accord with this trend, the president of the Supreme Court was elected by an assembly composed of elements chosen from the *cortes* as well as for their juridical wisdom. A strong judiciary would serve as a guarantee of Spanish law. Then Jiménez de Asúa declared that the financial provisions would guarantee the nation against a repetition of the fiasco of the dictatorship, when the funds of the state were dissipated.

The ideal of the Court of Constitutional Guarantees was based on the Supreme Court of the United States, although similar courts in Austria, Mexico, and France had furnished useful models. The court provided by the *dictamen* differed from the American institution in that it was not endowed with the power of declaring a law unconstitutional, and in this way preserved the sovereignty of the *cortes*. It could call the attention of the president to an improper law and he could send it back to the *cortes*. The decision of that body was final unless an appeal was made to the electorate through a referendum.

In the last instance you see how we are constantly appealing to the people in this case and, above all, in the other to resolve the conflict between the president and the popular chamber, because if both are elected by the people, only the people can be the judge in their conflicts.[23]

Jiménez de Asúa admitted that the complicated provisions for the reform of the constitution made it a rigid document, but held that the doctrine of flexibility was losing ground.

Finally he declared that the rapid drafting of the proposal was unparalleled in the constitutional history of other Euro-

[23] *Diario*, No. 28, 648; Mori, I, 197.

pean countries. It had taken three and a half months to frame the Weimar Constitution, and two months for those of Jugoslavia and Poland. He concluded:

We are making a constitution of the Left, and this constitution goes directly to the popular soul. The commission which composed it does not want the Spanish people, who went out into the street to win the republic, to have to go out some day to win its content. . . .

Our constitutional project is a conservative work, conservative of the republic.[24]

The debate on the totality of the project began immediately and continued through the session of September 9. The majority of the *votos particulares* had already anticipated the nature of many of the objections to the report of the commission. The specific ones can best be considered with the debate on the various articles. The discussion of the totality, however, was important in its indication of the divergences of opinion among the various minorities and the concessions that would have to be made by all in order to reach a common understanding.

The first to oppose the project was a priest, Molina Nieto, of the Catholic *vasconavarra* group. He was followed by Sánchez Albornoz of Republican Action, who declared that his party viewed with sympathy "the socializing and autonomist tendency of the constitutional project."[25] In the next session Basilio Alvarez, a republican and liberal priest, attacked the *dictamen,* and Luis Zulueta, a professor and journalist, answered him. Guerra del Río spoke in behalf of the Radical minority, indicating the parts of the project with which his group agreed or disagreed.[26]

The session of September 1 was opened by Alvarez Buylla. He opposed the project and was answered by Clara Campoamor in the name of the commission. Luis de Tapia approved

---

[24] *Diario,* No. 28, 648; Mori, I, 198. Compare these with the expanded exposition of the constitutional commission's report in Jiménez de Asúa, 41-79.

[25] *Diario,* No. 28, 652.

[26] *Ibid.,* No. 29, August 28, 1931, *passim.*

of the *dictamen* and was followed by Gordón Ordáx, representing the Radical-Socialist minority. The debate continued for a week, each deputy seeking to impress the chamber with his modesty in apologizing for his lack of ability and then in astounding them with his oratory and acumen. The speakers, in the order of their discourses, were Nóvoa Santos, representing the Galician Republican Federation; the Progressive leader in the *cortes,* Carlos Blanco; Franchy Roca, the leader of the Federals; De los Ríos for the Socialists; Gómez Roji for the Agrarians; Companys for the Catalans; José Ortega y Gasset for the *Agrupación al Servicio de la República;* Leizaola, Sáinz Rodríguez, and Melquiades Alvarez, the leader of the old Reformist Party. The debate was concluded by Botella, who spoke in behalf of the commission.

The discourse of Luis Jiménez de Asúa and the debate on the totality of the constitutional project indicated the nature of the problems that would arise in the consideration and approval of the articles. Most of the objections to the *dictamen* were later reiterated. The first problem was that raised by the question of national organization. The strong integral state, as conceived by the Socialists was opposed by the proponents of nineteenth-century liberalism. The latter desired either a federal or a unitary state. In this respect the Catalans were also somewhat divided. Some of them were devoted adherents to the federalism of Pí y Margall, others were willing to accept a compromise that would effect their agreement with the Republicans in the Pact of San Sebastian and grant their autonomy. This problem involved not only the name of the republic but also the more intricate one of the division of powers between the state and the regions.

There was little or no divergence in regard to the fundamental rights of man. The problem in this respect was involved in the extension of those rights to enfranchize the women of Spain and protect social as well as individual rights. The concession of the vote to women was opposed because it was feared that it would lead to a conservative reaction. The defense of the reform was based on the argument that the rights of women were equal to men as human beings in a pure democracy. The principal objection to divorce was that it was not appropriate in a constitution. Both divorce and education, however, were closely allied with the religious problem, while the question of language in education was related to the regional problem. The socialization of protection of private property was another question that promised to produce a heated debate.

A most critical problem was that of religion. It involved not only the separation of Church and state, with the consequent problems of the concordat with the Vatican and the support of the Catholic clergy. The dissolution of the religious orders, the nationalization of their property, and the related question of education were also important. Divorce may be considered as vitally related to the religious issue because marriage was a sacrament of the Church and the inclusion of divorce in the fundamental law of the land was regarded as civil interference in the sacramental institutions of the Church and opposed to its tenets.

The most important questions in the organization of the government of Spain were involved in the concept of the strong state. One *bloc* desired the bicameral system, as has already been indicated. The Socialists had won a preliminary victory in the constitutional commission, but they had yet to sustain the attacks of parliamentary oratory in order to guarantee the inclusion of the unicameral system in the constitution. The election of the president and the powers to be attributed to him raised another problem. It was held desirable to find a balance between the strong president who might encroach upon the powers delegated to the chamber and the alternative of subordinating him to the will of the *cortes*. The technical councils, devised by the Socialists for more effective legislation and as a substitute for the second chamber, were attacked by Gordón Ordáx, a Radical-Socialist, in the debates on the totality of the *dictamen* an indication that this novelty would not be unopposed.

All of these problems and others would undoubtedly pro-

duce tension in the chamber. The intensity of the feeling
among the deputies may be judged from the *rumores* that
greeted the orators in the preliminary debates when they expressed themselves on the more delicate topics. Pedro Sáinz,
an ex-deputy of the Consultative Assembly convoked by Primo
de Rivera, attempted to address the *cortes* on September 8,
and Besteiro had difficulty in maintaining order. Many deputies left the chamber at the instance of Pérez Madrigal, the *en-
fant terrible* of the *cortes* because of his diregard for order and
disrespect for speakers of the opposition.[27]

Nevertheless, despite delays and the pressure of current
business, the *cortes* was now confronted with the task of dis-
cussing the various *votos particulares* and amendments, and
approving the constitutional project article by article. There
were three basic documents to consider, the *anteproyecto* of
the *Comisión Jurídica Asesora,* the *dictamen* of the constitutional commission, and the *voto particular* of Juan Castrillo.
They represented the conservative juridical, the Socialist, and
the Progressive tendencies. The other minorities expressed
their opinions through the *votos particulares* of their members on the commission or the amendments of their deputies.
The Spanish press hoped for a rapid approval and promulgation of the constitution. The people and the Provisional
Government undoubtedly shared that desire. The hope
proved to be an elusive one, constantly postponed. The deputies had a monumental task ahead of them, that of approving
the articles one by one, and maintaining a coalition government while doing it. The problems involved and the interests
at stake could not be resolved as easily as the press desired.

[27] *Ibid.,* No. 34, September 8, 1931, 796.

XII

NATIONAL ORGANIZATION

THE SESSIONS of September 10 and the following day were devoted to the discussion of the totality of the preliminary and first titles of the constitution. This debate included the first twenty articles of the *dictamen* of the constitutional commission and involved the naming of the republic, the declaration that there was no state religion, the renunciation of war as an instrument of national policy, and the organization and powers of the state and autonomous regions. The debate was limited to three speeches on each title, instead of the usual six, because as Besteiro announced, an administration for the country had to be constituted and no time should be lost in personal exhibitions.[1]

These speeches are of importance only because they indicated the nature of two of the most difficult problems that the *cortes* had to solve. They were confined almost entirely to the regional and religious questions. Raimundo de Abadal, the first to oppose the project as the solitary representative of the *Lliga Regionalista* of Catalonia, held that the *dictamen* was one of a party. The fundamental law of a country had to regulate the juridical modes within which the different parties and tendencies acted, and therefore had to be something permanent. It should allow all parties and tendencies to protect the rights it guaranteed and solve problems according to the thought and will of the national electorate. This required an extraordinary tolerance. He respected the tendencies of the Socialists, but many Spaniards were alarmed at their attack on private property in the *dictamen*. In addition, it tended to make an irreligious society. This was a mistake because many of the great Catholic majority in the country were alarmed.

[1] *Diario*, No. 36, September 10, 1931, 839; Mori, II, 12.

He desired spiritual peace and an end of class and religious struggles.[2]

Tenreiro was the first orator to defend the *dictamen*. He represented Galician regionalism, was an excellent writer and an irreproachable gentleman, but added little to the discussion. He declared that all of the districts of Spain had their natural, historic, and economic characteristics, but above these regional differences was the unity inherited from Roman Spain. The most original note in his speech was his plea for the obligatory knowledge of the three peninsular languages: Castilian, Catalan, and Galician.[3]

Another representative of regionalism, Humberto Torres, of the Catalan Left, spoke next. His minority regarded the project as more unitary than the *anteproyecto*. The regional personality conceded by the *cortes* through the statutes would be precarious because the sovereignty of the autonomous states might be suspended. The process of sovereignty should be inverted, originating in the man and extending through the municipalities, grouped in regions. Spain had the local regional elements on which to erect a federative state. The Catalan Left desired such a state, inspired in the principles of liberalism.

Torres then spoke on the religious question. He held that Catholicism was the true official religion. All others were heterodox. The Catalan Left desired the subordination of the Church to the state, rather than the separation of Church and state. The chamber could count on the decided and enthusiastic collaboration of that party in the complete secularization of the state.[4]

The view of the extreme Catholic minority was expressed by Estévanez. He desired to discuss the origin of power, since the constitutional project merely affirmed the sovereignty of the people, without referring to the superior principle of its origin. He regarded the *dictamen* as atheistic. His words were

[2] *Diario*, No. 36, 840-842; Mori, II, 16-22.
[3] Mori, II, 12, 21.
[4] *Diario*, No. 36, 847-850.

lost at times amid the interruptions and heckling of various deputies. Besteiro requested that he moderate his expressions somewhat, and the speaker concluded with the statement that God was the origin and proprietor of the authority of society.[5]

In the next session Samper, a member of the commission, declared his complete solidarity with his colleagues, but pointed out two discrepancies in the project. Some of its precepts lacked a liberal sense and it was not elastic enough. Then García Gallego, a liberal canon who had opposed the dictatorship, considered the religious question. He replied to Estévanez by declaring that sovereignty resided in the people, basing his argument on theological reasoning. He held that separation of Church and state, with mutual liberty and independence, was not a heresy, but a fundamental base of Christian civilization. The relationship, however, should be traced in a concordat between the two powers.[6]

Ruiz Funes closed the debate, explaining the titles on behalf of the commission. He declared that the problem of national organization was the most difficult that Spain faced in that critical period. The commission had chosen the municipality as the unit within the national organization because it was impossible to defend either a highly centralized state or a federal state. This unit had an old democratic content and an important tradition in Spain. The provinces were composed of these units, and finally the region was erected above the provinces. The commission would have failed to face reality in Spain had it not recognized that, because the region was superior and anterior to the constitution they had elaborated. The precept that the law of the Spanish state should prevail over that of the region had been transcribed from the German constitution. The commission had tried to define the functions of the state and region, but the former was empowered to settle any differences between the regions.[7]

The deputies now considered the preamble of the constitu-

---

[5] *Ibid.*, 853-857.
[6] *Ibid.*, No. 37, September 11, 1931, 869-881; Mori, II, 39-41.
[7] *Diario*, No. 37, 881-884; Mori, II, 41-48.

tion. Various amendments were offered to the project of the constitutional commission. Antonio Royo Villanova rose to defend an amendment which aimed to substitute "the Spanish nation" for "Spain," while Pí y Arsuaga wanted the phrase to be "the Spanish people." Both of these proposals were defeated, but they were significant. Royo Villanova represented a group which was hostile to Catalonia. His phrase carried the sense of the unity of Spain, which he declared even the Federal, Francisco Pí y Margall, had used. The Catalans, however, followed the opposite doctrine of Prat de la Riba.[8]

Gil Robles answered Royo Villanova on behalf of the commission. It was one of the ablest speeches he delivered in the *cortes*.

We believe that the word "Spain," rich in national content and in juridical sense, is eminently more comprehensive than the words "Spanish nation." . . .

The aim of the commission was to maintain great cordiality, to bring all criteria to light, in order that the deputies might understand one another for the ideal of the country that belonged to all of them.[9] The venerable Pí y Arsuaga, leader of the official Federals as a disciple of his father, offered his amendment in the interest of a federal rather than a unitary state, but shortly withdrew it.

A third amendment, offered by Sánchez Albornoz, was accepted by the commission. The preamble to the constitution, approved on September 15, was drafted as follows:

Spain, in use of its sovereignty, and represented by the Constituent Cortes, decrees and sanctions this constitution.[10]

The commission had won its first victory for the integral state.

The first article of the constitutional project was based on a *voto particular* of various members of the *Comisión Jurídica Asesora* to the *anteproyecto*. It was conceived in the following terms:

[8] Jiménez de Asúa, 107-108; Mori, II, 49-58.
[9] *Diario*, No. 37, 893.
[10] Jiménez de Asúa, 108; *Diario*, No. 38, September 15, 1931, 924.

Spain is a democratic republic. The powers of all its organs emanate from the people.[11]

Each minority desired to name the republic according to its concept of the Spanish state, and there were numerous *votos* and amendments. The majority of them were defeated. The amendment of Joaquin Pí y Arsuaga, conceived in the interest of federalism, passed nearly unnoticed in the chamber and was withdrawn. It declared:

Spain is a democratic and federal republic.[12]

Fernando Valera offered a *voto particular* which was defeated, but it was important because a similar amendment was later approved by the chamber. He wished the article to state:

Spain is a republic of workers, liberal in principle, democratic in foundation, and social in orientation.

In his defense of this *voto*, Valera tried to prove three things: (1) the necessity of an additional article which incarnated the whole spirit of the constitution; (2) the failure of the initial article to fulfil this adequately; and (3) that the one he proposed completely indicated the spirit of the constitution and embodied the essence of the amendments which had been offered.[13]

Valera may almost be considered as the author of the name of the republic, for the next day the socialist minority offered a *voto particular* which incorporated his idea. It was signed by Jiménez de Asúa, Trifón Gómez, Bugeda, and De Francisco. The able defense of Luis Araquistain convinced the majority of the chamber. He declared that Valera's *voto* had been rejected because it was mixed with less accepted ideas. The idea it embodied had been defeated in the commission by a majority of one vote, on a day when not all the members of the commission were present. It was not an allusion to the Marxist concept of the class struggle. It did not take the worker

---

[11] *Diario*, No. 22, August 18, 1931, Appendix 4; Jiménez de Asúa, 109.
[12] Mori, II, 99.
[13] *Ibid.*, II, 100-109; Jiménez de Asúa, 110; *Diario*, No. 38, 924-929.

in the sense in which the word was generally interpreted, as a salaried employee or a manual worker. A worker was

. . . every person who discharges a function materially or spiritually necessary to the society where he lives; a worker is also one who exercises a profession predominantly intellectual, the man of science, the artist, the inventor, the technician, and the organizer of a syndicate or of an industry. All are workers who render a social service which society needs, from the most humble country peasant to the director of a bank, the soldier, or the astronomer.[14]

Only the social parasite would be excluded. Socialism did not need to enslave the vanquished classes. It aimed to integrate them "in a community of service, in an equality of duties and in a hierarchy of functions." The *voto* contained a postulate which belonged to contemporary civilization. Work was a social obligation. This was not exclusively socialistic nor the work of a group which wished to include unconstitutional material in the constitution. Similar precepts were included in Article 3 of the Russian and Article 2 of the Italian documents. Their object was to give to the Spanish constitution the most original character in the world,

. . . not in the sense of something new, unused, extraordinary, which has never occurred in history, but as the origin, as the beginning of a new attitude toward life, as an anticipation of the history to come.[15]

Spain should be a republic of men associated for the supreme end of work. The acceptance of this social obligation would prove to the people of Spain their decision to break definitely with an ominous past

. . . in which the directing classes, including a part of the new bourgeoisie, considered work as a servile stigma. And this cause, in my opinion, has been one of the principal causes of Spanish decadence.[16]

The new name of the Spanish Republic was approved almost

---

[14] *Diario,* No. 39, September 16, 1931, 941; Mori, II, 111.
[15] *Diario,* No. 39, 942; Mori, II, 114.
[16] *Diario,* No. 39, 943; Mori, II, 116.

immediately in a nominal vote, 170-152. The Socialists and Radical-Socialists broke into applause at the announcement of the result, and the Radicals momentarily left the chamber.[17]

Later the amendment of Victoria Kent was accepted in part by the commission and the words "liberal and democratic" were added to the approved *voto particular* of the Socialists. Arauz offered another amendment on behalf of the Federals, requesting the declaration that Spain was a federal republic. The Radicals, somewhat disgruntled because of the victory of the Socialists, were disposed to vote this amendment and Guerra del Río defended it. Besteiro considered the impassioned attitude of many of the deputies and suspended the session, declaring,

The presidency neither wishes nor can declare itself in one sense or the other; but prudence is necessary in order not to give the sensation that we do not know how to govern ourselves.[18]

The Federals were determined, and the final definition of the republic was still unapproved. The victory of the Socialists was not yet complete, but they were also determined to carry the *dictamen* to victory. At this critical juncture, Alcalá Zamora threw his prestige into the breach of the divided *cortes,* on September 17. After explaining the Pact of San Sebastian, he said,

The Pact of San Sebastian has the full potentiality, the perfect possibility for the complete satisfaction of federalism for the regions which desire it. That is to say, the road has been opened for the fullest possibilities of a federal constitution without imposing the rigidity of a type or the fetish of a name.

There was, in reality, no discord among the majority of the chamber. Words had neither enough importance nor value to poison the debate, divide the majority, and endanger the constitution. Therefore, "I believe that the word 'federal' is not indispensable in the constitution, because there is the federal substance." Names were unnecessary. "I saw it with

[17] *Diario,* No. 39, 954-957; Mori, II, 118-119.
[18] Jiménez de Asúa, 110; Mori, II, 119-120.

one, yesterday I bade it farewell with three, and today I meet it with four. . . ."

The insistence on the approval of the amendment did not agree with pure federal doctrine in theory or with federal interests in practice.[19]

The chamber was in an uproar when he concluded. The deputies passed before him to congratulate him. The crisis had passed and the prestige of Alcalá Zamora assured that the contending parties would be satisfied with a federal content without insisting on the use of the name. On the proposal of Besteiro, it was agreed that the commission should be entrusted to present a new draft of Article 1 which could be voted unanimously by the chamber, and the discussion was suspended.

Article 1 was not considered again until September 25, when it was presented in the new form proposed by the constitutional commission. Guerra del Río, the parliamentary leader of the Radicals, withdrew his amendment, but Samper defended a *voto particular* that was identical to the amendment. It was defeated and after the words "federative tendency" had been struck out at the suggestion of José Ortega y Gasset, the article was approved in the following form:

Spain is a democratic republic of workers of every class, which is organized in a régime of liberty and justice.

The powers of its organs emanate from the people.

The Spanish Republic constitutes an integral state, which makes possible the autonomy of municipalities and regions.

Later, when the whole constitutional text had been discussed, Terrero proposed the inclusion of various additional articles. One of these referred to the color of the republican flag. The chamber approved this addition, and in the revision in style of the approved constitution the commission added this sentence as more appropriate to Article 1 than in an epilogue.[20]

[19] *Diario*, No. 40, September 17, 1931, 986; Mori, II, 129.
[20] *Diario*, No. 45, September 25, 1931, 1251-1258; Jiménez de Asúa, 111. The article was changed in wording in the revision of style. The paragraph concerning the flag was, in its definitive form: "The flag of the Spanish Republic is red, yellow, and violet."

Meanwhile Article 2 had been approved without discussion. It was not accompanied by any *votos particulares* or amendments and was based on the first paragraph of Article 11 of the *anteproyecto*. It stated very simply:

All Spaniards are equal before the law.[21]

The third article, which disestablished the Catholic Church, had also been considered, but Jiménez de Asúa suggested that, since this concerned the religious problem, it would avoid repetition to discuss it with Article 24. This request was approved and the debate of Article 3 was postponed.[22]

The regional question was raised again in the consideration of Article 4. This provision had not figured in the *anteproyecto* but originated with the parliamentary commission. It made Castilian the official language of the republic without prejudice to the regional or provincial rights recognized in the laws of the state. Various *votos particulares* and amendments were withdrawn or defeated in the chamber, but the commission accepted an amendment of Miguel de Unamuno which declared:

Spanish is the official language of the republic. Every Spanish citizen has the duty of knowing it and the right of speaking it. The language of the majority of the inhabitants in each region may be declared coöfficial. Nevertheless, the use of no regional language will be imposed on anyone.[23]

Two intellectuals had already debated the question of calling the language Spanish or Castilian. Ovejero, Socialist professor of the Central University, defended an amendment which requested the substitution of "Spanish" for "Castilian." He declared that Castilian was known as the Spanish language all over the world. Twenty nations spoke this language and called the national literature Spanish. He declared that he offered the amendment in the interest of the spiritual unity of Spain.[24]

---

[21] *Diario*, No. 40, 989; Jiménez de Asúa, 112.
[22] *Diario*, No. 40, 989.
[23] *Diario*, No. 41, September 18, 1931, 1015; Jiménez de Asúa, 114.
[24] *Diario*, No. 40, 996; Mori, II, 133-142.

Gabriel Alomar, a well-known writer from Majorca, who was a Catalan in political ideals and a Socialist in revolutionary desires, attacked Ovejero's amendment.

> Spanish language! If the Spanish language is Castilian, evidently my Catalan tongue, Basque, and Galician, are not Spanish languages.[25]

There were only two languages which could be called imperial, Spanish and English. The English language was not called British. The greatness of a language lay in conserving its original name. Spain was enriched by three languages. The central was Castilian; the eastern was Catalan, with its two variations, Valencian and Balearic; and the western was Galician or *galaico-portuguesa*. If there was only a single Spanish language, Castilian, then those who talked Catalan did not speak a Spanish tongue.[26]

Ovejero's amendment was withdrawn. In the following session Unamuno defended his proposal. The Rector of Salamanca declared that *vasquence* was not the language of the majority in the Basque provinces. Those who tried to inoculate this tongue with drugs in order to give it a fictitious life would not succeed. He told the Catalans that they did not speak Catalan better than they did Castilian. Spain was not a nation, it was a nation reborn, in which the sad and poor differential personality of language should disappear. He wanted a single Spanish language, which might integrate and federate all the intimate essences, all the virtues of the languages which separated them.[27]

The chamber accepted Unamuno's amendment, but "Castilian" was used instead of "Spanish" as the name of the national language. Some deputies observed that the knowledge of a regional language might be required of certain functionaries. In order to find a satisfactory formula, the commission was charged with revising the article. The new draft was pre-

[25] *Diario*, No. 40, 996.
[26] *Ibid.*, 996-997.
[27] *Diario*, No. 41, 1015-1020; Mori, II, 149-159.

sented to the *cortes,* on September 25, and approved without discussion.

Castilian is the official language of the republic.

Every Spaniard has the duty of knowing it and the right of using it, without prejudice to the rights of the languages of the provinces or regions which the laws of the state recognize.

Neither the knowledge nor the use of a regional language may be required of anyone except in accord with special laws.[28]

The recognition of Madrid as the capital of the Spanish Republic had been approved on September 18 without debate. In the revision of style the word "Spanish" was suppressed as unnecessary. Article 6, in which Spain solemnly renounced war as an instrument of national policy, was approved in the same session. It had been incorporated into the constitutional text at the suggestion of Salvador de Madariaga. Royo Villanova proposed that this article be suppressed, but withdrew his amendment and the article was approved.[29] The discussion of the preliminary title was concluded.

The conflict between the federalists and those who desired an integral state was indicated in the discussion of the first and fourth articles. Autonomy had been one of the great problems considered in the Pact of San Sebastian, and it was feared that the constitution might set a precedent in the restriction of regional authority. The articles approved had not been nominally federal, although they had revealed a strong inclination toward the real concept of federalism. Some groups had rebelled against this tendency, led by Royo Villanova, the champion of *unitarismo.*

The real crisis of the regional question was raised in Article 8. It was based on a *voto* of Romero Otazo, Pedroso, Valdecasas, and Luña to the *anteproyecto,* and made the *municipio* the unit of both the provinces, directly subordinated to the central power, and the autonomous regions. The municipality had already been suggested as the unit of the integral state, but this article did not guarantee the autonomy of the region

[28] *Diario,* No. 45, September 25, 1931, 1258; Jiménez de Asúa, 114.
[29] Jiménez de Asúa, 115-117; *Diario,* No. 41, 1026-1032.

to the extent desired by the federal and regional interests.[30]

The debate on this question was begun September 22, with the discussion of Article 8. Various amendments were withdrawn or defeated. An amendment of Orozco proposed the explicit recognition of the region, but was defeated, 153-111.[31] Then Xiráu pointed out two aspects of the autonomy which Catalonia desired. These were the manner of organizing the regions and the division of the powers between the state and the region. He desired that the region be endowed with control of education, the civil and municipal régimes, and the police power and internal order. Unamuno, on the other hand, declared that Catalonia wanted a life fully autonomous, a sovereignty of its own.[32]

After much discussion the article was redrafted. The commission had accepted the spirit of an amendment offered by Jaén, Baeza Medina, and others, which referred to the autonomy of the territories of North Africa. The phrase alluding to the direct connection of the provinces to the central power was suppressed at the suggestion of Sánchez Albornoz and the article was approved in the following form:

The Spanish state, within the irreducible limits of its actual territory, will be integrated by municipalities, united in provinces, and by regions which constitute themselves in a régime of autonomy.

The sovereign territories of the north of Africa will organize themselves in an autonomous régime in direct relation with the central power.[33]

Article 9 was quickly approved. The commission had examined all of the amendments, and incorporated those which seemed most worthy into its project. Two declarations were thereby added. One guaranteed the autonomy of the *ayuntamientos* in the matters within their competency. The other provided that the *alcaldes* would be elected by the municipalities, either through the *ayuntamientos* or directly by the peo-

[30] Mori, II, 161; Jiménez de Asúa, 118.
[31] *Diario*, No. 42, September 22, 1931, 1056-1058.
[32] Mori, II, 162.
[33] *Diario*, No. 43, September 23, 1931, 1079; Jiménez de Asúa, 117-119.

ple. These additions were based on the *votos particulares* of Castrillo, Rodríguez Pérez, Valdecasas, and Alomar, and the amendment of Jaén. The approved article read as follows:

All the municipalities of the republic will be autonomous in the matters of their competence and will elect the *ayuntamientos* by universal, equal, direct, and secret suffrage, except when they function in a régime of an open council.

The *alcaldes* will always be designated by the direct election of the people or by the *ayuntamiento*.[34]

The following article was also quickly approved. The *anteproyecto* had not recognized the province, except as the association of municipalities. The draft of the constitutional commission was accepted in the first two paragraphs of the approved article and a third paragraph was added. It was based on the proposal of Lara as redrafted by Valle. This article provided that the provinces should be constituted by the municipalities, united according to a law which should determine their régime, functions, and the manner of electing their political administration. They should consist of the municipalities within their jurisdiction unless modifications were introduced by law. The third paragraph recognized the insular *cabildos* of the Canary Islands as equal in powers to the provinces. A fourth paragraph permitted a similar régime for the Balearic Isles.

The regional crisis arose with the question of the formation of the regions and the provision of their powers, involving articles 11-20 of the parliamentary *dictamen*. The base of this draft was contained in articles 4-11 of the *voto particular* of Romero Otazo, Pedroso, Valdecasas, and Luña to the report of the juridical commission. The *dictamen* of the constitutional commission provided that if one or more provinces, with definite cultural, historical, and economic characteristics agreed to constitute an autonomous region as a political and administrative unit within the Spanish state, they might draft a statute. The approved statute would serve as the basic law of the administrative and political organization of that

[34] *Diario*, No. 43, 1080-1083; Jiménez de Asúa, 119-120.

region. The Spanish state would recognize it and protect it as part of its juridical arrangement. Three conditions had to be fulfilled for the approval of the statute. The majority of the *ayuntamientos* or those whose municipalities contained two-thirds of the electoral census of the region was necessary to propose the statute It had to be accepted by at least two-thirds of the electors, and if the plebiscite was negative the subject could not be voted on again until after five years. Finally, the parliament of Spain had to approve it. The regional statutes would be approved by that body when they had been presented according to these conditions and contained no precepts contrary to the constitution or the organic laws of the state. In no case would the federation of autonomous regions be permitted.

The next two articles distributed the powers of the regions according to two classifications. Certain general matters that transcended regional limits and jurisdictions were reserved to the exclusive competence of the state. They included nationality, religious matters, foreign relations, the public debt and treasury of the state, matters relating to foreign commerce, legislation concerning intellectual and industrial property, extradition, the jurisdiction of the Supreme Court, sanitation, public security, the military and naval establishments, weights and measures, banking and coinage regulations, mining and agricultural legislation in defense of the national wealth and the coördination of the national economy, the regulation of communications and transportation, immigration and emigration, and the production and commerce in arms.

There was a second class of powers in which the state and the regions shared equally: the maintenance of public order, maritime fishing, civil law, social legislation, judicial organization, the regimen of social security and social assistance, the socialization of natural wealth and economic enterprises, and the geographic, statistical, and meteorological services. The regions would provide their powers in their statutes, subject to the restriction that all Spaniards had to be treated on the same basis as the natives of the region. All matters not explicitly specified in the statutes were reserved to the competency of the state.

When the harmony of local and general interests required, and that necessity was recognized by the Court of Constitutional Guarantees, the state could fix by law the principles according to which the autonomous regions had to adjust their legislative or regulatory dispositions. The laws of the republic were to be executed by the regional authorities, except when that execution was attributed to special organs or when the government of the republic dictated regulations for the execution of its laws. Finally, Article 20 provided that the law of Spain would prevail over that of the autonomous region.[35]

The constitutional commission had been deeply preoccupied by the regional problem and had tried to present a formula which would satisfy the Catalan representatives. Jiménez de Asúa believed that it would have attained this desire had it not been announced that Alcalá Zamora intended to present an amendment, formulated with the deputies from Catalonia. This proposal, signed by Dr. Juarros and others, was presented to the chamber and the commission studied it in several meetings. It was rejected because of the threefold classification of powers. Some were reserved to the exclusive competence of the state, others were reserved for state legislation and regional execution, and a third class was delegated to the regions. The commission defended the bipartite classification, to which the representatives of Catalonia would not agree.[36]

Alcalá Zamora left the Blue Bench to defend the amendment in the session of September 23. He declared that it signified the tangibility of the statute which had already been presented to the chamber on August 18, and which had been passed on to the constitutional commission to be studied.[37] The amendment was also similar to the criterion of the com-

---

[35] *Diario*, No. 22, Appendix 4, 1-3; Jiménez de Asúa, 131-135.

[36] Jiménez de Asúa, 141-142. The amendment of Dr. Juarros is given in full in Jiménez de Asúa, 142-151 and in Mori, II, 164-188. Its content is noted only in those modifications of the *dictamen* of the commission.

[37] *Diario*, No. 22, 448-449.

mission in its establishment of a régime within which the
regions could live, whether or not they desired autonomy.
The discrepancy between the *dictamen* and the amendment
was one of method. There could be no autonomy if the limits
of the regional powers disappeared and confusion ensued.
He described the threefold classification of powers and declared that the third class delegated complete autonomy to
the regions, under whose authority it was to be exercised,
with responsibility to the people of the regions only. The
criterion of the commission was more restrictive on the
autonomous expansion of the region, more unitary and centralist. The Catalan representatives had accepted the legislative unities entrusted to the state, and the amendment
assured the legislative unity of the state in ten or twelve
fundamental matters. These were subject to dispute if the
dictamen was accepted.[38]

A debate ensued in which Carner, Zulueta, Xiráu, and
Royo Villanova participated. It was continued in the following session without developing any formula for mutual agreement. Finally Besteiro announced that the deputies were
more divided in appearance than reality. Therefore the constitutional commission would meet with the leaders of the
minorities and Alcalá Zamora. The deputies approved the
proposal and the session was suspended.[39]

The situation appeared to be very grave. The attitude
of the Socialists was most interesting. They were not disposed
to vote for the amendment which Alcalá Zamora had defended for reasons of discipline, yet they could not oppose
Catalonia and an autonomous régime for that region. They
were also divided internally. In a meeting of the minority the
question of supporting the amendment was put to a vote
and it was approved by a majority of four. Many deputies
announced their abstention or rebellion against the discipline
of their parties. Finally, however, all the deputies were convinced that the victory or defeat of the amendment would

[38] *Ibid.*, No. 43, 1088-1095.
[39] *Ibid.*, No. 44, September 24, 1931, 1149.

not avoid a break in the harmony within the *cortes*. This explains the desire of the deputies to seek a formula that would satisfy all the minorities. Largo Caballero suggested the necessity of finding a harmonious solution. It was necessary to secure a larger representation of the minorities than was found in the commission. The Catalans agreed to Jiménez de Asúa's proposal that the minority leaders meet if Alcalá Zamora also attended. This enabled Besteiro to announce the meeting to seek a satisfactory formula.[40]

The group met under the presidency of Besteiro. Jiménez de Asúa was given the floor to propose a solution and suggested that the part of the amendment of Juarros providing for the tripartite system be accepted while Article 16 of that amendment should be replaced by Article 15 of the *dictamen*. This sustained the conviction of the commission that the constitutional text should not prejudge those powers that might be recognized as within the competence of the regions. The formula was accepted after debating it, article by article.[41]

That same evening the secretary of the *cortes* read the new draft of the commission. It consisted of Articles 11-21, with the changes noted above. The chairman of the constitutional commission announced that he considered it a duty to refuse to accept any of the amendments presented, in order that the debate might be accelerated. It was up to the chamber to decide in the last instance the amendments that should be incorporated into the *dictamen*.[42]

The debate on the new draft began on September 25. Unamuno attacked the proposed formula, and Jiménez de Asúa explained the modifications introduced. Sánchez Román opposed it because it relinquished the sovereignty of the state in the autonomous regions.[43] A number of amendments were presented as the formula was debated article by article and a few were taken into consideration. Largo Caballero

[40] Mori, II, 183-185; Jiménez de Asúa, 151-152.
[41] Jiménez de Asúa, 153.
[42] *Diario*, No. 44, 1160-1161.
[43] *Ibid.*, No. 45, 1174; Mori, II, 190; Jiménez de Asúa, 162.

rose to defend an amendment asking that social legislation be included in the powers reserved to the state. This was necessary in order to protect the international obligations of the state. Spain had adhered to the International Labour Office and was obliged to ratify and honor its obligations. The state had to effect and enforce the consequent social legislation, rather than leave this to the regions.

Lluhí responded that the amendment deliberately prejudiced the question of Catalonia. There was a strong labor organization there and the Catalans knew how to enforce social legislation. Nevertheless the amendment of the Minister of Labor was approved in a nominal vote, 132-118, redrafted, and finally incorporated into the dictamen.[44]

An additional article was added in the early hours of September 26. It was proposed by Alonso de Armiño and permitted the provinces, forming a region or a part of one, to renounce their autonomy and return to the status of provinces under the central power. It was necessary that the majority of the *ayuntamientos* propose this measure and at least two-thirds of the electors approve it. This provision became Article 22 in the definitive text. Thus, shortly before the end of the session at 7:40 on the morning of September 26, the last article of Title I was approved. The question of regional organization and the division of powers was solved as far as the constitution was concerned.[45]

[44] *Diario*, No. 45, 1206-1211, 1251; Mori, II, 199-211.
[45] *Diario*, No. 45, 1250-1251; Jiménez de Asúa, 175-176.

XIII

INDIVIDUAL RIGHTS AND GUARANTEES

THE SESSION following the approval of the first title of the constitution was rather colorless. The deputies had spent their energy and dissipated their enthusiasm in the heated contest over the regional question. The title containing the articles on nationality was approved without any extended debate and but few amendments. There were no individual, vested, or regional interests involved.

Article 23 provided that Spanish nationality should be extended to those of Spanish parentage; those of alien parentage who were born in Spain and desired to be nationalized; those of unknown parentage born in Spain; and those naturalized by law. A foreign woman who married a Spaniard conserved her nationality or acquired that of her husband. Her choice was regulated by laws in accord with international treaties. It was also provided that a special law would establish the procedure to facilitate the acquisition of Spanish nationality by persons of Spanish origin and of foreign residence. This was based on Article 22 of the *dictamen,* Article 9 of the *anteproyecto,* and two *votos particulares* of Pedroso to the *anteproyecto.* One *voto particular* of Castrillo and two amendments were presented, but the article was approved without any modification, except that introduced in the revision of style.[1]

The last provision of this title, Article 24, involved more debate and was considerably modified. The original report of the juridical commission provided that Spanish nationality should be lost by the acquisition of foreign citizenship or by entering the employ or armed service of a foreign state with-

[1] *Diario,* No. 46, September 29, 1931, 1263-1267; Jiménez de Asúa, 176-179.

out a license from the Spanish government. The parliamentary commission added a clause to include the citizens of those countries of Spanish or Portuguese speech which recognized a reciprocal right. Only three of the *votos* introduced in the *cortes* were incorporated into the constitution. Barriobero offered an amendment to exclude all friars, since they could not be regarded as citizens in a republic of workers. It was defeated by a vote of 113-82. The *voto* of Castrillo provided that nationals should lose their citizenship by accepting employment that involved authority with another government. Ruiz de Villa's amendment admitted natives of Portugal and the Hispanic-American countries to Spanish citizenship on a basis of reciprocity. The third proposition accepted by the commission was proposed in the *voto particular* of Botella. This provided that Spanish nationals who were naturalized in Portugal and the Spanish-speaking countries should retain their citizenship. The article was approved with these modifications.[2]

The chamber passed immediately to the consideration of the rights and duties of Spaniards. The first chapter of the third title was concerned with individual rights and guarantees. Article 25 declared that neither birth, social class, wealth, political ideas, nor religious beliefs could be the basis of privilege in Spain. The second paragraph recognized the equality of the rights of the two sexes. Finally, it was provided that the state should not recognize titles and distinctions of nobility. Article 23 of the *dictamen* of the commission was based on Article 11 of the *anteproyecto*. The acceptance of an amendment proposed by Victoria Kent resulted in the suppression of the second paragraph. The commission declared that its substance was contained in the first paragraph. The article was then approved.[3]

Debate on the next two articles, which dealt with the religious orders and the liberty of conscience, was postponed until the following week. The chamber next turned to Arti-

---

[2] *Diario*, No. 46, 1267-1284; Jiménez de Asúa, 179-181.
[3] *Diario*, No. 46, 1284-1292; Jiménez de Asúa, 181-183.

cle 28. It provided that crimes could be punished only by laws in force before their perpetration and that no one could be judged except by a competent authority and within legal limits. It was based on Article 13 of the *anteproyecto* and was approved without any modification.[4]

The next proposal provided for the abolition of corporal punishment and the death penalty. The latter could be applied only in time of war by the military authorities. The *anteproyecto* contained no such provision and it was suppressed after considerable discussion, with the understanding that it should be included in the revised penal code. Several amendments and *votos* were offered proposing the partial or complete abolition of the article, but an accord was reached as a result of a speech of Pedro Rico in support of the *voto particular* of Castrillo. Rico declared that such a provision would be equivalent to relinquishing the control of the Spanish Republic to the extremists of the Right and Left. It was not a question of the abolition of the death penalty but of the defense of the republic against the dangers which threatened it. Jiménez de Asúa took the opposing view, and Barriobero wished to include even the army in the urgent reform. Castrillo's proposal was finally accepted and the article was eliminated from the constitution.[5]

Article 29 guaranteed the individual against arbitrary arrest and imprisonment. No one could be detained except for a crime and would be liberated or handed over to the competent judicial authority within twenty-four hours of the arrest. The prisoner would then be notified of the sentence within three days, after which time he would be freed or imprisoned. The authorities and executing agents were made responsible for illegal arrest, and it was further provided that the action to prosecute any infraction of the law would be public, without the necessity of any security. The article was approved with one slight modification of the corresponding

[4] *Diario*, No. 46, 1292; Jiménez de Asúa, 222-223.
[5] *Diario*, No. 47, September 30, 1931, 1306-1320; Mori, II, 222-223; Jiménez de Asúa, 223-241.

Article 28 of the constitutional project, which, in turn, was nearly a literal transcription of Article 14 of the *anteproyecto*.[6]

The following article did not exist in either the *dictamen* or the *anteproyecto*. It provided that Spain should subscribe to no international agreement which aimed at the extradition of political or social delinquents, and was proposed in an amendment offered by Eduardo Ortega y Gasset. It was accepted by the commission despite the opposition of Clara Campoamor and Jiménez de Asúa, on the ground that it conflicted with existing international treaties. These, they held, provided for extradition for high treason and had already been recognized in the approved Article 7. The League of Nations had made a universal law on the question of extradition, and social delinquents were not included in the category of political ones for protection. Hence the proposed article was opposed to Article 7, and would necessitate the reform of the constitution. Gomáriz defended the amendment which he had signed, declaring there was no conflict and that they were protecting the rights of Spaniards. The proposal was approved in an ordinary vote as Article 30.[7]

Article 31 guaranteed to every Spaniard the right to move freely in the national territory and to choose his residence and domicile in it, without being compelled to change them except by virtue of an executory sentence. The right of emigration and immigration was recognized and the home was declared inviolable. No one could enter the home of either a Spaniard or a foreigner without a warrant. In cases of search or arrest, all papers and effects were to be registered in the presence of the interested party, a member of his family, or two neighbors. These guarantees were nearly identical with those provided in the two preliminary projects. Eduardo Ortega y Gasset proposed an amendment which provided that no foreigner could be expelled from Spain except in accord with the guarantees established by a special law.

[6] Jiménez de Asúa, 241-244.
[7] *Ibid.*, 244-249; *Diario*, No. 47, 1320-1323.

The commission offered a formula proposing that the expulsion of foreigners should be regulated by a special law. This satisfied Ortega y Gasset and the article was approved.[8]

The next four articles were quickly approved with but few amendments and little debate. They guaranteed the inviolability of correspondence; the freedom of choice of profession and the recognition of the liberty of commerce and industry, except for economic and social reasons of general interest; freedom of speech and the press; and the right of petition. They were evolved directly from the ideas of nineteenth-century liberalism expressed in the preliminary project of the juridical commission. The only differences between the two projects and the definitive constitution resulted from the revision of style by the constitutional commission.[9]

Such a vital question as the electoral franchise, however, was not settled so easily. It involved the age for suffrage and the concession of the right to vote to the women of Spain. Article 20 of the *anteproyecto* had extended the franchise to all citizens, while Article 34 of the same report set the electoral age at twenty-three and did not discriminate between the sexes. The Socialists had succeeded in reducing the required age to twenty-one in Article 34 of the *dictamen,* but they also approved of the concession of the vote to women. Various *votos particulares* and amendments were offered, and the commission accepted the criterion maintained in some of them as a basis for redrafting the article. A *voto* of Trifón Gómez supporting the socialist point of view was defeated, 135-112, and the electoral age was raised to twenty-three.[10]

Woman suffrage was considered to be vitally connected with the security of the republic. The first encounter on this important reform involved the two feminine members of the chamber. An amendment of Guerra del Río, the Radical leader, had been defeated, 153-93. It guaranteed the franchise to both sexes.[11] Following this, on October 1, the debate be-

[8] *Diario,* No. 47, 1323-1326.
[9] *Diario,* No. 47, 1327-1331; Jiménez de Asúa, 252-256.
[10] *Diario,* No. 47, 1331-1336; Mori, II, 223-224.
[11] *Diario,* No. 47, 1342-1344.

tween Victoria Kent and Clara Campoamor ensued. The former believed that the moment was not propitious for granting the right of franchise to the women of Spain. It should be postponed.

> In this moment we are going to give or deny the vote to more than half of the Spanish individuals and it is necessary that the persons who feel the republican fervor, the democratic and liberal fervor, should rise here to declare: it is necessary to postpone the feminine vote.[12]

She requested this not because she doubted the capacity of women to vote, but because it was a question of opportunity for the republic.

> If we postpone the feminine vote, no injustice is committed, in my opinion. I understand that woman, in order to become imbued with an ideal, needs some period of association with the ideal itself. Woman does not throw herself into the questions which she does not see clearly, and because of this I understand that some years of association with the republic are necessary; that the women may see what the republic has brought to Spain that the monarchy did not bring. . . .

In some years

> . . . woman will be the most fervent, the most ardent defender of the republic; but . . . the president has just received petitions of Spanish women who, in good faith, believe at this moment that the ideals of Spain must go by another road. . . .[13]

Spanish women could not be judged by university girls or by women workers. Victoria Kent declared:

> If the Spanish women were all workers, if the Spanish women had already finished a university course and were liberated in conscience, I would rise today before the whole chamber to ask for the feminine vote.

---

[12] *Diario*, No. 48, October 1, 1931, 1351; Mori, II, 224.

[13] Mori, 225. She was referring to the flood of petitions and representations from Catholics of both sexes, especially women, which were pouring into the secretariats of the chamber and president of the Provisional Government. *Cf Diario, passim.*

After a few years the women would be the most enthusiastic defenders of the republic but "today, gentlemen, it is dangerous to concede the vote to woman."[14]

Clara Campoamor was as spirited in her defense of woman suffrage. Did not women influence the political life of the men? Did the deputies have the right to close the doors on women in the matter of suffrage?

No; you have the right which the law has given you, the law which you make, but you do not have the natural right, the fundamental right, which is based on respect for every human being, and what you do is to restrain a power; let woman manifest herself and you will see that that power cannot continue to be restrained.

She regarded it as a serious political error to prevent women from voting. At this point Besteiro had to ask the chamber to maintain order. Miss Campoamor said:

I request the chamber to listen to me in silence; it is not with attacks and it is not with irony that you are going to conquer my strength; the only thing that I have here before you, gentlemen, that merits consideration and perhaps emulation precisely is the defense of a right which my nature and my faith force me to defend with tenacity and firmness.[15]

It was not a question of principle but of ethics to recognize woman as a human being. Since the time of Fichte, in 1796, the postulate had been accepted in principle that only the man who did not consider woman as a human being was capable of affirming that all the rights of man or of the citizen should not be the same for woman as for man. She cited the study of Luzuriaga on literacy in Spain. It showed that in 1910 illiteracy was diminishing more rapidly in women than in men. The decrease had continued, and women not only had the elemental cultural grade of men but surpassed it. Would the deputies vote that half of the human being was incapable? The women wanted the suffrage with their

[14] *Diario*, No. 48, 1352.
[15] *Ibid.*, 1353.

masculine half, "because there is no degeneration of sexes, because we are all children of man and woman and we receive equally the two parts of our being." And then she concluded:

I, gentlemen, feel myself a citizen before a woman, and I consider that it would be a profound political error to leave woman on the margin of that right, the woman who trusts in you.[16]

Thus the issue was planted before the deputies. It was a question of protecting the republic against a possible reaction toward the Right as a measure of practical politics, or of postponing the concession of a natural right to the women as liberals and democratic republicans. All of the republicans except the Progressives tried to avoid the risk involved in the desire for the liberal purification of the country. The most strenuous opposition came from the Radical minority. Guerra del Río did not deny the right of woman to vote, but he considered that it was not the time to put that right to the test. The chamber became very excited. The Radicals tried to face reality, as they conceived it, in the conservative and religious traditions of Spanish women. The Socialists struggled for the triumph of their ideals in fashioning a perfect state. The Federals and the Catalans supported them. When the issue was put to the test of a nominal vote, the Socialists were victorious, 161-121, and the right of the Spanish women to vote was conceded. When the result was announced the ladies present broke into *vivas* and applause.[17]

Opinion continued to be divided as to the wisdom of this decision and the possible effect woman suffrage would have on the future of the political life of Spain. The next general election held the answer. Would the women support the ideals of social liberty that the Constituent Cortes was framing into the fundamental law of the land? Would they be loyal to the traditions of Spain and throw their newly won liberty into the balance of reaction? Even after the vote,

[16] *Ibid.*, 1353-1354.
[17] *Ibid.*, No. 48, 1359-1361; Mori, II, 231-238.

Jiménez de Asúa, a Socialist, confessed his perplexity as to the consequences of the reform. Prophecy was difficult. In England, when the Conservative Party expected the women to vote with it, they had supported the Labor Party. When the Germans thought the women would swing to the Left, they had voted with the Nationalists. It was only safe to hope that the women of Spain would exercise the greatest responsibility in casting their votes.[18]

The chamber was fatigued by the preceding debate and the next few articles were passed without prolonged discussion. Article 35 of the parliamentary project provided that the state should require the personal service of every citizen for civil or military duties, as the law should require. The parliament was empowered to fix the military contingent annually. There was only one amendment to modify this article. It was proposed by Claudio Sánchez Albornoz and referred, in reality, to the whole constitution. It suggested that the phrase "parliament" be replaced by *"cortes,"* not only in this article but in the whole text. This was accepted by the chamber, and Article 35 became Article 37 of the Constitution. It was, in fact, identical with Article 21 of the *anteproyecto*.[19]

Article 38 recognized the right of peaceful assembly without arms. Both the project of the constitutional commission and the *anteproyecto* prescribed the necessity of obtaining previous permission of the authorities before holding meetings in the open air. The phrase " in the open air" was debated and, as the result of an amendment of Victoria Kent, the article was redrafted. The matter was left to the regulation of a special law.[20] The next article guaranteed the right of association or "syndication" for the different ends of human life, according to the laws of the state. The various syndicates and associations were obliged, however, to register themselves according to the law devised. The parliamentary

[18] Jiménez de Asúa, 259-260.
[19] *Diario*, No. 48, 1363-1365.
[20] *Ibid.*, No. 48, 1367-1369; Jiménez de Asúa, 262.

project was based on the *anteproyecto,* which the commission had completely redrafted, but it was identical with Article 39 of the approved constitution.[21]

The following article was also quickly approved. One amendment, that of Martínez Moya, aimed to exclude foreigners from the public service, but it was defeated. The approved Article 40, based on the *anteproyecto* as revised by the constitutional commission, provided that all Spaniards, regardless of sex, were admissible to public employment and office, according to their merit and capacity, except for incompatibilities prescribed by law.[22]

Before the constitutional debate was suspended for the consideration of other matters, the session of October 1 was devoted to the preliminary discussion of one other provision, Article 41. The corresponding Article 39 of the *dictamen* declared that public functionaries should be appointed and promoted according to law. The constitution guaranteed their permanence. They could be removed and suspended only for justified causes previously specified by law. The second paragraph guaranteed that no public official could be persecuted or molested for his political or religious opinions. Finally, these officials were permitted to organize professional associations. These would be regulated by a law and could appeal to the courts against the decisions of superiors which injured the rights of the functionaries.

Several amendments and *votos particulares* were offered to this article. A third paragraph was added as a result of the acceptance of an amendment of Royo Villanova. It proposed that the responsibility of the state should be subsidiary to that of the officials for damages resulting from the infringement of their duties. Gordón Ordáx asked that no functionary be molested or persecuted for his social ideas. Both of these were accepted by the commission. The last paragraph had been modified by the commission as a result of a *voto* proposed by Botella Asensi. The *anteproyecto* provided for

[21] *Diario,* No. 48, 1369-1371; Jiménez de Asúa, 263.
[22] *Diario,* No. 48, 1371-1372.

professional associations only, and Botella wished to expand it to include syndicates, although those public officials who were invested with authority were denied the right to strike. A long and impassioned debate ensued. Then another deputy, Villanueva, presented the original *dictamen* of the parliamentary commission as a *voto particular*. The chamber accepted his proposal by a vote of 135-118, and the final paragraph was approved as it had been presented to the *cortes*.[23]

The final article of this chapter was approved in the same session. It concerned a matter of vital importance to those who had endured the unconstitutional procedure of the dictatorship, the suspension of the constitutional rights and guarantees specified in articles 29, 31, 34, 38, and 39. Article 42 specified that these might be suspended in all the national territory, when the security of the state, "in cases of notorious and imminent gravity," required. It was necessary to delegate this power to the government, but the deputies took precautions to qualify the exercise of the power and prevent its abuse. If the *cortes* was in session it should approve the suspension proposed by the government. On the other hand, if the *cortes* was not assembled, the government was obliged to convoke it within eight days, and if the government failed in its duty, it would assemble automatically on the ninth day. The *cortes* could not be dissolved while the suspension was in effect, unless the *cortes* had reached a decision on that suspension. If the *cortes* was dissolved, the government would immediately notify the Permanent Deputation, established by Article 62. This body would approve the suspension with the same powers that were exercised by the chamber. It was further provided that the suspension could not exceed thirty days, and any extension of the period required the previous accord of the *cortes* or the Permanent Deputation. The law of public order would prevail during the period of the suspension in the territory to which the suspension applied. The government was not permitted to alienate, deport, or exile

[23] *Ibid.*, 1373-1378, No. 49, October 2, 1931, 1397-1413; Jiménez de Asúa, 265-268.

Spaniards more than 250 kilometres from their home in any case.

The parliamentary *dictamen* was based on the *anteproyecto*, and various amendments were offered in the chamber. Only one was taken into consideration. It was offered by Gordón Ordáx and defended by Baeza Medina. It involved the final paragraph concerning the deportation or exile of Spaniards and was the basis for the addition of this clause to the constitutional text. The other changes resulted from the revision of style.[24]

The chamber had now completed the approval of the first forty-two articles of the constitution. It had considered all of the individual and political guarantees in the preceding week, except those concerning the religious orders which had been postponed. None of the articles approved had provoked any unusual debate except the qualifications of age and sex for electors. Woman suffrage had been granted. The individual and political guarantees were those universally accepted in democratic countries. They guaranteed that Spain would be a liberal and democratic republic. They had been inherited from nineteenth-century liberalism, and no liberal in Spain disputed their inclusion in the constitution. The only anxiety was that they be sufficiently guaranteed and protected from possible infringement or the restraint of the freedom of action of the individual.

[24] *Diario*, No. 49, 1413-1424; Jiménez de Asúa, 268-273.

XIV

SOCIALISM AND PRIVATE PROPERTY

THE SOCIALISTS had succeeded in overriding the moderates and had extended the suffrage to the women of Spain. They had also modified the Marxist concept of the class struggle in making Spain a republic of workers. The charter of individual liberties, included in Title III, had assured an equality of opportunity and personal liberty in the nascent republic. The question of collective rights and the concept of the general welfare produced a bitter struggle in the chamber, arousing the vested interests of Church and property to the defense of Spanish traditions.

The first article of the chapter entitled "Family, Economy, and Culture" had been postponed for later consideration and Article 42 was the next to be discussed. It concerned the vital question of property and was raised at the end of the session of October 2. The debate was postponed, however, until the following week because many of the deputies had to leave Madrid to participate in the partial elections for vacancies in the *cortes*. Besteiro announced that Articles 42, 44, and 45 of the *dictamen* had to be approved by the end of the session of October 6, and that every effort would be made to accelerate the discussion of the constitution and its definitive approval.

All of the session of October 6 was devoted to Article 42. The original *dictamen* of the parliamentary commission differed radically from the *anteproyecto*. The latter provided that the state should protect both individual and collective property, in accord with laws regulating its social function. Property could be forcibly expropriated for reasons of social utility. Indemnization was guaranteed, but a special law was to be enacted to define the procedure. Property might also be socialized. The constitutional commission expanded these concepts considerably. It declared that natural resources within the national territory belonged originally to the state in the name of the nation. The state recognized private property in direct proportion to its social utility as administered by the proprietor, but it would proceed with its socialization in a gradual manner. In addition, the state had the right to impose those modifications on private property which were necessary for the public interest. All property could be forcibly expropriated for social utility, with the indemnization provided by law. In cases of social necessity this expropriation might be effected without indemnization. Finally, all public services and enterprises affecting the national interest were to be nationalized in the shortest possible time.

The *dictamen* reflected the ideology of the Socialists on the parliamentary commission, while the *anteproyecto* represented the more conservative and juridical attitude of the *Comisión Jurídica Asesora,* although it recognized the claims of social utility. It was natural that the more extreme measures proposed by the Socialists should arouse the anxiety of the conservative classes and provoke a flood of *votos particulares* and amendments. The chamber was profoundly divided.

Castrillo opened the debate with a defense of the individualistic concept of private property. Bugeda replied in the name of the constitutional commission. The article, he declared, was not completely socialist in content, but reflected the compromise of the majority of the parties which formed the commission. The first paragraph should frighten no one. It aimed only to establish the origin of property in order that the reforms might be accomplished, however transcendental they might be. They were not ignorant of the currents of thought in the contemporary world. These indicated, despite the manifestation of Castrillo in defending his *voto particular,* "that individualism has failed in the world. We are witnessing the crisis of capitalism, whether those who represent that tendency desire it or not."[1] They had not wished to carry purely socialist concepts to the constitution in accord with reality. The nineteenth century was characterized by the struggle for political power, the twentieth by the struggle for the economic liberation of all men. Therefore, in speaking of the origin of property in this sense, they were in accord not only with those who supported their program, but with those of the opposed doctrines.

The opposition arose principally from the Catholics, who held that type of property which, in Bugeda's opinion, had not "signified more than abuse." It should be given a socializing, human, comprehensive content, capable of resolving in an instant all of the tragic problems which afflicted the social economy of the world.

We do not conceive a free economy today, but one enslaved to the necessity of the social function which it represents.[2]

Bugeda cited articles of the constitutions of Germany, Serbia, Chile, and Peru, to prove that the necessity of establishing the concept of public power in the question of private property was a tendency of the contemporary world. He then declared that "all those constitutions, which are not of a socialist type, carry in their provisions the conception of a useful function. . . ."[3] It was necessary to require the greatest sacrifices and submission of the private proprietor without eliminating him. The idea of gradual socialization of private property by the state would eradicate the irritating and eternal inequality which until then had separated some classes from the others. The state would arrange the harmonious and necessary coördination of production, and indemnization was provided in all cases of necessary socialization. The nationalization of public services and enterprises was necessary because the great companies had fallen into such a condition that they had to seek aid from the government during the

---

[1] *Diario*, No. 50, October 6, 1931, 1433; Mori, II, 242.
[2] *Diario*, No. 50, 1433-1434.
[3] *Ibid.*, 1434.

dictatorship. Confiscation of property, however, was prohibited, and nationalization and socialization, the submission of an economy to the central power, could not be interpreted as confiscation.[4]

The debate continued between Castrillo and Bugeda, followed by Ossorio y Gallardo, who defended the classic concept of individualism. Samper introduced a *voto particular*
based on the *anteproyecto*. It proposed the modification of
the first paragraph to read

The state recognizes the right of individual and collective property.

He desired to change the phrase "property must be socialized" to "property can be socialized." The parliamentary
project imposed an exclusive régime, the Radicals desired
a more elastic one, lest the problem be prejudiced for a
future *cortes*.[5] Gil Robles rose to defend the agrarian and
Catholic interests. He was in accord with neither the extreme individualism advocated by Castrillo nor the socialist
concept embodied in the article under discussion. Private
property was a natural right:

. . . private property organized individually, at least in part, because only through that organization may that concrete interest
of property be given, which is the true stimulus of all activity and
all progress.[6]

This did not signify that property was an absolute right.
The Catholic doctrine of property was based on two fundamental affirmations: first, that the individual element should
predominate in all of the improvement and administration
of property; second, that the collective element should predominate in everything related to the profit or utility of the
goods produced. He represented a minority that held that
property was

. . . a right limited by all of those social ends and considerations

[4] *Ibid.*, 1435-1436; Mori, II, 242-249.
[5] *Diario*, No. 50, 1436-1440.
[6] *Ibid.*, 1441.

which arise from the substantial equality of human nature and of all the duties of sociability which it is necessary to fulfil within human collectivity. . . .[7]

This speech, adroitly inspired with the hope of arousing the conservative interests to the defense of a less extreme view than that advocated by Castrillo, was constantly interrupted by members of the Socialist minority. The presiding officer warned Gil Robles that his oration ran the risk of becoming a dialogue with the Socialists, and requested that he should address the chamber rather than the Socialists. Aizpún then charged that the article was exclusively socialistic and declared that the *vasconavarra* minority could not support it.[8]

Besteiro had already surrendered his position as presiding officer to participate in the debate. He expressed his own views rather than the criteria of the minority he represented. He feared they were trying to make too perfect a constitution. The national problems would be solved more slowly in Spain than in other states. The Socialists had made a concession in the recognition of private property in relation to its utility, but historically private property was a necessity. They recognized that socialization had diverse forms and followed various paths.

The immense majority of the proprietors of Spain were blinded by private interests. They neither grasped the implications and new necessities of production nor the sufferings of the great human masses. Those who framed the constitution had to effect not a political but a social revolution. It could "be bloody or not, according to the position in which we find our adversaries." He continued:

Ah! but if you close the doors to us then we shall have to tell you that the republic is not really our republic, and it will not be your republic except by means of insurrection.[9]

Then he asked that they should speak no more of comparisons between Russia and Spain.

[7] *Ibid.*, 1442.
[8] *Ibid.*, 1442-1443.
[9] *Ibid.*, 1445.

The cases are completely different. Russia undertook the task of producing the social transformation completely from the authority of the state.

The position of Spain was less favorable for attempting such an enterprise.[10]

This appeared to be a threat to resort to desperate means if the socialist concession was not accepted. Moreover, it was delivered by the real leader of the Socialist Party, although he had declared it a personal view. Ossorio y Gallardo, the bland, suave, cordial gentleman, the conservative, answered Besteiro. He reminded him that no one had closed a door on the Socialists. Samper's *voto particular* opened an unlimited means of socializing property. The antithesis between the *dictamen* and the *voto* was not as great as it might appear to "a hasty reader or a preoccupied spirit." No one in the chamber defended the classic economic liberalism. Private property was to be respected and defended in the very measure in which it served society. He would define property as "the right of using, enjoying and disposing of goods according to their nature in the service of society and for the profit of the owner." In this manner the social interest and private interest would always be combined. But "we are frightened—at least I am frightened, I confess terror—at a constitutional text which says that property will be gradually socialized. . . ." Was it necessary to maintain such a drastic provision when the other had the same possibilities? Finally, Ossorio y Gallardo asked Besteiro,

Can you make affirmations in a constitution which, without bringing anything essentially new to other recognized and indisputable possibilities, contribute to sow an inquietude, serve as a defense for certain egoisms, refuse justified and respectable alarms, and break economic situations?[11]

Besteiro rose to rectify his speech. He feared that the Spanish Republic might be more reactionary than he desired.

[10] *Ibid.*, Mori, II, 253-254.
[11] *Diario*, No. 50, 1446-1447.

The constitution should signify a direction for the evolution of the state. States should not be created in which the people believed themselves to be free when in reality they were slaves. The debate continued and no compromise seemed possible. Then Alcalá Zamora left the Blue Bench to address the chamber, and a real crisis was provoked.

The President of the Provisional Government spoke briefly. He held that property was an enterprise and that the proprietor was only an agent. The agent might be removed and the enterprise transformed for reasons of social utility. He turned to the Socialists and declared there was a difference between the sacrifice by which someone profited and the contingency or threat which rendered everything valueless. Therefore, he offered an alternative. He favored the *voto particular* of Samper in preference to the *dictamen,* but he asked that the Socialists draft a formula which would reflect the attitude of the whole chamber and reconcile the discrepancies.[12]

The chamber was going to proceed to a nominal vote on the *voto particular* when Botella interrupted. He declared:

. . . as has already happened several times, the President of the Government, with the indisputable authority which he has in the chamber, rises just before the vote, and expounds his view in a form that all must respect, but this commission cannot do less than tell you that under this system it feels in a disadvantageous position.

Botella was interrupted with applause and great protests in the chamber. Some of the members of the commission declared that that body had not authorized him to make such a statement. The vice-president, Barnés, tried to restore order, but the protests and the tumult continued. Castrillo and Botella almost came to blows. Various deputies had to restrain them. When the chamber was quieted the *voto particular* was defeated, 167-157.[13]

[12] *Ibid.,* 1452-1453; Mori, II, 255-266.
[13] *Diario,* No. 50, 1453-1456.

Ruiz Funes proposed that unindemnified expropriation should be undertaken only upon the initiative of a fourth of the deputies and after the approval of a law by two-thirds of the members. But his suggestion was also defeated, 161-146, and the discussion was suspended.[14]

The constitutional commission met immediately to consider the issue raised by Botella. It drafted a note to be read in the chamber that night. Various amendments had been withdrawn or rejected when Jiménez de Asúa rose to read the following:

The commission, without entering into the basis of the incident which occurred in the chamber in the session of this evening, declares that Botella spoke in its name and by its express charge, and that the members who manifested a discrepancy with his words could do so only on their own responsibility.[15]

The chamber again broke into an uproar. Alcalá Zamora hastily left the Blue Bench to join his minority, while the more conservative deputies rose to applaud him. The uproar continued until the President began to speak.

Alcalá Zamora declared that he was merely trying to propose a formula, regardless of whether the *dictamen* or the *voto particular* was taken as a base. The formula he desired was one in which the whole world of socialism would be realizable, "and in that moment there arose an attack against me, an explosion of animosity." He could not occupy his position in full authority without the complete confidence of the chamber. He did not wish to retain a position when he lacked the support, however slight the defection, of two forces which at that time, at least, constituted a majority. Jiménez de Asúa had attacked him in an indirect manner. He had "been treated iniquitously," and could not continue as President of the Provisional Government. The chamber should form the combination which appeared most suitable to the deputies.[16]

[14] *Ibid.*, 1457-1460.
[15] *Ibid.*, 1467.
[16] *Ibid.*, 1467-1469.

Besteiro and Prieto tried to dissuade Alcalá Zamora from resigning, but the latter was determined. He returned to the Blue Bench but sat at the foot rather than in his accustomed place. After trying to gain the floor several times, Jiménez declared that he had not intervened to cast aspersions on anyone. Then he, too, resigned as president of the constitutional commission and left the chamber.[17]

The session was suspended while the government met to deliberate on the ministerial crisis which had arisen and Besteiro tried to persuade Jiménez de Asúa to withdraw his resignation. Within forty minutes the crisis was resolved and the chamber was reassembled. Besteiro announced that both Alcalá Zamora and Jiménez de Asúa had changed their minds and would continue in their respective offices. It seemed a petty matter, but Alcalá Zamora declared later that it was evident that he could not be sustained by a vote of confidence and that he resigned to prevent a division.[18] This emphasized the magnitude of the sacrifice that the president was prepared to make. Nevertheless his greater political experience, his position as leader of the most conservative of the republican parties, and his undoubted prestige had been used before to influence the decision of the assembly toward a policy of moderation. And at this juncture, in a matter of such vital importance to their program, the Socialist minority was resentful. Botella was a Radical-Socialist, but he had dared to say what was probably on the lips of many Socialists at that moment.

Several amendments were rejected, but one offered by the *Agrupación al Servicio de la República* and signed by González Uña, Valdecasas, José Ortega y Gasset, and others, was now taken into consideration by a vote of 151-143. It was based on Article 30 of the *anteproyecto,* in that it and the corresponding Article 45 of the constitutional project were incorporated as the first paragraph of Article 42. The debate continued, and finally the commission was charged with re-

[17] *Ibid.,* 1469-1473; Mori, II, 255-278.
[18] *Diario,* No. 50, 1472; Mori II, 259, 272.

drafting the text of Article 42 on the basis of González Uña's amendment. The session was suspended at 3:50 in the morning.[19]

When the chamber reassembled, on October 7, the new formula was read and was almost immediately approved as Article 44 of the constitution.[20] It is of sufficient importance, in view of the crisis it had provoked, to be quoted in full:

All of the wealth of the country, whoever its owner may be, is subordinated to the interests of the national economy and charged with the sustenance of the public offices, in accordance with the constitution and the laws.

The property of every kind of goods can be the object of necessary expropriation for cause of social utility by means of adequate indemnization, unless a law approved by the votes of the absolute majority of the *cortes* may dispose otherwise.

Property can be socialized with the same requisites.

The public services and the exploitations which affect the common interest can be nationalized in the cases in which social necessity may require it.

The state can intervene by law in the exploitation and coördination of industry and enterprises when the rationalization of production and the interests of national economy require it.

In no case shall the penalty of confiscation of goods be imposed.[21]

Thus the compromise between the Socialists and the vested interests of property was effected. The aim of the more extreme minorities in the *cortes* to proceed immediately to the gradual socialization of private property was thwarted. Their desire to secure the principle of the responsibility of proprietors through the recognition of the social utility of property was granted, but the provision that public services and enterprises affecting the general interest be nationalized was also modified. Instead of immediate nationalization, it was provided that it would be effected only in cases of social

[19] *Diario,* No. 50, 1478-1481, 1487-1488; Jiménez de Asúa, 291-295.

[20] *Diario,* No. 51, October 7, 1931, 1492.

[21] Jiménez de Asúa, 291. Compare this with any copy of the definitive constitution.

necessity. Expropriation for social purposes and socialization could be effected, but only with the approval of the absolute majority of the *cortes* and with indemnization assured. In short, the forces of the Right had ably defended the vested interests of property in Spain. Private property was recognized as subordinate to the national interest, but it was guaranteed against any kind of confiscation.

A week later the *cortes* approved Article 45, which concerned another kind of property. The *anteproyecto* had neglected to provide for the protection of the artistic and historic wealth of the country. The parliamentary project, however, in Article 43, provided that treasures of this nature should be under the protection of the state, which was empowered to prohibit their exportation and alienation by decrees regarded as opportune for their defense. A number of amendments were presented to this article when it was considered in the chamber, and the commission, after examining them in one of its morning sessions, drafted a new formula which was accepted by the chamber. The original concept was somewhat expanded. The artistic and historic wealth, regardless of ownership, was declared to constitute the cultural treasure of the nation and was placed under the protection of the state. The state could not only prohibit its exportation or alienation, but could decree the necessary legal expropriation in its defense. In addition, the state should organize a registry for this wealth and should assure its careful custody and perfect conservation. Those places notable for their natural beauty or for their recognized artistic and historical value should also be protected.[22]

Meanwhile, on October 7, two other articles concerned with the economic life of the nation were approved. The first provided the desired guarantees for the protection of labor and various forms of social security. Castrillo withdrew his *voto particular* and the majority of the amendments were withdrawn or defeated. Pérez de Ayala defended an amendment

[22] *Ibid.*, 295-296; *Diario*, No. 58, October 16, 1931, 1799.

which proposed the reduction of the article into a shorter formula. It declared:

Labor, in any of its forms, is a social duty.

The condition of the laborer is the most precious title of citizenship for the Spanish Republic. The social legislation will protect the right to work, will defend the laborer against the risks and dangers inherent in his activity, and will assure his full participation in the product of his effort.[23]

The majority of the deputies, however, desired a more certain guarantee of the securities offered to the laborer, and this amendment was defeated in a nominal vote, 195-129. Victoria Kent proposed an amendment which declared that there should be no difference in remuneration between the sexes, as a result of the "equality of labor." This was defeated. The only addition accepted was that of Dr. Juarros. The *dictamen* specified that the labor of women and children should be regulated. Juarros observed that the word *niños* should not be used, because the children would be exempt from all work during the period of their schooling. He proposed the use of *adolescentes*. The commission accepted the sense of the amendment, but not the terminology, which was held to be a trifle too pedantic. In the correction of style the commission substituted the word *jovenes* (youths) and introduced other slight modifications. Otherwise Article 46 of the definitive constitution was almost identical with both the *dictamen* and the *anteproyecto*.[24]

Article 46 reflected the social and economic thought of the contemporary world. It represented a social point of view in its provisions for security, and in this the technical approach of the liberal juridical commission was sufficient even for the socialists. The article provided: "Labor in its diverse forms is a social obligation," and would enjoy legal protection. The republic would guarantee every laborer the conditions necessary for a worthy existence. It concluded with an enu-

[23] *Diario*, No. 48, October 1, 1931, Appendix 11.
[24] *Diario*, No. 51, 1492-1511; Mori, II, 274; Jiménez de Asúa, 296-299.

meration of the guarantees and forms of social security to be provided by legislation: infirmity, accident, unemployment, old age, disability, and death; the labor of women and children and the protection of maternity; the length of the working day and the minimum wage; annual vacations with remuneration; the conditions of Spanish laborers abroad; cooperative institutions; the economic and juridical relation of the factors which integrate production; the participation of the workers in the direction, administration, and benefits of enterprises and everything that might effect the protection of the laborers.[25]

The following article was approved in the same session. It had not been included in either of the preliminary projects, but had originated in an amendment of the Federal deputy, Arranz. It was offered to Article 44 of the *dictamen* and was postponed for later discussion.[26] The amendment was explained as follows:

. . . it refers to a humble laborer, worthy of all protection, who is not considered as having a fixed wage, who lives exclusively by his labor, by the cultivation of the land, whether he may be a small proprietor, whether he may be a farmer, whether he may be a tenant, but who cannot be under the protection of the legislation which holds for the salaried laborers by any concept.[27]

The amendment provided:

The republic also assures the small peasant proprietor a worthy existence; and to that end will legislate, among other matters, on the family patrimony, untaxable and exempt from every kind of impost; on agricultural credit, based on personal security alone; on indemnization for loss of harvests; on production and consumption coöperatives; on old age security; on practical schools of agriculture and agricultural and cattle forms of experimentation; on irrigation works and establishment of ways of communication between all the villages.[28]

[25] Jiménez de Asúa, 296-297.
[26] *Diario,* No. 51, 1496.
[27] *Ibid.,* 1511.
[28] *Ibid.,* No. 35, September 9, 1931, Appendix 1.

In its definitive form, Article 47 was modified to begin

The republic will protect the peasant. . . .

An additional paragraph was added as a result of an amendment of Leizaola, requesting that the republic should protect the fishermen in similar terms. The article was approved and the way was cleared for the debate of the religious question.[29]

[29] Jiménez de Asúa, 300; *Diario*, No. 51, 1512-1513.

XV

THE RELIGIOUS CRISIS

THE RELIGIOUS problem was the most intricate and difficult that the chamber had to solve in the framing of the constitution. It involved not only the separation of Church and state and the policy that should be followed in regard to the religious orders, but the questions of divorce and education as well. Divorce was an attack on the sacrament and the ecclesiastical control of marriage. The proposal of lay education struck at the very foundation of the clerical control of the schools of Spain, which the Republicans and Socialists wished to replace with a united educational system under the control of the state.

Actual debate on the provisions relating to the religious question did not begin until October 8, when Fernando de los Ríos delivered an able speech. He did not speak for the Socialist minority to which he belonged, but independently. In his opinion the smallest common divisor for the solution of the religious problem consisted of the liberty of cults and relative secularization. The Provisional Government had not compromised the full moral autonomy of the chamber to decide the policy of the state toward the Church. The state should be neutral in the matter of faith and confession in the realm of sentiment and belief, but if it was neutral, it could sustain no church.

No. The churches must be sustained by the faithful; and this is the dominant position in the world.[1]

The Minister of Justice then proceeded to combat the historic argument that the budget of the clergy was based on a compensatory obligation of the state for having made the

---

[1] *Diario,* No. 52, October 8, 1931, 1522; Mori, III, 16.

property of the clergy an object of amortization and was equivalent to the interest on this obligation. In reality, the clerical budget had developed as a budget of public service in Spain. He proceeded to elaborate various plans for the solution of the problem of the support of the thirty-five thousand persons dependent on the clerical budget.

Separation of Church and state would strengthen the Church spiritually rather than weaken it. The thing that frightened and preoccupied him was the teratological development of the Church. Its organs were united with the state, and as a result of that union it used the political power which the state gave it and the concurrence of its organs with those of the state to scourge the consciences of the dissidents. The separation of the Church and state signified that the state would not collaborate in the realization of the ends of the Church, but would leave it complete liberty to organize itself internally. He regarded the recognition of the Church as a corporation of public law a juridical mistake and a grave political error. The two institutions should leave each other to the pursuit of their respective ends. An independent Church signified a renunciation of the rights of patronage and presentation by the state. But the latter should retain the right of veto as opposed to the right of patronage in order to protect is own ends.

He then turned to the question of the religious orders. There were 36,569 nuns and 8,369 monks in Spain. The constitution might take one of two positions in regard to the orders and congregations. They could be eliminated, or the question could be postponed for consideration by a special law. If the law of congregations was passed it should be conditioned in the constitution so that it would limit the number, character, capacity, and activity of the orders. It had to impede their economic, industrial, and commercial activity. He turned to the Catholics of the chamber and declared:

We come here, then—do not be surprised—with an arrow fastened in the depth of the soul, and that arrow is the rancor that the Church has aroused through having lived for centuries confounded with the monarchy and making us constantly the object of the deepest vexations: it has not respected either our persons or our honor; it has respected nothing, absolutely nothing, including the supreme hour of sorrow, in the moment of death, it has separated us from our parents.

Therefore, he asked

. . . that you be very careful with the words that you pronounce: do not renew our sorrow, do not strike drums of war, because in the war you will be and would always be conquered in the name of the Spanish liberal emotion.[2]

Gil Robles spoke for the Catholics of Spain. They desired the neutrality of the state as opposed to the concept of Article 3, which in their opinion signified a lay state. They preferred that this article should declare that there was no official religion rather than no state religion. They accepted the concept of liberty of conscience and were willing to admit the absolute separation of Church and state as two complete and perfect entities, with one condition,

. . . that we have to define in the name of a doctrine which we cannot surrender, and that is the full recognition of the juridical personality of the Church as a perfect and independent society, a recognition that implies respect for its private ends, for its own regimen, for all its hierarchic entities, and for the free disposition of the means necessary for the fulfilment of the ends. With the recognition of this personality, I have no reason to enter into the distinction whether or not it should be a corporation of public law.[3]

He then attacked De los Ríos on two points, his reference to ecclesiastical properties and his statement regarding a concordat with the Vatican.

The important consideration, then, appeared to involve the religious orders. Gil Robles declared that the *dictamen* on this point was an absolute negation of the liberal and democratic spirit that infused the rest of the constitution.

[2] *Diario*, No. 52, 1527; Mori, III, 27.
[3] *Diario*, No. 52, 1529; Mori, III, 29.

The precept of the constitution which dissolves the religious orders and decrees the nationalization of their properties goes against
the essence of individual liberty, against the right of association,
against the principle of equality; three principles which you have
regulated in the articles which are already approved by this very
assembly.[4]

As he proceeded there were interruptions and cries from
various sides of the chamber. Undaunted, he declared that
the *dictamen* of the commission was the accusation of a
prosecutor against the religious orders, and a sentence. They
were being condemned without trial or defense. It was a
project of religious persecution and the Catholics could not
accept it. He spoke in the name of millions of Catholics who
thought as he did. The Catholics might be persecuted but
they would be triumphant. He concluded:

. . . and I, gentlemen, in the name of a religious emotion and a
patriotic love, say that I will struggle with you in the great battles
for my ideals, but that I shall always have the understanding to
view you, finally, as no more than brothers.[5]

The debate on the totality of the religious problem continued through the next two sessions. It is not necessary to
follow the course of the debate, for the discourses of De los
Ríos and Gil Robles had already indicated the principal
issues involved, and the later speeches revealed the attitude
of the various parties. The Socialists and Radical-Socialists
supported the parliamentary project, which aimed at the
creation of a lay state, liberty of conscience, and the suppression of the religious orders and nationalization of their property. The Radicals, the dominant minority in the Republican Alliance, desired the separation of Church and state;
the conversion of the religious institutions into corporations
of public law, leaving the state the power of proceeding
against them or dissolving them when their actions made it
necessary; and agreed that the expulsion of the Jesuits was
a matter of the utmost importance.[6]

[4] *Diario*, No. 52, 1530; Mori, III, 32.
[5] *Diario*, No. 52, 1532; Mori, III, 36.
[6] Mori, III, 12, 38.

The Progressives desired to vote the most moderate proposition possible, within a régime of complete liberty of conscience. Their leader, Alcalá Zamora, participated in the debate on October 10. He declared that he realized he was not supported by the chamber, that he stood alone, but he considered the religious problem one of justice and politics, rather than of dogma. He differed from the *vasconavarra* and Catholic minorities because they seized upon liberty of conscience as a remedy in the hour of distress. He, on the other hand, proclaimed it as a guarantee for all dissidents. The *dictamen* of the majority of the chamber was opposed to democracy, liberty, and justice. It was religious prejudice. He enumerated the various restrictions that were placed on the Catholics while the deputies were loudly proclaiming the equality of all Spaniards. He opposed the dissolution of the religious orders and declared:

... if a sectarian formula prevails, I have still a grand mission to fulfil, not only aided by many persons, and many of them heterodox, freethinkers, unbelievers, in the service of the republic; I have to turn to the Catholic masses of the country to tell them: do you see what you feel as an injustice, and I affirm that it is? But outside the republic, never. Within the republic, supporting the injustice and aspiring to modify it; not increasing lines of monarchist reaction, nor lines of dictatorial folly, within the republic.[7]

The Catalan deputies appeared likely to divide. The speeches of Abadal, Jiménez, and Samblancat indicated some divergences of opinion within the ranks of that minority. Humberto Torres, of the Catalan Left, supported the proposed dissolution of the religious orders and an extremist criterion in general. Some of the Federal deputies were also disposed to defend the *dictamen* as it stood, including Barriobero, but all of the minority did not share this conviction.[8] On the Right were the *vasconavarras,* who desired to rescue all they could in defense of Catholicism in Spain. Gil Robles

[7] *Diario,* No. 54, October 10, 1931, 1611.
[8] Mori, III, 13, 61, 82.

was a member of this minority, but he hoped to unite the various conservative minorities in defense of Catholic interests. To that end, he was willing to concede the separation of Church and state and liberty of conscience. He had declared that the dissolution of the religious orders was, in reality, persecution of the Catholics.

The consideration of the various articles concerning the religious question was begun on October 13. Article 3 had been postponed and was the first to be discussed. The parliamentary project provided that there was no state religion. Gil Robles had already indicated the disagreement of the Catholics with this declaration and a long discussion now ensued. The *anteproyecto* was identical with the *dictamen* in this respect, but the idea of a lay state in Spain was anathema to the Catholics. Many amendments and *votos particulares* were offered. Most of them were defeated or withdrawn. Ramos, however, offered an amendment which was finally incorporated into the *dictamen* and the formula proved so satisfactory that it was passed by a nominal vote of 267-41. It was identical with the concept offered by Gil Robles, but he voted against it. Article 3, as approved, declared:

The Spanish state has no official religion.[9]

This was the first blow at the Church. Even the Catholics recognized that it was inevitable. But they had been able to win a compromise with the more extreme concept of the lay state.

This debate on the totality of the articles dealing with the religious problem had indicated the necessity of modifying Article 24 of the parliamentary project, with the aim of limiting the provision dissolving the religious orders. The majority of the deputies preferred to restrict the dissolution to those congregations which appeared particularly pernicious. The rest would be submitted to a law which would reduce their activity to the strict sphere of their own ends.

[9] Jiménez de Asúa, 112-113; *Diario*, No. 36, September 10, 1931, Appendix 3; No. 55, October 13, 1931, 1654, 1660-1662.

The *anteproyecto* had provided that after its separation from the state, the Church should be considered a corporation of public law. The other religious confessions, however, were extended the same privilege if they solicited it and their constitution and the number of their members offered guarantees of subsistence. The more radical constitutional commission had modified the juridical provision. All the religious confessions were to be considered as associations subject to the general laws of the country. The state could in no case sustain, favor, or aid the churches, associations, and religious institutions economically. Finally, it declared that the state would dissolve all of the religious orders and nationalize their property.[10]

It was the last paragraph that aroused the protest of the conservatives and moderates. The commission agreed to modify the *dictamen,* basing its new draft on an amendment offered by the Radicals. The groups affiliated with Republican Action and the *Agrupación al Servicio de la República* seemed inclined to accept this proposal. The Socialists, on the other hand, refused to accept the new formula and agreed to maintain the *dictamen* as a *voto particular* and submit it to the consideration and vote of the *cortes.*[11]

When the chamber assembled on October 13, Jiménez de Asúa introduced the *voto particular* of the Socialists, and a debate developed. Azaña declared that if the Socialist Party was going to assume the power immediately and declared the necessity of having its text to govern, he would vote for it. The problem was more political than religious. Companys, leader of the Catalan Left, took the same position as the Minister of War. Alvaro Albornoz, a Radical-Socialist, had already expressed the approval of the original *dictamen* by that minority. Baeza Medina now reiterated that approval and expressed a desire for an immediate vote. The Radicals asked for time to reflect on the matter and succeeded in having the session suspended.[12]

[10] Jiménez de Asúa, 184-187.
[11] *Ibid.,* 188; *Diario,* No. 55, 1663.
[12] *Diario,* No. 55, 1663-1674, *passim.*

The discussion was continued just after midnight. The commission had prepared a third draft which was now read to the chamber:

All of the religious confessions will be considered as associations subject to a special law.

The state, the regions, the provinces and the municipalities will not maintain, favor, nor aid economically the churches, associations and religious institutions.

A special law will regulate the total extinction, within a maximum period of two years, of the budget of the clergy.

Those religious orders which impose by statute, in addition to the three canonical vows, another special one of obedience to an authority distinct from the legitimate authority of the state, are dissolved. Their property will be nationalized and dedicated to beneficent and educational ends.

The other religious orders will be subjected to a special law adjusted to the following bases:

1. Dissolution of those which in their activity constitute a danger for the security of the state.
2. Registration of those which remain in a special registry subject to the Ministry of Justice.
3. Incapacity of acquiring and conserving, by themselves or by an agent, more property than that which, previously justified, is destined for their living or the direct fulfilment of their private ends.
4. Prohibition of activity in industry, commerce, and education.
5. Submission to all of the tributary laws of the country.
6. Obligation to render annually an account of their properties in relation to the ends of the association.

The properties of the religious orders can be nationalized.[13]

This differed from the second draft of the commission in the modification of the second paragraph to include the political subdivisions and regions as well as the state. It was also more explicit in regard to the extinction of the clerical budget. Finally, it added education to the list of occupations prohibited to the religious orders.[14]

[13] *Ibid.*, 1674-1675.
[14] Jiménez de Asúa, 188-189; Mori, III, 156.

Various amendments and *votos particulares* were now proposed. One of Cornide suggested the establishment of the legal situation of the Catholic religious orders by means of a concordat. The Catholics and conservatives rallied to its defense, but it was defeated, 194-43.[15] The *vasconavarras* fought a gallant battle in defense of the religious orders, but amendment after amendment was defeated. They had no allies except the Catholics and Agrarians. The commission accepted only the *voto* of Valle Gracia which proposed that the law regulating the religious orders be voted by the Constituent Cortes. Finally, at about seven o'clock on the morning of October 14, the article was approved by an overwhelming vote of 178-59. The Catholic parties remained staunch until the end.

Upon the approval of Article 26, the chamber and the galleries broke into applause which the *vasconavarras* answered with *vivas* for liberty. There was great confusion and some personal encounters occurred. Leizaola was the object of a personal attack, and the president of the chamber had difficulty in calming the tumult. He warned the deputies of the necessity of maintaining serenity and dignity, even when fatigue excused their lack of restraint. Any personal grievance, he announced, would be considered by the chamber and corrected. Leizaola tried to intervene but Besteiro declared that he had not the necessary serenity to speak and should postpone his remarks. Leizaola replied, "I have all the serenity necessary to say that I have not opened my mouth and I have received a punch."[16]

This triumph of the Left in the approval of Article 26 had two serious consequences. The most serious was the ministerial crisis produced by the resignation of Alcalá Zamora and Miguel Maura from the Provisional Government. The President of the Ministry had left the chamber in great disgust. He had already expressed himself in regard to the course he expected to follow. The chamber had failed to heed his

[15] *Diario*, No. 43, Appendix 8; No. 55, 1683-1684.
[16] *Ibid.*, No. 55, 1719-1721; Jiménez de Asúa, 214.

intervention in the cause of moderation. Therefore he called the ministers together and presented his resignation in an irrevocable manner, although Prieto tried to dissuade him, reminding him of the occasion when Alcalá Zamora had induced Prieto to maintain the solidarity of the government. This had happened only a few days before.[17]

The ministry decided that the crisis could be resolved only by Besteiro, who represented the highest authority in the state as the President of the Constituent Cortes. When the deputies assembled on the evening of October 14, Besteiro announced Alcalá Zamora's resignation and declared that the solution of the crisis was entirely in the hands of the *cortes*. He was confident that the chamber would give "a new proof of the high spirit" which animated it and would resolve the difficulty with the greatest possible facility. Lerroux asked that the deputies should not give the impression that Spain lacked authority, and suggested a vote of confidence in Besteiro. The chamber rang with applause. Besteiro accepted the responsibility and expressed the hope that the continuity of this labor for the prestige of the republic and the future of Spain, although momentarily broken, would quickly be reëstablished. The session was then suspended in order that the minorities might deliberate upon the selection of a new chief of state.[18]

The Socialists, as the most numerous group in the chamber, were offered the choice of the new president, but they were not willing to accept the political responsibility and refused. Lerroux, who was a most experienced politician and a statesman of great prestige, also declined the honor. As a result, Manuel Azaña was chosen as President of the Provisional Government. Although he had had little experience in the field of politics, he had won quite a reputation as a result of his administration of the Ministry of War. In addition, opinion generally conceded that his speech in the *cortes* the day before had contributed to the solution of the question

[17] Mori, III, 208.
[18] *Diario*, No. 56, October 14, 1931, 1725-1726.

of the religious orders. He had become the man of the hour.

The Ministry was reconstituted with a few changes. Casares Quiroga was transferred to the portfolio vacated by Maura, the Ministry of Government, and Giral, rector of the Central University, became Minister of Marine. Azaña retained the Ministry of War.[19]

The session was reopened shortly before nine o'clock. The new government was applauded as it entered the chamber. Besteiro presented the new president to the deputies, and Azaña addressed the chamber. The discourse is of some importance as an indication of the change in policy of the government. Azaña's administration of the War Office had been a vigorous and effective one. He was farther to the Left than Alcalá Zamora and his elevation to the highest office in Spain, following the approval of Article 26, indicated a distinct radical trend in Spanish politics.

He paid a tribute to his old colleague and predecessor, announced the changes in the formation of the new ministry, and outlined the policy he expected to follow. He proposed two things. First, the government would collaborate with the *cortes* for the most rapid approval of the definitive constitution. Everyone was convinced of this necessity, but the *cortes* had much to do besides framing a constitution. In the second place, the government would bring the agrarian law up for debate and consider the grave and important problem of the budget. Spain would be governed for all the Spaniards, and the government would strive to maintain the dignity and prestige of the republic.

We will govern with the firmness, the security, the loyalty, and the horizon as open as if we had before us a long series of years and all the long work of the republic depended on our fortune.

Azaña concluded with the following words:

Never, gentlemen, in my hands will the authority of the public power remain diminished, never in my hands will the government of my country be the object of contempt, or of mockery, or of

[19] Mori, III, 211-212.

scorn; never in this ministry will there be a weakness to serve the public good. The republic is of all Spaniards, governed, ruled, and directed by all republicans, and woe to the one who tries to raise his hand against it!

He was a man of force and action, and he was as good as his word.[20]

Alcalá Zamora told reporters that he would continue his parliamentary battle for revision with complete liberty. He had resigned because he disagreed with the constitution and believed he could revise it more easily as a deputy than as president. He had clashed with the chamber on four occasions: first, on the question of responsibility, then on the Catalan question, on the incidental difference with the constitutional commission, and finally, on the religious problem.[21]

The second result of the approval of Article 26 was the withdrawal of the Catholic deputies from the Constituent Cortes. The following note, justifying their action, was issued:

The development of the parliamentary debates, and in particular the last session, in which a violent and sectarian solution was imposed on the religious question, has demonstrated to the representatives of the Catholic groups and other independent Catholic deputies, the impossibility of harmonizing, as was their desire, the activity of the forces which they represent with the integral nuclei in the bloc of the Government on the constitutional question.

As a consequence, the Agrarian and *vasconavarra* minorities and the independent Catholic deputies have agreed to abstain from participation in this debate, and leave to the rest of the chamber the whole responsibility and the result of the discussion.

This decision, of which an account will be given to the electors, leaves both minorities free for a future activity within the chamber.

Royo Villanova, an Agrarian, could not join the exodus because of the mandate of his electors, although he appeared to

[20] *Ibid.*, III, 213-218; *Diario*, No. 56, 1727-1729.
[21] Mori, III, 220.

agree with this course of action. Gil Robles, on the other hand, was not a party to the agreement but was forced to withdraw in accord with party discipline.[22]

The solution of the religious question had forced an issue in the *cortes*. Before the constitution had been half approved two groups had undertaken a campaign for its revision. The Progressives, led by Alcalá Zamora and Miguel Maura, remained within the *cortes* as a conservative obstacle to the desires of the groups of the Left for a radical solution of the problems that confronted the government, while they actively engaged in a campaign against the swing to the Left among the electors. Another group, the most conservative of all, the Agrarians, Catholics, and *vasconavarras,* disdained to accept responsibility for the action of the *cortes,* although they gradually drifted back into the sessions. Yet they were equally interested in the revision of the constitution and the defense of the vested interests of land and Church that they represented. The activity of the Catholic Party, National Action, was increased and every preparation was made to take advantage of a reaction among the electors and to accelerate a possible trend to the Right.

One article remained before the approval of the religious provisions of the constitution was completed. It was based on Article 12 of the *anteproyecto.* Both this article and the corresponding Article 25 of the *dictamen* guaranteed liberty of conscience and the right of freely professing and practising religion in Spain, with due regard for the requirements of public morals. The constitutional commission modified the work of the juridical commission to provide that the various religious sects could hold their religious exercises in their respective temples only, instead of both "privately and publicly," although both projects restricted these exercises in the interest of public order. Both provided also that no one should be compelled to declare officially his religious beliefs, but the *anteproyecto* added, "unless for statistical reasons." The parliamentary commission added a paragraph to

[22] *Ibid.,* III, 206-207.

the effect that religious opinion should not constitute a modifying circumstance in the exercise of civil or political rights,
except as provided in the constitution for the election of the
president of the republic.[23]

The discussion of this article occupied a portion of the
session of October 15. Nine days before, the commission had
adopted a new *dictamen,* including the secularization of the
cemeteries in a second paragraph. Most of the numerous
votos and amendments proposed desired to secure the possibility of public manifestations for the various sects. This concept had been accepted by the majority of the members of
the commission before the discussion of the article began.
The formula presented by Ruiz Funes was incorporated into
the constitution. A later modification was introduced in connection with Article 86. It was agreed, in the debate of this
article, that the President of the Council of Ministers should
be subjected to the same incompatibilities as the president of
the republic. Thus ecclesiastics and ministers of all confessions were excluded from both offices. This addition was included in the revision of style.[24]

[23] Jiménez de Asúa, 220.
[24] *Diario,* No. 57, October 15, 1931, 1734-1743; Jiménez de Asúa, 217-222,
352. *Cf.* Article 70 of the definitive constitution.

XVI

THE FAMILY AND EDUCATION

FOLLOWING the constitutional solution of the religious problem, the *cortes* turned to the related questions of the family and education. It was essential, in accord with the twentieth-century social concepts, for the state to protect and regulate both the family and education in the collective interest of society and for the fullest development of the individual. The protection of the family involved the question of divorce, the obligation of parents to children, both legitimate and illegitimate, the investigation of paternity, and the necessary security for the infirm, the aged, maternity, and infancy. It was only upon the sound foundation of the protection of the fundamental unit of society that the deputies could hope to establish a strong and enduring state.

Yet the desire to solve the problem was confronted with the omnipresent Church. The religious orders had gathered the foundlings and reared them in monastic seclusion, enjoying the benefits of their labor, as long as they remained within the orders, and receiving the beneficence of their gratitude, support, and loyalty when they went out into the lay world. The intrusion of the state in the protection of the family would end the clerical monopoly of the illegitimate, and the establishment of divorce was a direct attack on sacramental marriage. As long as the Church protected the family and matrimony was a sacrament in Spain, the Catholic clergy perpetuated their power and received the support of the faithful. It was necessary, then, following the disestablishment of the Church and the dissolution of the religious orders, to place the family under the protection of the state, make matrimony and divorce civil matters, and rear the citizens of Spain as loyal citizens of the state.

The consideration of this vital question was undertaken on October 15. Article 41 of the *dictamen* was based on Article 27 of the *anteproyecto,* but greatly expanded the conservative concepts of the juridical commission. The parliamentary project placed the family under the special protection of the state and declared that matrimony was founded on an equality of rights for both sexes. Then it added a provision that had no precedent in the *anteproyecto:* Matrimony could "be dissolved by mutual consent, by the free will of the wife or on the petition of the husband, with allegation, in the latter case, of just cause."[1] The second paragraphs of both projects were nearly identical. They provided that parents were obliged to feed, assist, educate and instruct their children. The constitutional commission chose to use "assist" or "attend" as a more practical provision than the juridical proposal "to have them in their company." In either case the state would require the fulfilment of these duties. The third paragraph of the *dictamen* provided that children born out of marriage should have the same rights and obligations as those born in it. Civil laws would regulate the investigation of paternity. The *anteproyecto,* on the other hand, left the regulation of illegitimacy to a special law. The parliamentary commission also added a social concept that had been omitted in the juridical report. The final paragraph of Article 41 declared that the state was obliged to protect and assist infancy and maternity.[2]

A number of *votos* and a "plague of amendments" were offered to this article. Ruiz Funes proposed a *voto particular* that was incorporated into the *dictamen* by a vote of 146-101.[3] It provided that although marriage could be dissolved by divorce, the question should be regulated by law. Ossorio y Gallardo undertook to defend an amendment of the absent *vasconavarra* and agrarian deputies. Leizaola and Gil Robles had proposed that the matter of divorce be totally excluded from the constitution and relegated to a law.[4]

[1] Jiménez de Asúa, 273.
[2] *Ibid.,* 273-274.
[3] *Diario,* No. 57, 1743.
[4] *Ibid.,* No. 24, August 20, 1931, Appendix 11.

Ossorio y Gallardo devoted a considerable portion of his time to lamenting and criticizing the withdrawal of these minorities. He declared that they knew as deputies that they had come to battle for their programs and that they might win or lose. There was no reason for them to become angry at having lost. Besteiro called him to order and requested that he consider the defense of the *voto particular*. Ossorio then stated that he had long been opposed to divorce and had fully indicated his disagreement with the project on that point. His view was a purely social one and aimed at the protection of a social contract. The family was the unit of the nation of social perpetuity. No intimacy could be profound without perpetuity, and the very idea of change provoked change. The majority of divorces were petty, the reasons for them absurd. He did not know how the family could be firmly protected in a society in which the dissolubility of marriage was permitted. No constitution regulated divorce. It was a matter for civil law.[5]

Clara Campoamor replied for the commission, defending divorce on the grounds of liberty and laicism. No contract could be admitted which perpetually bound two beings. When marriage failed to realize the ends of love and spiritual affinity it was torture and degradation for the couple. Children might suffer from divorce but they were released from the scenes between their parents. Ossorio y Gallardo spoke again in a jocular manner and declared his opposition to both the dissolubility of civil and canonical marriage.[6]

The question of divorce was the principal theme in the debate that followed. It was a matter on which the conservatives were sensitive. The Socialists incorporated their views in an amendment defended by Sanchís Banús. It was inspired by the law of divorce of Uruguay and provided three methods for obtaining a divorce: by mutual consent, without the necessity of alleging any other cause; by the free will of the wife; and by the petition of the husband, who would have to show just cause for the action. This embodied a restate-

---

[5] *Ibid.*, No. 57, 1742-1746; Mori, III ,226-230.
[6] *Diario*, No. 57, 1746-1751; Mori, III, 230-241.

ment of the original *dictamen*. Jiménez de Asúa had first proposed it in the commission, but it had been replaced by the *voto* of Mariano Ruiz Funes.[7]

In his defense of the Socialist proposition Sanchís Banús declared that a stable monogamy was the most perfect form for the sexual organization of society. They advocated divorce solely for the good of the state. The regulation of divorce was an obligation of the state, because the social function of matrimony involved the health of the children. They hoped to eliminate the hysterical aspect from matrimony by giving the wife a means of breaking the conjugal tie.[8]

Castrillo explained the reasons of the commission for refusing to accept the socialist amendment and the previous *dictamen*. It was necessary to include divorce in the constitution. The majority of the commission held that if divorce were established at the instance of the wife without demanding the allegation of a just cause, it would convert hysteria into law. Such a concept was not even included in the Soviet code of 1918, which was naturally saturated with Marxism as interpreted by the revolutionaries of 1917. Jiménez de Asúa rallied to the defense of his proposal, and the debate became more intense.[9]

On the following day, after a final plea of the liberal canon, López Dóriga, for the regulation of divorce in a prudent law, the amendment of Sanchís Banús was taken into consideration by a vote of 169 to 153. The Radical-Socialists supported the Socialists in this vote and then offered an amendment signed by Gordón Ordáx and defended by Baeza Medina. It provided for the complete equality of husband and wife in the matter of divorce and was accepted as the formula for the definitive constitution.[10]

The third paragraph was modified by the commission on the proposal of Valdecasas, and the chamber accepted the change. The duties of the parents were prescribed rather

[7] Jiménez de Asúa, 274-282.
[8] *Diario*, No. 57, 1759-1764; Mori, 243-252.
[9] *Diario*, No. 57, 1764-1769.
[10] *Ibid.*, No. 58, October 16, 1931, 1777-1783; Jiménez de Asúa, 282-283.

than the rights of the illegitimate children. Dr. Juarros defended an amendment requesting that the requirement of a prematrimonial certificate as well as the investigation of paternity should be included, and that provisions for adequate legislation be made. The commission did not accept the amendment.[11]

The fifth paragraph was based on an amendment offered by Sbert, which proposed the guarantee of the equality of the rights of legitimate and illegitimate children.[12] Then, at the suggestion of Dr. Coca, the sick were added to the list of those meriting the assistance of the state. The article was redrafted and approved in the following form:

The family is under the special protection of the state. Matrimony is based on equality for both sexes and can be dissolved by mutual consent or on the petition of either of the couple with allegation, in this case, of just cause.

Parents are obligated to feed, assist, educate, and instruct their children. The state will insure the fulfilment of these duties and oblige their execution by subsidy.

Parents have the same obligations to children born outside matrimony as to those born in it.

Civil laws will regulate the investigation of paternity.

Neither the legitimacy or illegitimacy of birth can be alleged nor the civil state of the parents be mentioned either in the acts of inscription or in any registration.

The state is obliged to protect and assist the sick, old age, maternity, and infancy, adopting the Declaration of Geneva or the Table of the Rights of the Child.[13]

The last few articles of the second chapter of Title III were concerned with education. This question was related to the problem of the control of education by the Church and the organization of a single, unified system of instruction. The great contribution of Giner de los Ríos and his followers had been an attempt to free Spanish thought from clerical domination through the establishment of an inde-

[11] Jiménez de Asúa, 283-285; *Diario*, No. 58, 1788-1790; Mori, III, 257-262.
[12] Jiménez de Asúa, 283; *Diario*, No. 50, Appendix 17; No. 58, 1792.
[13] *Diario*, No. 58, 1793-1794, 1798-1799; Jiménez de Asúa, 272-273.

pendent system of education. Now the dissolution of the religious orders and the provision denying them the function of teaching made it necessary to provide for a system of education under the control of the state. The Provisional Government had already taken steps to create new schools and provide additional teachers. The dominant aim in the *cortes* was to make Spanish education lay in character.

The discussion of the educational problem was begun on October 20. The deputies had had the week-end recess in which to relax and restore energy after the heated debates on the problems of religion and divorce the preceding week. Article 46 of the *dictamen* was the next to be considered. It was based on Article 31 of the *anteproyecto* with some important modifications. Both asserted that the service of national culture was an essential attribute of the state. The juridical report declared that primary instruction should be gratuitous and obligatory. The *dictamen* expanded this concept by providing that primary education should be given in the *escuela única,* which would be lay as well as gratuitous and obligatory. Teachers would be given the status of public officials. The *anteproyecto* had a paragraph which was omitted. It gave a student the right to religious instruction, although a teacher could not be obliged to provide this instruction against his conscience. Both projects promised that legislation should be enacted to facilitate access of all classes to the institutions of higher learning, to the end that it should be conditioned only by aptitude and vocation. The *dictamen* mentioned this provision as an aid to Spaniards in economic necessity. It also recognized the right of the churches to teach their respective doctrines in their own establishments, subject to the inspection of the state. The *anteproyecto* recognized and guaranteed the liberty of the professors in a paragraph which was omitted in the *dictamen.*[14]

The constitutional commission examined its project on the eve of the debate of this article and found two defects in it. The establishment of the *escuela única* in primary education

[14] Jiménez de Asúa, 302-303.

was not technical enough and only mentioned laicism in regard to primary education. The commission wished to extend the lay signification to all of the grades of education. Therefore Article 46 and the two following articles were redrafted. The new draft omitted the definite provision of laicism for the primary grades and added an inclusive provision of laicism. In addition, the liberty of the professors was recognized and guaranteed, as provided originally in the *anteproyecto*.[15]

Jiménez de Asúa felt that the chamber considerably improved the project of the commission, as a result of the approval of the amendments of various teachers and professors of the socialist minority. An amendment of Sabrás and Llopis defined the *escuela única* as "educational institutions joined by the system of the unified school." This definition was apparently based on the German concept of the *Einheitsschule* as described by Lorenzo Luzuriaga in his work, *La escuela única*. Sábras also offered an amendment to include the *profesores y catedráticos* who taught in state institutions in the category of public functionaries. Llopis stated the method and orientation of education in an amendment:

. . . it will make work the axis of its methodological activity and will be inspired by ideals of human solidarity.[16]

The most vigorous opponent of the *dictamen* was none other than Rojo Villanova, the solitary Agrarian. He supported an amendment which proposed that a paragraph be added to Article 46, providing that the state should maintain official establishments of education in all grades throughout the national territory. This did not restrict the activity of the institutions established by the autonomous regions, provincial deputations, and *ayuntamientos*. In defending his proposal, Royo Villanova declared that he regarded the educational question as more important than the religious question. In his opinion, this amendment would resolve the apparent antagonism between Catalan and Spanish educa-

[15] *Ibid.*, 303-304.
[16] *Ibid.*, 304-305; *Diario*, No. 59, October 20, 1931, 1818-1824.

tion.[17] This was another effort to infuse unitary ideas into the constitution, and again Royo Villanova met with a rebuff. Valera replied in the name of the commission and affirmed that the amendment was more appropriate to Article 48. The debate continued and the amendment was defeated.[18]

The Catholics had offered an amendment in defense of the continuance of the educational work of the religious orders because they offered gratuitous instruction to the children of the laboring classes. There was no one to defend the amendment after the withdrawal of the Catholics, and it was retired. They could hardly have successfully opposed lay education anyway, because the religious orders were forbidden to engage in teaching.[19] Their absence, however, may explain the ease with which Article 48 of the definitive constitution was approved without a nominal vote. Basilio Alvarez, a priest, was the only deputy to ask that his vote he counted against it. The text had been newly drafted on the basis of the amendments of Llopis and Sabrás.[20]

Article 47 of the *dictamen* was considered on the following day. It was based on Article 32 of the *anteproyecto* and provided, in the first paragraph, that the state should have the exclusive power to grant professional titles and establish the requisites for obtaining them. A law of public instruction would determine the educational policy for the different grades, the duration of the periods of scholastic activity, the content of the plans for teaching, and the conditions under which education in private establishments might be authorized. The *anteproyecto* prescribed only the "minimum" content of the plans for teaching and, in the second paragraph, extended to every Spaniard the right to found and sustain educational institutions, in accord with the law. The person in charge of these institutions, however, had to have the aptitude legally prescribed. Finally, the *dictamen*

[17] *Diario*, No. 51, Appendix 8; Mori, III, 264-265.
[18] *Diario*, No. 59, 1813-1816.
[19] *Ibid.*, No. 43, Appendix 7; No. 59, 1812.
[20] *Ibid.*, No. 59, 1836.

provided that the state should exercise the power of inspection in all of the national territory to make sure that these dispositions and those contained in the preceding article should be fulfilled. The *anteproyecto* had a similar provision to guarantee that the policy and function of education should be effected in accord with the legal norms.[21]

The constitutional commission modified the *dictamen* and offered a second draft. The principal change was the declaration that the state had the exclusive power to grant professional titles even when the graduates came from the educational institutions of the autonomous regions.[22] Only one of the various *votos* and amendments offered to this article was accepted. It was the *voto particular* of Valera, Alas, and Botella. As a result, the last paragraph of the second draft in regard to the inspection of education was deleted. Its inclusion was considered more appropriate in the final article concerning education. Article 49 was then approved by acclamation.[23]

The following provision in the *dictamen,* Article 48, had no antecedent in the *anteproyecto*. It involved the important question of the language in which instruction was to be offered in the regions, and the debate that had arisen over Article 4 was renewed. The discussion was continued through the sessions of October 21 and 22.

The original article was inspired by Claudio Sánchez Albornoz, although his colleague Mariano Ruiz Funes proposed it in the commission. It declared that the teaching of Castilian was obligatory in all the primary schools of Spain. If the autonomous regions, however, organized education in their respective languages the state would maintain centers of instruction of all grades in the official language of the republic in those regions.[24]

Sánchez Albornoz later discussed the matter with Catalan professors and became convinced that it was dangerous and

---

[21] Jiménez de Asúa, 305-306.
[22] *Ibid.,* 307.
[23] *Ibid.; Diario,* No. 60, October 21, 1931, 1858.
[24] Jiménez de Asúa, 309-310.

conducive to separatism to establish this dual system in those regions in which instruction in the vernacular language had been provided. Therefore, as a thorough centralist, he composed a new formula on October 9. It did not satisfy the Catalans, but after repeated discussions a compromise was effected. The new draft provided that the state "could maintain" instead of "will maintain" institutions in the regions using their own language. The Radical deputies, Clara Campoamor and Emiliano Iglesias, disagreed with this text, and Botella drafted a *voto particular*. This provided instruction "in Castilian" instead of the teaching "of Castilian." It also returned to the imperative "will maintain" of the original *dictamen*.[25]

The problem of language was thus revived in the commission. Sánchez Albornoz tried to effect an understanding with the Catalans and Jiménez de Asúa coöperated to that end. Another formula was drafted which was acceptable to the Catalans, but the commission decided to leave its approval to the *cortes*. This body, therefore, had to choose between the second draft of the commission, the *voto* of the Radicals, and the amendment of Sánchez Albornoz. In addition, De Francisco offered an important amendment, which the Socialists preferred, and other proposals were offered by various deputies.[26]

The *cortes* took the *voto* of Valera, Alas, and Botella into consideration. It proposed the inclusion of the inspection of education in Article 50.[27] Various amendments were withdrawn or rejected, and the *voto* of Clara Campoamor and Iglesias was then discussed. Iglesias defended the proposal vigorously, but it was defeated in an ordinary vote, 192-78.[28] Castrillo defended his *voto* and Xiráu, the Catalan deputy, took the opposing view. The Progressive held that the Catalan proposal of two universities in the region would prove an extremely disturbing factor in Spanish higher education,

[25] *Ibid.*, 310-311.
[26] *Ibid.*, 311-312.
[27] *Diario*, No. 60, 1858.
[28] *Ibid.*, 1860.

productive of political discord between the state and the region. The Catalan, on the other hand, maintained that Catalan should have at least an equality in higher learning, and insisted on a single bilingual university.[29] Castrillo's proposition was defeated.

On the following day the debate occupied the entire session. Francisco's amendment was considered. It provided that instruction in Castilian should be obligatory in all of the educational centers of Spain, without prejudice to the use of the regional languages. The regions could organize their instruction in accordance with the powers recognized by the state in their respective statutes. This formula, which would have left the question to be solved by the state and *cortes* through separate understandings with the regions, was defeated in an ordinary vote, 149-91. Sánchez Albornoz then defended his formula and declared that it aimed at the maintenance of the spiritual unity of Spain through the obligatory knowledge and recognition of Castilian. He declared:

Only by means of the concession of the greatest liberty and the greatest respect to the regional languages shall we be able to please all within this state which we are building together.[30]

The commission accepted the formula.

Unamuno, however, was not convinced and immediately offered an amendment. It made the study of the Castilian language and its use as an instrument of education obligatory in all the centers of Spain. He proposed the extension of complete liberty to the regions in the matter of instruction in the regional tongues, but in these centers instruction in the official language of the republic would be maintained in institutions of all grades.[31] This tended toward the absolute sovereignty of the state and Castilian in national education. Miguel Maura had also signed the Unamuno amendment and both defended it warmly. Azaña

[29] *Ibid.*, 1870-1873; Mori, III, 293-299.
[30] *Diario*, No. 61, October 22, 1931, 1887; Mori, III, 304.
[31] *Diario*, No. 61, 1887; Mori, III, 306.

participated in the debate to defend the formula offered by
Sánchez Albornoz and declared he would vote for it. Both
of these deputies were members of Republican Action.
Finally, after a prolonged discussion, Unamuno's amendment was defeated, 179-93. Crespo vainly defended a federal
amendment, which the commission had already refused to
consider. It was defeated 90-72. The meager vote on this
amendment indicated the fatigue of the assembly. But it
had reached its decision of accepting the compromise formula
of Albornoz, which was shortly approved in an ordinary
vote, 143-67.[32]

Article 50 was definitely approved in the following form:

The autonomous regions can organize instruction in their respective languages, in accord with the powers which are conceded in their statutes. The study of the Castilian language is
obligatory, and this will be used also as an instrument of education in all the centers of primary and secondary instruction of
the autonomous regions. The state can maintain or create in
them educational institutions of all grades in the official language
of the republic.

The state will exercise the supreme inspection in all the national territory to assure the fulfilment of the dispositions contained in this article and in the two preceding.

The state will be attentive to the cultural expansion of Spain,
establishing delegations and centers of study and education
abroad and preferably in the Hispanic-American countries.[33]

The final paragraph was added as the result of the acceptance
of an amendment proposed by Ovejero.[34] Another warmly
contested issue had been compromised, and the third title
of the constitution had been approved.

[32] *Diario*, No. 61, 1901-1902.
[33] Jiménez de Asúa, 308.
[34] *Diario*, No. 58, Appendix 3; No. 61, 1878-1881.

XVII

THE CORTES OF THE REPUBLIC

THE CHAMBER was nearly empty when the Constituent Cortes began its task of constructing the legislative branch of the Second Spanish Republic, on October 23. The previous sessions on hotly contested issues had been too great a strain for the emotions and attentiveness of the deputies. The great interest now lay in a rapid promulgation of the definitive constitution rather than in the differences among the various minorities on the structure of the government. Only three of the ten titles of the parliamentary project had been approved. The paramount issues that had aroused the electors in the early months of the republic had been debated and resolved, yet the nature of the political structure had to be determined before these solutions could be adequately effected and administered. The mandate of the Constituent Cortes was not eternal, and a permanent governmental structure had to be established.[1]

The debate on the totality of the fourth title, providing the legislative body of the republic, was begun in an atmosphere of almost passive acquiescence on the part of the majority of the deputies. Three of them—García Gallego, Azcárate, and Otero Pedrayo—had asked for turns to speak against the *dictamen*. Ruiz de Villa had likewise been scheduled to defend the parliamentary project. But none of the four was in the chamber when the session was opened. Algora rose to lament the fact that the excessive consideration of the president was forcing the entire chamber to wait on one deputy. It seemed that the *cortes* had lost all interest as soon as the Catalan question had been decided. He asked that the chamber be consulted as to procedure because the

[1] Mori, IV, 9.

deputies were not disposed to wait while a speaker was sought in the passages of the building.[2]

Ruiz de Villa finally arrived and defended the *dictamen* on behalf of the Radical-Socialists. It provided for a single chamber and this minority was decidedly in favor of the unicameral system. When the orator had concluded, the three speakers who were to support the opposed criterion of a bicameral system and attack the *dictamen* were still absent. Various deputies gallantly offered their services as speakers, including Lluhí and Royo Villanova. The latter was ever ready to speak and was a strong partisan of the traditional two-chamber system. He believed that the republic should be frankly parliamentary. To that end it was necessary to define the relation of the *cortes* and the president. In any event, the latter had to be elected by the parliament and it was therefore essential that there should be two chambers.[3]

An issue was thus placed before the chamber. The great question relative to the legislative structure was whether the unicameral or the bicameral system should be adopted. The *anteproyecto* had provided for two chambers, while the parliamentary project had provided for a single chamber. The issue divided the chamber into two groups. On the one hand, the conservative Republicans, heirs of the traditional liberalism of the nineteenth century, defended the criterion of the juridical commission. On the other, the proponents of the twentieth-century social concepts favored the *dictamen,* which had been impressed with socialist doctrines. The two important speeches in the preliminary debates which illustrated this antagonism were delivered by Fernández Clérigo and Juan Castrillo.

Fernández Clérigo declared that Republican Action could

[2] *Diario,* No. 62, October 23, 1931, 1906.

[3] *Ibid.,* 1906-1914. Both of the preliminary projects used the word *parlamento* rather than *cortes,* because of the connotation of the traditional term. The amendment of Sánchez Albornoz to Article 37 provided that *cortes* should be used throughout the text of the constitution.

not support the provision of a second chamber. It had its value in facilitating the election of the chief of state, but that was not the only means of avoiding a plebiscite. He wished to associate representatives of the municipalities with the chamber for the election of the president. This system would solve the problem by eliminating both the direct popular election of the chief executive and the second chamber. Royo Villanova was mistaken in his assertion that few republics had adopted the unicameral system. Most of the post-war constitutions had provided this type of legislative body.

On the other hand, the crisis of the bicameral system is notorious, the crisis of the senate is well known in all Europe, and I do not need to recall more than the restrictions against the functioning of the House of Lords, which have been established in a country as democratic as England.[4]

Castrillo replied that the life of the republic could not evolve with the normality which they all desired without the second chamber. In the opinion of the Progressive minority, the presidential veto should be suppressed and the senate should serve as the check on the lower chamber. It would be organized on a professional basis and would not be similar to the monarchical institution provided in 1876. The technical councils which the Socialists wished to substitute for the senate could not be effective as a check in the free play of the powers of the state.

Spain is, unfortunately, gentlemen, one of the countries which suffer most constantly the infirmity of bureaucracy; this is the country in which functions are created after the artificial organs are created in order that they may fulfil these functions.[5]

It was necessary to have a check on the lower chamber in order that an appeal might be made to the country in case the mandate of the deputies was exceeded.[6]

[4] *Ibid.*, 1914-1916.
[5] *Ibid.*, 1918.
[6] *Ibid.*, 1916-1919; Mori, IV, 15-20.

The first article concerning the legislative power was considered the following week, on October 27. The *anteproyecto* had not been taken as the basis for formulating the *dictamen,* since the latter had adopted the opposed criterion. The *voto particular* of Matilde Huici, Manuel Pedroso, Viñuales, and others to the fourth title of the *anteproyecto* was taken as the base for the *dictamen.* Article 49 of the latter provided that the legislative power resided in the people, rather than the nation, the phrase used in the *voto.* It was to be exercised through the Congress of Deputies. A number of *votos particulares* and amendments were proposed by Gil Robles and Leizaola, Samper and Villanueva, Castrillo, Valle, Ayuso, Royo Villanova, and Terrero. They coincided in proposing that the bicameral system be substituted for the unicameral.[7]

Alcalá Zamora rose valiantly to defend the cause of the senate, in connection with the *voto* of Samper and Villanueva. He wanted a democratic senate in which all of the national energies would be represented and which would maintain a moderative power. He declared that the single chamber was reactionary, that the true motive for supporting it was the desire to assure the systematic predominance of a policy which its proponents believed to be the salvation of the country. If a single chamber was dominated by a majority of conservative tendencies it would produce a reaction which was impossible in a bicameral system. He cited the three classic arguments for the senate: the criterion of social structure, the criterion of federal representation, and that of double deliberation. These arguments were more forceful in Spanish life than in any other state and were stronger at this time than in any other epoch. Spain was a country of traditional individualism. It was still powerful while orientating itself to a process of socialization. Spain also had a strong federal tendency that had to be considered.

Alcalá Zamora regarded the senate as indispensable be-

[7] Jiménez de Asúa, 318.

cause the alternatives, the technical councils and presidential omnipotence, had patently failed. The councils were coexistent with the chamber and acted before the latter deliberated. They prepared legislation, while the senate contradicted it. The power of the president was either useless or dangerous, and he obviously could not serve as a substitute for the senate. He declared:

There must not be a constitution of a party; there must not be a constitution of tendencies; there must be a constitution in which we can all live together.

Then he warned the deputies that with a single chamber an ambitious president might usurp the legislative power.[8]

Mariano Ruiz Funes replied for the commission, but the great defense of the single chamber was delivered by the socialist Minister of Finance, Indalecio Prieto. He opposed any compromise because constitutions framed in this manner meant nothing. He did not hesitate to speak plainly:

. . . the essential defect of the Constituent Cortes has been its lack of courage, its timidity, that compromising desire which is destroying the ideal of the republic.

He did not fear the danger of civil war, but he did fear the danger of

. . . internal treason to the republic, a total destruction, a deception of the masses, a republican fraud, in the road of the fraud of making a republic of the arch-bourgeois type, conservative, timid, reactionary, negative of all the sincere democratic advances and of all the social progress. . . .

The senate would betray the designs of Spanish democracy, and the single chamber was fully legitimate in a true democracy.[9]

Galarza declared that the Radical-Socialists accepted the idea of a single chamber, but the Radicals, represented by Armasa, insisted on two chambers. The last speaker, Ayuso,

[8] *Diario*, No. 63, October 27, 1947-1955; Mori, IV, 23-39.
[9] *Diario*, No. 63, 1957-1960; Mori, IV, 40-47.

a Federal, was ideologically inclined toward the bicameral system. The *voto particular* was now brought to the decisive test of a nominal vote. The Socialists and Radical-Socialists were successful in defeating the bicameral idea, 150-100. Alcalá Zamora's prestige had once again failed to influence the chamber toward compromise and the moderation he advocated.[10] The other amendments of the advocates of the senate were withdrawn and Article 51 was approved by a vote of 150-83. The decision had already been made in the vote on the *voto* of Samper and Villanueva. The article declared:

The legislative power resides in the people, who exercise it by means of the *cortes* or Congress of Deputies.[11]

Article 52 of the constitution, which was based on the unicameral idea, was quickly approved on the following day. It was identical with the parliamentary project, which was based on the *voto particular* of Huici, Pedroso, and others. It declared:

The Congress of Deputies is composed of representatives elected by universal, equal, direct, and secret suffrage.[12]

The next article of the parliamentary project determined the eligibility and length of the term of the deputies. All citizens who were twenty-three years of age and fulfilled the conditions of the electoral law were eligible to serve as deputies regardless of sex or civil state. They would represent the nation, and their mandate was to last for five years from the date of the general elections. At the end of that period the congress would be totally renewed, but the deputies were reëligible indefinitely. These provisions were identical with the Huici-Pedroso *voto*. The commission, however, accepted an amendment proposed by Terrero, of the Radical minority. In accord with this proposal, it was provided that new elections should be held within seventy

[10] *Diario*, No. 63, 1960-1966.
[11] *Ibid.*, 1970-1971; Jiménez de Asúa, 317.
[12] Jiménez de Asúa, 319-320; *Diario*, No. 64, October 28, 1931, 1975.

days of the end of the term or the dissolution of the *cortes*. The new body would assemble within thirty days after the election. The commission also reduced the term of the deputies to four years. With these modifications, Article 53 was quickly approved.[13]

Article 52 of the parliamentary project determined the provisions of incompatibility of the deputies. It declared professional military men ineligible, unless they were retired, and left the determination of the other cases and the compensation of the deputies to a special law. Various amendments were offered requesting the suppression of the provision of incompatibility of the military. That of Ruiz Lencina was accepted and the rest were necessarily withdrawn. Thus the approved Article 54 left all cases of incompatibility to be determined by law.[14]

An additional article was now proposed. It had no precedent in either the *anteproyecto* or the *dictamen* and originated in a socialist amendment. It aimed to incorporate the parties into the mechanics of the political code. Originally every deputy who ranked lowest in his minority after the chamber was constituted should be automatically deprived of his credentials. The commission regarded this as too rigid, and a compromise was effected. As a result a formula was proposed as Article 53 of the project. A party was permitted to require that its candidates, at the time of their election, should sign a resignation, with the date blank. It would then be used in case of unjustified desertion. This article, however, never reached the chamber. It was suppressed in the commission and the Socialists did not even wish to carry it to the *cortes* as a *voto particular*.[15]

Article 55 was approved without discussion. It was based on the Huici-Pedroso *voto* to the *anteproyecto* and provided that the deputies were inviolable for their votes and opinions while exercising their offices.[16]

---

[13] *Diario,* No. 64, 1975-1976; Jiménez de Asúa, 320-322.
[14] *Diario,* No. 64, 1976; Jiménez de Asúa, 322-323.
[15] Jiménez de Asúa, 323-324.
[16] *Ibid.,* 325; *Diario,* No. 64, 1977.

The procedure in regard to deputies charged with some civil or criminal offense was determined in Article 55 of the *dictamen*. They could be arrested only for a flagrant crime, and information of the arrest would be communicated immediately to the chamber or Permanent Commission. A court that found it necessary to indict a deputy would notify the *cortes* at once, explaining the pertinent reasons. If the chamber failed to agree on the matter within sixty days, the judge could proceed as he desired. Every arrest or indictment of a deputy, however, was without effect if the *cortes* or Permanent Commission recommended his release. Both of these bodies could recommend that the proceedings be suspended until after the expiration of the parliamentary mandate of the accused deputy. Any recommendation of the Permanent Commission would be revoked if the *cortes* assembled and did not expressly ratify it in one of its first twenty sessions. These provisions were also based on the Huici-Pedroso *voto particular* and were approved by the chamber with only two slight modifications. A *voto particular* of Alomar, Iglesias, and Valle was incorporated into the *dictamen*. It asked that the silence of the chamber be interpreted as a denial of the concession of the supplication. The commission refused to accept this interpretation, desiring to regard the silence of the chamber as favorable to the continuance of the procedure, but the chamber adopted the *voto*, 84-48. Jiménez de Asúa proposed that the Permanent Commission be called the Permanent Deputation, the classic term. This was immediately accepted and Article 56 was approved.[17]

Two articles of the parliamentary project furnished the basis for Article 57 of the constitution. This article endowed the *cortes* with the power to determine the validity of the election and the capacity of the elected members. It was also to adopt the rules of order necessary for its interior organization. Article 57 was a slight modification of Article 56 of the *dictamen*, eliminating a non-essential

---

[17] Jiménez de Asúa, 325-329; *Diario*, No. 64, 1977-1978.

enumeration of powers. The next article of the *dictamen*, which provided for investigating commissions in exceptional cases, was suppressed by the commission as unnecessary. The new draft was approved without discussion.[18]

Article 58 provided that the *cortes* should assemble without being convoked, on the first day of February and October of each year. It would function for three months in the first period and two in the second. This had been modified in the commission. The first draft, based on the Huici-Pedroso *voto particular,* provided for only one annual meeting of the *cortes,* which opened on October 2 of each year and lasted four months.[19]

The government and the Congress of Deputies were granted the power to initiate laws by Article 60. This provision was derived from the *voto particular* of Huici and Pedroso to the *anteproyecto,* although slightly modified in the parliamentary commission. The only proposal to change it in the chamber was offered by Gil Robles, but because of his self-imposed absence the *voto* was withdrawn and the article was approved without debate.[20]

The *cortes* also approved the following article without debate. The parliamentary commission modified the Huici-Pedroso *voto* and Article 61 was identical with Article 60 of the *dictamen.* The *cortes* could authorize the government to legislate by decree upon matters reserved to the legislative body. These authorizations, however, could have no general character, and the decrees were to be strictly limited to the bases established by the deputies for each concrete matter. The congress could, in fact, judge whether the decree was adapted to these bases. But in no case were the expenditures to be increased in such a manner.[21]

The following article was nearly identical with the *dictamen* which had been inspired by the Huici-Pedroso *voto,* although the commission had modified it by an enumera-

[18] Jiménez de Asúa, 330-331; *Diario,* No. 64, 1978.
[19] *Diario,* No. 64, 1980; Jiménez de Asúa, 331-332.
[20] *Diario,* No. 64, 1980; Jiménez de Asúa, 333-334.
[21] *Diario,* No. 64, 1980-1981; Jiménez de Asúa, 334-336.

tion of powers. It established the Permanent Deputation of the *cortes*. The twenty-one members of this body were to be chosen from the political minorities in proportion to their numerical force, and the president of the *cortes* was to preside over it. Its powers were to be exercised during the recess or dissolution of the *cortes*. It was the guardian of the legislative power during these periods and was to function in cases of the suspension of the constitutional guarantees, legislative decrees, the detention or arrest of deputies, and those in which it was empowered to intervene by the *reglamento* of the chamber. The only change involved the substitution of "Permanent Deputation," a phrase used by the Constitution of Cádiz, for "Permanent Commission."[22]

The president of the council and the various ministers were extended a voice in the congress, whether or not they were deputies. Article 63 also required that their attendance should not be excused when it might be required. This was approved without debate. The commission, however, had modified the Huici-Pedroso *voto* considerably in framing this article. The *voto* had not permitted the ministers to speak in the chamber unless they were deputies.[23]

The congress was empowered to pass a vote of censure against the government or any one of the ministers. It had to be proposed in writing, with the pertinent reasons and the signatures of at least fifty active deputies. The proposal had to be communicated to all of the deputies and could not be debated or voted until five days after its presentation. An absolute majority of the deputies was required for the approval of the censure and the consequent resignation of the government or the minister involved. The same guarantees would hold in any measures which indirectly implied a vote of censure. This article was based on the Huici-Pedroso *voto* and was modified by the commission in only one respect. The number of deputies required to

[22] *Diario*, No. 64, 1980-1981; Jiménez de Asúa, 336-338.
[23] *Diario*, No. 64, 1981; Jiménez de Asúa, 338-339.

initiate a vote of censure was reduced from a fourth of the constituents of the chamber to fifty. Terrero presented an amendment which further modified the original proposal. The vote of censure was extended to include the political conduct of a minister as well as the government.[24]

Article 65 provided that international conventions ratified by Spain and registered with the League of Nations, possessing thereby the character of international law, should be considered an essential part of Spanish legislation. Spanish laws were to be adjusted to these treaties. If any treaty which affected the juridical regulations of the state was ratified, the government would present the necessary projects for the execution of its precepts to the *cortes* in the shortest time possible. No law contradicting a convention or treaty could be passed unless the treaty had been previously denounced in accord with the prescribed procedure. In this case, the denunciation had to be sanctioned by the *cortes*. The parliamentary commission had modified the Huici-Pedroso *voto* by inserting a second paragraph which provided that every international treaty had to be considered by the technical council concerned before its presentation to the *cortes*. A *voto particular* of Alomar and Xiráu and an amendment of Martínez Moya proposed that this paragraph be omitted. The matter was debated and the *cortes* agreed to retain it by a vote of 96 to 82. Later, the technical councils were suppressed, and the commission eliminated the paragraph in the final revision of the constitution.[25]

The final article of the fourth title had no antecedent in either the *anteproyecto* or the *dictamen*. It originated in the *voto particular* of Juan Castrillo. The commission refused to take the *voto* into consideration, and a prolonged discussion developed. Finally the session was suspended to permit the commission to draft a formula. When the chamber reassembled, the text of the commission was read and

[24] *Diario*, No. 64, 1981; Jiménez de Asúa, 339-341.
[25] *Diario*, No. 64, 1981-1983; Jiménez de Asúa, 341-344.

a *voto particular* offered by Castrillo, Samper, Valle, and Villanueva was also proposed. The *voto* was defeated in a nominal vote, 156-100.[26]

The next day a second draft of the commission was read:

The people can bring to their decision, by means of the "referendum," the laws voted by the parliament. To this end, it will suffice that 20 per cent of the electoral body solicit it. The constitution, its complementary laws, those of ratification of international conventions, and tributary laws will not be the object of this recourse. The people themselves can present a proposition of law to the *cortes,* exercising the right of initiative; it will suffice for this that 20 per cent of the electors request it. A special law will regulate the procedure and the guarantees of the "referendum" and the initiative.[27]

The Socialists had accepted this but had included the popular initiative. The commission finally agreed to reduce the required percentage to fifteen per cent, following a proposal of Guerra del Río. The suggestion of Alba was also accepted and slightly modified the enumeration of the subjects exempt from a referendum. Only those treaties registered with the League of Nations were included in this category.[28]

An additional article was then inserted as Article 59 of the constitution. It was proposed originally by Alcalá Zamora and was incorporated into the *dictamen* and approved without discussion. It provided:

The dissolved *cortes* will assemble in full power and recover its authority as the legitimate legislative power of the state if the president should not fulfil the obligation of convoking and electing another within the period.[29]

The fourth title was completed with the addition of this article.

After the victory of the socialist concept of the single

[26] *Diario,* No. 64, 1983-2008; Jiménez de Asúa, 344-346.
[27] *Diario,* No. 65, October 29, 1931, 2012.
[28] *Ibid.,* 2014; Jiménez de Asúa, 345.
[29] *Diario,* No. 65, 2014.

chamber in the question of the organization of the *cortes,* the deputies relaxed into a lethargic state and approved the articles as a matter of routine or absented themselves from the chamber. Fifteen articles were approved on October 28 in a dull session. There were no issues at stake, until the question of initiative and referendum was raised. Then the deputies in attendance awoke from their stupor and a lively debate developed. The primary consideration now, however, was the rapid approval and promulgation of the constitution, the definitive consolidation of the republic.

XVIII

THE EXECUTIVE POWER

THE *cortes* now undertook the consideration of Title V. It was to be expected that the executive power should be invested in a president and that he should personify the nation. His salary and honors were left to be determined by a special law, but they were guaranteed against any change during the president's tenure. These provisions, included in Article 67, were identical with the parliamentary project, which in turn was based on the Huici-Pedroso *voto particular*. The article was approved without discussion.[1]

The question of the election of the president involved a great deal more debate. The *dictamen* provided that he should be elected by universal, equal, direct, and secret suffrage. It was obviously impossible to elect the president in a joint assembly of the two chambers, as provided in the *anteproyecto*. The Huici-Pedroso *voto,* however, had established an indirect election in which the *cortes* would participate in the choice of the president. It provided an assembly composed of the deputies and three representatives from the *ayuntamientos* of each province. The Constituent Cortes was to elect the first chief executive.[2]

When Article 66 of the *dictamen* was considered on October 29, it was confronted with numerous *votos particulares* and amendments. All of these, except the *voto* offered by Botella, which was complementary to the text of the *dictamen,* aimed to avoid the designation of the president by the direct vote of the people. Some proposed an assembly to choose the chief executive and others provided that the *cortes* should perform the task. Ruiz Funes and Alomar,

[1] Jiménez de Asúa, 346; *Diario,* No. 65, 2014-2015.
[2] Jiménez de Asúa, 347-348.

for instance, offered a *voto* which proposed that the president should be elected by the *cortes* and *compromisarios* (presidential electors) chosen by the municipalities in a number no greater than that of the deputies in the *cortes*.[3]

The two opposed extremes were the weak president, subject to the potential domination of the *cortes,* and the strong president, elected by direct suffrage. The compromise lay between the extremes in some method similar to that proposed by Ruiz Funes or the Huici-Pedroso *voto particular*. It was the general aim to guard the presidential power against absorption by the *cortes*. The desire of the constitutional commission to establish a strong president through a direct popular vote was not immune, on the other hand, to the risk of a possible dictatorship through the personal prestige of the chief executive. The system of election by the chamber and an equal number of *compromisarios* provided an indirect system which would avoid both dangers.[4]

The *voto* of Ruiz Funes was defeated in a nominal vote, 237-41, after a short debate. Villanueva, speaking in the name of the commission, had refused to accept it because such a system was held to have all the disadvantages and none of the advantages of the bicameral system.[5] Nevertheless, Gabriel Alomar, seconded by Trifón Gómez, Castrillo, and Ruiz Funes, presented a minority report of the commission in the same session. This reproduced the previously defeated *voto particular* with slight variations.

The president of the republic will be elected by the *cortes* jointly with a number of *compromisarios* equal to that of the deputies. The *compromisarios* will be elected by universal, equal, direct and secret suffrage, according to the procedure which the law may determine.[6]

The debate developed around this *voto particular*. The

[3] *Ibid.*, 348-349; *Diario*, No. 65, 2015.
[4] Mori, IV, 57-58, 60; Jiménez de Asúa, 349.
[5] *Diario*, No. 65, 2916-2919.
[6] *Ibid.*, 2023.

commission refused to accept it. Alcalá Zamora pointed out the difficulty of finding an impartial power to examine and pass on the powers of the *compromisarios*. The *cortes* would tend to be influenced by political considerations, and he suggested that the Court of Constitutional Guarantees should examine and resolve the matter. Besteiro proposed that the commission modify its text in accord with this suggestion. The Socialists, represented by Saborit, supported the *voto* despite their desire for a direct election. It appeared better strategy to accept the compromise. Guerra del Río declared that the Radical desire for a second chamber had been thwarted and the only recourse was an election by the people. The Radical-Socialist, Baeza Medina, also supported the popular election of the president. Xiráu declared in the name of the Catalans that the impossible French type of election had already been discarded. Therefore the only alternative was an election through the *compromisarios*. The Federals, having suffered a reverse in their desire for two chambers, regarded any intervention of the *cortes* in the election of the president as dangerous, and defended the Radical-Socialist concept of a democratic and popular election. Republican Action also supported the direct election of the president, in order that his authority might be superior to that of an executive chosen by partisan politics in the *cortes*. The Galicians defended the *voto particular* and the debate was terminated.[7]

The text of the *voto* as redrafted by the commission was then read. It delegated the power of examining and approving the powers of the *compromisarios* to the Court of Constitutional Guarantees. The *voto particular* was approved in a nominal vote, 150-130.[8] The article was not approved, however, until the following day, when the debate was continued. The nominal vote had not been decisive enough to prevent the opponents of the *voto* from hoping that they might yet defeat it. José Ortega y Gasset

[7] *Ibid.*, 2023-2031.
[8] *Ibid.*, 2032-2034.

asked why it would not be possible to elect the president by electors chosen from different districts than those used in the parliamentary elections. This would have eliminated any intervention of the *cortes* in the election of the president, and that appeared to be the great objection to the *voto particular*. The discrepancies between and within the minorities became more obvious as the debate continued. Alcalá Zamora proposed various additions to the amendment offered by José Ortega y Gasset, but all of these were defeated in an ordinary vote. Article 68 was then approved by the narrow margin of fourteen votes, 146-132.[9]

Article 67 of the *dictamen* was identical with the Huici-Pedroso *voto particular* and provided that only those citizens of forty years of age and in full possession of their civil and political rights should be eligible for the presidency. This was approved without any modification by the *cortes* and became Article 69 of the definitive constitution.[10]

The following article concerned the question of those to be considered ineligible for the presidency. The article of the constitutional commission was nearly identical with the Huici-Pedroso proposal. It enumerated the various classes to be debarred from the office. These included naturalized citizens; active or reserve soldiers and all those who had been retired less than ten years; all ecclesiastics, including ministers of the various confessions and monks; and the members of any royal family, regardless of their relationship to the head of the family. The proposal was obviously directed to prevent the danger of a possible presidential reaction through the domination of the military, religious, or monarchist interests. Only two amendments were offered in the chamber. Dr. Pittaluga proposed the suppression of the paragraph declaring the ineligibility of naturalized citizens. This was approved by the *cortes* and the paragraph was deleted. The other amendment was proposed by Basilio Alvarez, who asked that the whole article be suppressed.

[9] *Ibid.*, No. 66, October 30, 1931, *passim*.
[10] *Ibid.*, No. 67, November 3, 1931, 2080; Jiménez de Asúa, 351.

This would have permitted priests or monks to become candidates for the presidency. The deputies defeated the amendment and Article 70 was approved.[11]

Basilio Alvarez was the only priest left to defend the cause of the clergy. The Catholic *vasconavarras* had withdrawn and the liberal López Dóriga had been recalled by the Archbishop of Granada. That personage demanded that he explain his political attitude in the *cortes,* not to his electors, but to the public of his diocese. López Dóriga sustained the test satisfactorily and was warmly greeted when he returned to the Constituent Cortes.[12]

Article 69 of the *dictamen* was based on an identical provision in the Huici-Pedroso *voto.* It declared that the presidential term should last six years. The same person could not be elected twice in succession. There were no counterproposals to this article, but it was slightly modified as a result of Salvador de Madariaga's request for greater clarity in the second part of the article. He suggested that the president should not be reëlected until six years had transpired after the end of his previous term. This proposal was incorporated into the approved Article 71.[13]

The two following articles, 70 and 71, of the *dictamen* were likewise quickly approved, without discussion. Both were modifications of the Huici-Pedroso proposal, Articles 6-7. The first provided that the presidential oath should be taken before the *cortes,* after which the presidential term would officially start. The second declared that the election of the new president should be held thirty days before the expiration of the preceding mandate. They became Articles 72 and 73 respectively of the definitive constitution.[14]

The exercise of the executive power in case of the incapacity or absence of the president was considered in the next article. Articles 72 and 73 of the *dictamen* were based

[11] *Diario,* No. 67, 2080-2085; Jiménez de Asúa, 352-353.
[12] Mori, IV, 75.
[13] *Diario,* No. 67, 2086; Jiménez de Asúa, 354.
[14] *Diario,* No. 67, 2086; Jiménez de Asúa, 355-356.

on Articles 8 and 9 of the Huici-Pedroso *voto particular,*
and provided that a vice-president should be elected at the
same time as the president. He would assume the duties of
the latter in case of his permanent incapacity, removal,
resignation, or death. A new election would be held within
fifteen days. In one of its morning sessions, the commission
adopted the criterion proposed by Ruiz Funes, of suppressing the vice-president and permitting the president of the
cortes to exercise the presidential function. As a result, the
two articles of the *dictamen* were combined in a new draft.
The article was redrafted in the *cortes* on the basis of suggestions of Royo Villanova, Iranzo, and Castrillo. Article
74 was then read and approved. It provided that in case of
the temporary incapacity or absence of the president, the
president of the *cortes* should replace him. He in turn
would be replaced by the vice-president of the *cortes.* If
the presidency became vacant the president of the *cortes*
would assume its functions and a new election would be
called within eight days, to be celebrated within thirty days.
Even though it was disbanded, the *cortes* would conserve
its powers in this election.[15]

The president was endowed with the power of naming
and dismissing the president of the government and, in accord with the premier, exercised the same authority over
the ministers. In any case, they were forced to resign if
the *cortes* explicitly denied them its confidence. This article
was based directly on the *dictamen* and the Huici-Pedroso
voto particular, with slight modifications in style, proposed
by the amendment of Suárez Uriarte.[16]

The powers of the chief executive were next considered.
Article 75 of the parliamentary project was also based on
the Huici-Pedroso *voto particular.* The parliamentary commission modified the latter by excluding the restrictions on
the power of the president to declare war. Later, however,
a second draft, incorporating various proposals, was sub-

[15] *Diario,* No. 67, 2086-2089; Jiménez de Asúa, 357-359.
[16] *Diario,* No. 67, 2089-2090; Jiménez de Asúa, 359-361.

mitted to the chamber. Political and commercial treaties and those affecting the national treasury were to be valid only when approved by the *cortes*. Projects of adherence or agreement with international organizations of labor had to be submitted to the *cortes* within a year and, when approved, had to be registered with the League of Nations. Other treaties and conventions were likewise to be registered and no secret clauses or treaties would be valid. The other powers conferred on the president were similar to those provided in the *dictamen*. He could declare war and make peace in accordance with the above restrictions. He could confer military and civil offices and professional titles in accord with the law. He could authorize ministerial decrees, signed by the corresponding minister and previously approved by the ministry. He could also take any measure necessary for the defense of the integrity and security of the nation, rendering an immediate account of this activity to the *cortes*. A debate developed in which Alcalá Zamora, Clara Campoamor, and Salvador de Madriaga participated, and various amendments were withdrawn. Finally Madariaga drafted a new text in which the power of the president to have illegal decrees submitted to the *cortes* was suppressed. Article 76 was then approved.[17]

Article 77 limited the power of the president in the declaration of war. It could be declared only under the conditions prescribed by the League of Nations and only after those defensive measures which had no belligerent character and the judicial recourses of arbitration and conciliation had been exhausted. Treaties of arbitration and conciliation with other states would be applied unless they conflicted with the general conventions. Then the president could be authorized by law to sign the declaration of war. This accord was based on Article 76 of the *dictamen* and the last five paragraphs of Article 11 of the Huici-Pedroso *voto*. The principal modifications arose from a formula presented by Salvador de Madariaga. A second draft was

---

[17] *Diario*, No. 67, 2090-2094; Jiménez de Asúa, 361-365.

based on this formula and the article was approved.[18]

The following article originated in an amendment of Salvador de Madariaga which was accepted by the chamber. It provided that the president could not withdraw the membership of Spain in the League of Nations, unless it was previously announced in accord with the covenant of the League and with previous authorization of a special law approved by an absolute majority of the *cortes*.[19]

Article 79 empowered the president to promulgate the decrees, regulations, and instructions necessary for the execution of the laws. It modified the parliamentary project only by suppressing this power in the interest of the proper progress of the administration. This modification was proposed by Royo Villanova. He thanked the commission for accepting it and was greeted with applause.[20]

The question of the power of the president to issue statutory decrees on matters reserved to the competency of the *cortes* was raised in the next article. These could be issued only in the interest of the defense of the republic or in exceptional cases when the chamber was not in session. Such decrees, however, had merely a provisional character and were limited to the time required for the *cortes* to resolve or legislate on the question. Article 78 of the *dictamen* was based on Article 14 of the Huici-Pedroso *voto particular*.[21]

Botella presented a *voto* proposing the suppression of this article, and after other proposals were withdrawn the commission redrafted the article in the sense that these decrees had to be approved not only by the unanimous consent of the government, but also by two-thirds of the Permanent Deputation. Valdecasas presented the original *dictamen* as a *voto particular,* but the commission defended the second draft and Article 80 was approved in an ordinary vote, 109-28.[22]

The next provision of the *dictamen* was suppressed as

[18] *Diario,* No. 67, 2094-2097; Jiménez de Asúa, 365-367.
[19] *Diario,* No. 67, 2097-2099; Jiménez de Asúa, 367-368.
[20] *Diario,* No. 67, 2098; Jiménez de Asúa, 369.
[21] Jiménez de Asúa, 369-371.
[22] *Ibid.,* 371-372; *Diario,* No. 67, 2099-2104.

unnecessary when the commission redrafted Article 80. It had provided for the intervention of the permanent commission only if the decrees came into conflict with the constitutional order. The approved article, however, required the previous approval of the Deputation, and its defense of the constitution as provided in Article 79 of the *dictamen* was not essential.[23]

There was little difference between the *dictamen* and the first two paragraphs of Article 81 of the definitive constitution. The first authorized the president of the republic to convoke an extraordinary congress when he deemed it opportune. The second concerned the suspension of the ordinary sessions of the congress. The *dictamen* provided that the *cortes* might be suspended twice each parliamentary year. Article 81 was amended to limit the suspension to a month during the first session and to fifteen days in the second.

Various amendments and *votos* were proposed in the chamber, but the majority of them were concerned with the power of the president to dissolve the *cortes*. The *dictamen* permitted the president to propose the dissolution of the parliament to the people, if the reasons for suspension persisted and he regarded it as necessary. If the result of the referendum should be negative, the president would be forced to resign. The commission concluded, however, that this text was unsupportable. It would have reduced the president to a mere figurehead. Finally, Alomar, Ruiz Funes, and Araquistain composed a *voto particular* which they presented in the chamber and which was accepted, 102-27. It provided that the *cortes* might be dissolved no more than twice during the presidential term, subject to three conditions. The dissolution was to be announced by a motivated decree and a convocation of the new elections within sixty days was to accompany the decree of dissolution. In the case of a second dissolution, the first act of the new *cortes* would be to examine and resolve upon the necessity of the

<hr />

[23] *Diario*, No. 67, 2104; Jiménez de Asúa, 372-373.

dissolution. If the vote of the *cortes* was unfavorable the president would be forced to resign.[24]

On the following day, November 4, Castrillo offered an amendment, proposing the clarification of the paragraph concerning the recall of the president. He requested that it specify the quorum. As a result, it was provided that the president could be forced to resign only by an absolute majority of the *cortes*. The article was then approved in an ordinary vote.[25]

Article 82 of the definitive constitution originated in the parliamentary commission. Article 81 of the *dictamen* provided that the president might be recalled before the expiration of his term, on the proposal of the parliament and the approval of this proposal in a popular referendum. The parliamentary proposal would require a majority of two-thirds. When this decision was made the president could not exercise his powers, but if the people voted against his removal then the parliament would be dissolved.[26]

An amendment of Rey Mora and a *voto particular* of Valdecasas coincided in proposing the suppression of the article. The chamber rejected them. The commission, however, had already agreed on the necessity of modifying the procedure for adopting a recall, since the direct election of the president had been defeated. Hence, a formula was drafted which changed the whole import of the *dictamen*. The initiation of the recall would be taken on the proposal of three-fifths of the members of the congress, and from the time of that proposal the president would not be permitted to exercise his functions. Within eight days an election of *compromisarios* would be held and these would meet with the deputies to render a final decision on the recall by an absolute majority of the assembly. If the proposition for the recall was rejected, the *cortes* would be dissolved, but if the assembly approved the proposal it would immediately

[24] *Diario*, No. 67, 2105-2109; Jiménez de Asúa, 373-375.
[25] *Diario*, No. 68, November 4, 1931, 2113-2119.
[26] Jiménez de Asúa, 377.

elect the new president. This article was approved by a vote of 123 to 76.[27]

The following article concerned the proclamation of the laws sanctioned by the *cortes*. They had to be promulgated within fifteen days of the time he had been officially notified of the approval of the law. If the *cortes* deemed the law urgent by approving it by a two-thirds vote it should be promulgated immediately. The president might ask the *cortes* to deliberate upon ordinary laws, but if they were approved by a two-thirds majority he would be obliged to promulgate them. This article was identical with the *dictamen* and Article 17 of the Huici-Pedroso *voto particular.* Two proposals were presented in the *cortes.* Both Gil Robles and Castrillo demanded the suppression of the power of the president to exercise a suspensive veto. These *votos* and two other amendments were withdrawn and the article was approved.[28]

Article 84 of the constitution was also identical with the parliamentary project and the Huici-Pedroso *voto,* except for variations in style. The acts or mandates of the president would be considered null and without force unless they were countersigned by a minister. Their execution implied penal responsibility, and the ministers who signed the presidential acts assumed full political and civil responsibility and shared in any criminal responsibility which might be involved. This article was approved with very little debate.[29]

The final provision of the fifth title, Article 85, was concerned with the penal responsibility of the president. The *dictamen* was based on the Huici-Pedroso *voto particular.* It provided that the chief executive should be criminally responsible for the infraction of his constitutional obligations. An impeachment was instituted in the *cortes* by a three-fifths vote, and the president was tried by the Court of Constitutional Guarantees. If this court decided to ad-

[27] *Ibid.,* 376-378; *Diario,* No. 68, 2119-2121.
[28] *Diario,* No. 68, 2121-2125; Jiménez de Asúa, 378-380.
[29] *Diario,* No. 68, 2125; Jiménez de Asúa, 380-382.

mit the accusation the president would immediately resign, a new election would be held, and the case would be tried. If the accusation was denied, the *cortes* would be dissolved and a new election would be convoked. The determination of the procedure for the exaction of the criminal responsibility of the president was left to a special law of a constitutional character. The *voto particular* of Samper and Villanueva was retired, but Cornide defended his amendment. He desired that the ministers should be held responsible. Jiménez de Asúa answered him, upholding the theory that political responsibility had no other penalty than ostracism. The amendment was then withdrawn and the article was approved 124-36.[30]

Title V was now approved and the chamber passed immediately to the discussion of the next section. It also concerned the executive power, providing for the duties and responsibilities of the government. Article 86 of the constitution was identical with both Article 85 of the *dictamen* and Article 66 of the *anteproyecto*. It declared that the government consisted of the president of the council and the ministers. There were no proposals to modify it and it was approved without debate.[31]

The second provision of Title VI, Article 87, declared that the president of the Council of Ministers should direct and represent the general policy of the government. This sentence was identical with both the *dictamen* and the *anteproyecto*. As a result of the approval of the *voto particular* of Castrillo to this article, a sentence was added to the first paragraph. It established the same incompatibilities for the premier as for the president of the republic. The second paragraph assigned the direction and policy of the public services to the heads of the various ministerial departments. The article was approved without any further debate.[32]

Article 88 was also approved without debate. Ayuso was the only deputy who asked that his vote be registered against

[30] *Diario,* No. 68, 2126-2129; Jiménez de Asúa, 382-387.
[31] *Diario,* No. 68, 2129; Jiménez de Asúa, 388.
[32] Jiménez de Asúa, 388-389; *Diario,* No. 68, 2129-2130.

it. It gave the president of the republic the power to name one or more ministers without portfolio and was identical with the parliamentary project. The *anteproyecto* had been taken as a base for the article, but it specified that the nomination in this case be proposed by the president of the council.[33]

The next four articles of Title VI were approved before the session of November 4 was suspended. They were all identical or similar to the corresponding articles of the *dictamen,* except for inconsequential variations in style. They were all based originally on the *anteproyecto.* The salaries of the ministers were to be fixed by the *cortes.* They were prohibited from engaging in any profession or in the direction of any private enterprise or association. Their principal duties were the elaboration of legislative projects to be submitted to parliament, the dictation of decrees, the exercise of regulatory power, and the deliberation on all matters of public interest. They owed a double responsibility to the *cortes:* collectively for the policy of the government, and individually for their own ministerial activity. In addition, they were individually responsible, both civilly and criminally, for any infraction of the constitution and laws. In a case of delinquency the *cortes* would bring the accusation before the Court of Constitutional Guarantees in the form prescribed by law.[34]

The powers of the executive had been carefully restricted to prevent the possibility of a reappearance of a dictatorship. His power of dissolving and suspending the *cortes* and his power to issue decrees were carefully specified, with due regard for the integrity of the *cortes.* In cases of open conflict between the executive and legislative powers the people could, as the final recourse, render the judgment. To prevent the capricious use of this appeal to the people, it was provided that the loser in any such decision should be forced to resign. The power of the president to appoint the ministers was

[33] Jiménez de Asúa, 389-390; *Diario,* No. 68, 2130.
[34] Jiménez de Asúa, 390-394; *Diario,* No. 68, 2130.

necessarily recognized, but the responsibility for their policies was exacted by the chamber. The president of the republic was placed in a position which removed him from politics, and if he descended into the arena of political activity he was subjected to the risk of losing his high office as a result of a conflict with the legislative body. The ministers were the political agents of the *cortes,* responsible for the administration of the affairs of the state, and their president was the real political head of the Spanish nation.

XIX

THE TECHNICAL COUNCILS AND
THE JUDICIAL POWER

THE PARLIAMENTARY project had a seventh title which was suppressed in the course of the parliamentary debates. The three articles of the title, Articles 92-94, were based on four articles of the Huici-Pedroso *voto particular*. They provided for the enactment of a special law which should determine the organization and procedure of autonomous technical councils in the different sectors of administrative activity, and in the cultural and economic interests of the nation. The government would submit any matter of importance which affected the matters within their competency and every project of law to their examination. The council concerned would furnish information which would be included with the legislative project presented to the *cortes* and might propose a different regulation of the matter concerned. They might draft projects of law for presentation to the *cortes* on the request of the government. These councils were also designed to be of assistance to the congress. That body could request one of the councils to prepare a definite law, which would serve as a basis for the work of the corresponding parliamentary commission. When the information differed from the governmental project of law the commission would consult a delegate from the council concerned.[1]

When these articles were formulated in the commission two extreme positions were maintained. One was favorable to the councils and was defended by Trifón Gómez. The other was unfavorable and was supported by Gabriel Alomar. The title was drafted as a compromise between the two extremes. The question was discussed in the chamber on November 5.

[1] Jiménez de Asúa, 394-395.

Jiménez de Asúa requested that there should be a debate on the section as a whole in order that the various minorities might have the opportunity of indicating their positions. Besteiro announced that the chamber had agreed that there should be no general debate because the title contained only three articles, but at his suggestion the *cortes* reversed its decision.[2]

Mariano Ruiz Funes opened the debate with a plea for the incorporation of a Council of State. Such a body would be merely administrative and would insure unity and continuity of governmental policy and administrative independence. He declared:

... it signifies the protection of the rights of the individual before the excess of power and the separation from all those damages which are unjustly caused by acts of the government."[3]

Alomar, of the Catalan Left, led the attack on the technical councils with the proposal that the title be completely suppressed.

We believe, gentlemen, that democracy has, in short, two great enemies, which are the forms which are useful for reaction to combat it. Those two enemies are, necessarily, corporatism and technocracy.

The first represented the struggle of interests against ideals and the second was worse. The intrusion of specialists in the free play of sovereignty was unnatural to politics. It was the intervention of a will foreign to the ideals and will of the people. He did not wish to exclude completely the function of the technicians, but rather to reduce that function. They should not be given a special emphasis in the constitution, in an irrevocable and liturgical category which removed them from their true sphere. They should be administrative rather than constitutional organs used as a substitute for a senate. They should be subordinated as parts of the executive power, regulated by decrees and administrative orders.[4]

[2] *Diario*, No. 69, November 5, 1931, 2169-2170.
[3] *Ibid.*, 2170-2171; Mori, IV, 114-116.
[4] *Diario*, No. 69, 2171-2172; Mori, IV, 116-117.

The debate was then suspended to permit the deputies to devote themselves to an interpellation on economic matters. This debate had important consequences, for Juan March, the "Croesus of Spain," and a deputy, intervened in the debate to answer certain allusions of Baeza Medina and to reply to Galarza, the Director General of Security. March tried to explain his rise to wealth and Galarza accused him of an attempt to bribe a judge during the dictatorship, when he had been accused of engaging in contraband trade. Galarza was a member of the Commission of Responsibilities and the question had to be clarified, for, as one deputy declared, the chamber could not associate with a man against whom such an accusation had been leveled.[5]

On November 6, the chamber met in a secret session to determine the question of March's responsibility, and another prominent deputy became involved. Cordero charged that some member of the Commission of Responsibilities had carried reports of the secret proceedings of that body to one of the persons concerned. The honor and responsibility of twenty men could not be placed in the hands of such a fool. Emiliano Iglesias rose to defend Juan March and was in turn charged with having offered Simó Bofarull 25,000 pesetas if the report of the commission was favorable to March. A commission was named to consider this new charge, and reported that Iglesias should be regarded as incompatible with the Constituent Cortes of the republic. The chamber approved the expulsion by a vote of 152 to 1.[6] The Radical leader, Guerra del Río, was implicated by an allusion of the expelled deputy, but managed to extricate himself with an alibi. On November 10 the commission reported on the case of Juan March, declaring him incompatible also. He was expelled by a vote of 191 to 4. Iglesias declared that he was the victim of a personal attack and had been unjustly persecuted. Juan March was detained in his house by the police and placed under surveillance.[7]

[5] Diario, No. 69, 2183-2193; Mori, IV, 118-135.

[6] Diario, No. 70, November 6, 1931, 2213; Mori, IV, 139-143.

[7] Diario, No. 70, November 10, 1931, 2231; Mori, IV, 144-148.

During the week-end recess, the socialist minority had tried to find a solution for the problem raised in the seventh title. Two criteria were maintained. Julián Besteiro wished to establish a Corporative Council in the constitution, while Fernando de los Ríos desired to detail more precisely the character and attributes of the technical councils. Besteiro's Corporative Council would contain representatives of the regions, producers and working classes. Its principal function would have been to advise the president of the republic in the exercise of the suspensive veto. The Socialists rejected this proposal, however, and De los Ríos formulated an amendment proposing a Council of State, regulating this body more minutely than was prescribed in the *dictamen* for the technical councils.[8]

The chamber returned to the discussion of the question on November 10. Alomar and Xiráu offered an amendment proposing the total suppression of the title. It was rejected by a vote of 71 to 36.[9] The chamber had already taken the *voto particular* of Ruiz Funes into consideration. Then Ayuso offered an amendment proposing the suppression of the title. Botella explained that he desired to eliminate the councils from the constitution rather than abolish them completely. The Ayuso amendment was accepted in a nominal vote, 136-109.[10]

In the course of the debate which was produced by the amendment of De los Ríos, the Minister of Justice rose to defend his proposal. He charged that the inefficiency of Spanish administration in the nineteenth century was responsible for the constitutional failure. With the evolution of economic concentration, the extension of public services, and the formation of workers' syndicates, it was evident that the old state administration did not suffice for the demands of modern state life. It was, therefore, necessary to insert a new organ between the two democratic ones, the electors and the legis-

[8] Jiménez de Asúa, 398-399.
[9] *Diario*, No. 25, Appendix 13; No. 71, 2218.
[10] *Ibid.*, No. 71, 2218-2221.

lative body. The technical councils provided for a permanent advisory organ for both the government and the *cortes*. This was an era of planned economy, as had been demonstrated in Russia, Germany, and Italy. A democracy which did not limit itself and call science to its aid would be inefficient and was doomed to failure.[11]

Fernando de los Ríos had redrafted his amendment on the basis of the *voto* of Ruiz Funes. It provided for a consultative Council of State and advisory technical councils. The latter could initiate laws in the chamber and elaborate projects presented by the government. They also provided the *cortes* with information and elaborated projects presented by that body. Finally, they were to prepare reports on technical problems that were requested by the government or *cortes* and propose *anteproyectos* of laws and regulations. Each council would designate a member to carry its report to the chamber with the corresponding legislative project. Their relation with the other legislative organs would be strictly functional. They were to be organized by a special law, with the condition that representatives of professional and labor syndicates be included.[12]

The commission studied this amendment and modified it by suppressing the right of initiating laws. They were prepared to defend it. Meanwhile, however, Ayuso's amendment had been accepted and the title was suppressed. The address of De los Ríos was, therefore, in the manner of an obituary, but it produced such an impression that Gomáriz proposed that the matter be again studied by the commission. This body would report a formula establishing the possibility of creating advisory administrative organs. The commission presented a new text, which was approved 143-112, on November 11, and became Article 93 of the constitution. It provided that a special law should create and regulate the procedure of the economic advisory organs of the administration, the government, and the *cortes*. They would include

[11] *Ibid.*, No. 71, 2223-2225; Mori, IV, 150-154.
[12] Jiménez de Asúa, 400-401.

a Supreme Consultative Council of the republic in matters of government and administration. The first paragraph was incorporated as a result of an amendment of Gomáriz, Baeza Medina, and others.[13]

Thus the technical councils disappeared as an essential part of the constitution, but the possibility of creating advisory economic organs was maintained. The principal objection had been that the incorporation of such administrative organs into the constitution was not appropriate.

Meanwhile the chamber had begun the debate on the totality of Title VII concerning justice. When the question of the administration of justice was first considered on November 10, Fernández Clérigo rose to oppose the *dictamen*. He made an eloquent plea for the establishment of an independent judicial power, free from the intervention of politics. He considered that the most adequate model for Spain was the Austrian system.[14] On the following day, Salazar Alonzo pointed out the failure of the *dictamen* to provide for the appointment of judges, and other deficiencies in regard to the removal, promotion, and salaries of the judges. Justice could not be properly administered without adequate provisions regulating judicial conduct and guaranteeing able judges.[15]

Barriobero offered a number of suggestions for improving the project. The administration of justice should be completely revolutionized. This revolution should be reactionary because justice had been well administered in the past. The *dictamen* did not adequately specify the responsibility of judges and magistrates. The personnel of the magistracy was insufficient to attend to the necessities of justice, and it was necessary to eliminate those details which annoyed litigants and resulted in unnecessary expenditures. Professional lawyers should be added to the scholarly men who had been selected

[13] *Ibid.*, 394, 401-404; *Diario*, No. 71, 2227-2228, No. 72, November 11, 1931, 2236-2252.
[14] *Diario*, No. 71, 2228-2230, Mori, IV, 158-162.
[15] *Diario*, No. 72, 2255-2258; Mori, IV, 163-168.

as judges in the past, and the rights of citizens should be protected from abuse by the police.

It is necessary that some norms should be established in order that in every case justice should follow the citizen and that he may enjoy its assistance in all the moments of his life.

He conluded with an extended list of principles which he believed should be included in Title VII.[16]

The speech of Barriobero was concluded on November 12. The law regulating the Spanish banking system was also being discussed in the chamber and occupied more of the energy and attention of the deputies than the constitution. The most important constitutional questions had been settled and the routine and technical discussion of the administration of justice wearied many of the deputies and the sessions were not well attended. The totality debate was therefore concluded in a peaceful legal atmosphere as the jurists expounded their favorite concepts. Elola cited the details of many cases which had appeared before the Supreme Court of the United States as an example of the domination of magistrates by plutocratic oligarchies.[17]

The approval of the articles of the seventh title began on November 12. Article 95 of the parliamentary project was based on Article 73 of the *anteproyecto*. It provided that justice should be administered in the name of the people and that the judges should be independent, subject only to the law. Ossorio y Gallardo immediately offered an amendment proposing that justice should be administered in the name of the nation, and that the judicial power should be autonomous. Its internal régime would be attributed to its own organs. The *cortes* could not intervene in judicial decisions, but might accuse the personnel and procedure of the courts of criminal offenses. To this end the president of the Supreme Court would have a seat in the *cortes*.[18]

[16] Mori, IV, 169-172, 201-210; *Diario*, No. 72, 2258-2261; No. 73, November 12, 1931, 2285-2289.

[17] *Diario*, No. 73, 2299.

[18] *Ibid.*, 2304; Jiménez de Asúa, 405.

The juridical commission, over which Ossorio y Gallardo had presided, also specified the autonomy of the administration of justice, but the constitutional commission had suppressed that paragraph. The eminent jurist defended his amendment and declared that there could be no autonomy of justice as long as it depended on the Ministry of Justice. Judicial authority was subjected to politics. It should have perfect autonomy in relation to the other organs of power. The Ministry of Justice and the assumption of its functions by the Supreme Court were quite different. The Minister of Justice was a politician in judgment and reality. The President of the Supreme Court was not a politician and would govern through a judical council.[19]

The Minister of Justice, Fernando de los Ríos, rose to defend his authority. He explained various reforms that he wished to introduce in the administration of justice and declared he would admit autonomy but only in a relative manner:

. . . there is no possibility of a full autonomy within the state organization; if there should be full autonomies within the state organization, the juridical unity of the state would disappear.

It was necessary, he admitted, to eliminate the possibility of favoritism or of any attempt to keep the judges in a servile frame of mind. He subscribed neither to the amendment of Ossorio y Gallardo nor to the *dictamen*. Justice was administered in the name of the state because neither the people nor the nation formed a juridical unity. Ossorio's amendment was then defeated. The chamber acceded to the concept of the Minister of Justice, and it was provided that justice should be administered in the name of the state.[20]

The second paragraph of Article 94 of the constitution provided that the republic should assure the gratuity of justice to litigants in economic necessity. This provision was proposed by Barriobero on November 13, and presented one of

[19] *Diario*, No. 73, 2304-2306; Mori, IV, 210-216.
[20] *Diario*, No. 73, 2306-2310; Mori, IV, 217-219; Jiménez de Asúa, 406.

the most difficult problems that had faced the chamber, according to Jiménez de Asúa. When the amendment was put to the test of an ordinary vote,

Nearly all of the republican sectors of the parliament stood up, in an affirmative sign, while the Socialists remained seated, conscious of the gravity of the proposal. It was a very serious moment. Socialism could not vote publicly against such a principle and, nevertheless, it assumed the burden of its inadmissibility in this hour.

The Minister of Labor indicated that the Socialists should rise and they did so, producing quite a bit of disorder and confusion in the process, but heeding the discipline of their minority. The amendment was approved. The Socialists still considered that the *voto* was dangerous, and Jiménez de Asúa and De los Ríos composed a formula which was included in the second paragraph of Article 94.

The republic will assure litigants in economic necessity the gratuity of justice.

The chamber recovered its serenity and approved the formula unanimously.[21]

The following article was approved with less confusion but required a great deal of debate. Article 96 of the *dictamen* provided that the administration of justice should include all existing jurisdictions and that they should be regulated by law. The penal jurisdiction of the armed forces was limited to the discipline of military and naval jurisdiction. No special rights could be established for persons or places except in cases of martial law, in accord with the law of public order. These provisions were similar to Article 74 of the *anteproyecto* except for certain variations in phraseology.[22]

The commission, however, agreed in a morning session to redraft its project and carry a new formula to the chamber. It differed from the original text in the suppression of the unitary character of the administration of justice and the

---

[21] *Diario*, No. 74, November 13, 1931, 2334-2341; Jiménez de Asúa, 406-408.
[22] Jiménez de Asúa, 408-409.

use of the phrase "armed institutions" in order to include the Civil Guards in the military jurisdiction. Finally the military *fueros* were limited to the time of war instead of cases of martial law.[23]

This second draft was based on the various amendments and *votos* offered and they were withdrawn. Sacristán asked that the inclusion of the mercantile jurisdiction be suppressed, and this phrase, which appeared in both of the drafts of the commission, was deleted. Then Rodríguez Pérez presented a *voto particular,* proposing the maintenance of the military *fueros* in a period of martial law and adding military crimes to those rights. The commission opposed the *voto* but the chamber accepted it. Finally an amendment of Elola was approved and a fourth paragraph was added to Article 95. It suppressed the courts of honor, both civil and military. Jiménez de Asúa had opposed this as unnecessary and improper, in view of the fact that the *cortes* itself had acted as a court of honor. Elola had based his amendment on a similar suppression in the Weimar Constitution.[24]

Salvador de Madariaga was one of the proponents of an amendment which proposed the addition of another article after Article 95. It aimed to divide the administration of justice into two different services, the governmental and the judicial. The deputies refused to take the amendment into consideration.[25]

The parallel debate of the banking regulations had continued, and the major portion of each session was devoted to this project. Hence, the week-end intervened before the *cortes* considered Article 96, on November 17. It concerned the president of the Supreme Court. Article 97 of the *dictamen* provided that this official should be designated by the president of the republic on the proposal of an assembly constituted by at least fifty representatives of the *cortes,* the magistracy, the faculties of law, and the colleges of lawyers.

[23] *Ibid.,* 409-410; *Diario,* No. 74, 2342.
[24] *Diario,* No. 74, 2342-2353; Jiménez de Asúa, 410-411.
[25] *Diario,* No. 72, Appendix 3; No. 74, 2353-2354.

The *anteproyecto* had included representatives of the Forum in addition to the above. The second paragraph stated the qualifications for the office: Spanish nationality, forty years of age, and a license in law. The president of the Supreme Court was subjected to the same incapacities and incompatibilities as the other judicial functionaries. The magistracy was to be held for a term of ten years, but the retiring president might be reëlected. The last three paragraphs of the two projects were nearly identical.[26]

The chamber had agreed to include representatives of the National Academy of Jurisprudence in the electoral assembly by decided to omit them when it was later agreed to leave the constitution of this body to the determination of a special law. The chamber approved Article 96 with this modification. The Federal minority was the only one to vote against it. Barriobero had offered an amendment proposing that the Supreme Court should be composed of a magistrate for each region. The judges would select their president and would constitute the judicial power and serve for five years. They were responsible to the Congress of Deputies.[27]

Article 97 of the constitution had no precedents in either of the projects and originated in an amendment of Fernando de los Ríos. A proposal of Madariaga had already been rejected. The president of the Supreme Court was authorized to prepare and propose laws of judicial reform and codes of procedure, and to propose that magistrates and prosecutors should not practice law. Finally, the president of the Supreme Court and the Prosecutor General of the Republic were to be added to the parliamentary commission of justice, without being required to hold seats in the chamber.[28]

The following article was identical with both of the preliminary projects. It was approved without any modification. Article 98 declared that judges and magistrates could not be pensioned, removed, suspended, or transferred except by

[26] Jiménez de Asúa, 412-413.
[27] *Ibid.*, 413; *Diario*, No. 73, Appendix 4; No. 75, November 17, 1931, 2377-2387.
[28] Jiménez de Asúa, 413-414.

laws which would contain the guarantees necessary for the effective independence of the courts.[29]

The question of civil and criminal responsibility of judges, magistrates, and prosecutors in the exercise of their functions was considered in Article 99. Such responsibility could be exacted before the Supreme Court and a special jury. Municipal judges and prosecutors who did not belong to the judicial career service were excepted from these provisions. The magistrates of the Supreme Court and the prosecutor of the republic were responsible to the Court of Constitutional Guarantees.[30]

This article was based on the second draft of the commission, Article 99 of the *dictamen*, which provided only that judges were responsible to the Supreme Court and excepted municipal judges. It differed slightly from the *anteproyecto*. This designated the Supreme Court as the one to exact civil responsibility and the Court of Constitutional Guarantees as the one before which cases involving criminal responsibility were to be heard. The second draft had attempted to interpret the spirit of the various amendments and *votos particulares* to the article. The special jury which participated in the trial of the various judicial officials originated in an amendment of Alcalá Zamora, although similar amendments were offered by Barriobero, Puig de Asprer, and Portela.[31]

Article 100 considered the action of the lower courts when they were confronted by unconstitutional laws. The judges were to suspend their proceedings and consult the Court of Constitutional Guarantees. The article was identical with the *dictamen* and varied from the *anteproyecto* only in phraseology. Two amendments were offered in the chamber. Elola considered the articles more appropriate among the provisions concerning the Court of Constitutional Guarantees. Royo Villanova proposed that no judge should be obliged to enforce laws he regarded as contrary to the constitution. Both

[29] *Ibid.*, 414-415; *Diario*, No. 75, 2396-2399.
[30] Jiménez de Asúa, 415-416.
[31] *Ibid.*, 416-417; *Diario*, No. 75, 2399-2406.

were defeated, and the article was approved on November 18.[32]

The question of recourses against illegal administrative acts or dispositions committed in the exercise of regulatory power was left to the determination of a law. It was also to include those discretionary acts which were in excess or an abuse of the power of the administration. Article 101 was redrafted by the commission and proposals of Ruiz Funes and Quintana were withdrawn. The preliminary projects stipulated only that a law should establish the recourses against the illegality of administrative acts.[33]

These articles had been approved without a great deal of discussion, but Article 102 aroused a heated debate. The *anteproyecto* had permitted the *cortes* to grant amnesties and general pardons, while individual pardons would be granted by the Supreme Court, on the proposal of the judge who passed the sentence. The president of the Supreme Court was required to submit annually to the *cortes* the reasons for the pardons granted. The parliamentary commission modified this article considerably. It left the right of granting amnesties to the *cortes,* but abolished general pardons.[34]

Jiménez de Asúa summarized the various amendments offered to this article before it was considered in the chamber. One class, represented by that of Jaén, requested that pardons might be sought by petition as well as on the proposal of the judge concerned. The second class asked that general pardons be granted. The third, like that of Del Río, requested that the president of the republic be the authority to grant a pardon from the penalty of death. The commission had rejected the proposals for general pardons, but had taken the two other classes of amendments into consideration in a second draft. Hence, pardons could be granted on the proposal of the judge concerned, the prosecutor, the Board of Prisons, or by petition. The president of the republic could

---

[32] Jiménez de Asúa, 417-418; *Diario,* No. 69. Appendix 3; No. 72, Appendix 6; No. 76, November 18, 1931, 2413-2418.

[33] *Diario,* No. 76, 2418-2425.

[34] Jiménez de Asúa, 419-420.

pardon political and military crimes of extreme gravity on receiving information from the Supreme Court and on the proposal of the government.[35]

The attack on the *dictamen* originated among those who desired general pardons. The great protagonist of this group was Luis de Tapia. He made an eloquent appeal as a poet and lawyer and declared his amendment would "erase from the constitution the only cruel corner which it contains, it is the corner in which it affirms that never again will general pardons be granted."[36] Jiménez de Asúa replied that he opposed all pardons but that the general pardon was the worst of all. It cast the wolves into the middle of the flock, and most of those pardoned were returned to prison. The debate continued, but Tapia's amendment was defeated and the article was at last approved. The only modification was one of phraseology proposed by Guerra del Río.[37]

Before the next article was approved the session was suspended and the night session was devoted exclusively to the debate on the capacity of Margarita Nelken Mansbergen to serve as a deputy from Badajoz. She was a Socialist and her admission gave the women of Spain three representatives in the Constituent Cortes. She lacked one requisite to enable her to qualify as a deputy. She was not of Spanish nationality. The report of the commission on credentials did not consider this technicality, but the *voto particular* of Casanueva was unfavorable and the Radical deputy, Diego Hidalgo, opposed her admission unless she was nationalized. The chamber was divided by the question. Victoria Kent rose to defend her capacity. She declared whatever the chamber decided would be absolutely legal, because it was sovereign. This led to a philosophical debate on sovereignty, but Castrillo finally proposed that she make a solemn declaration of her Spanish citizenship by word or writing, which would qualify her. The commission accepted the formula and it was drafted and approved as follows:

[35] *Diario*, No. 76, 2425.
[36] *Ibid.*, 2428.
[37] *Ibid.*, 2428-2439; Jiménez de Asúa, 422-433.

The chamber, in use of its sovereignty, concedes to Mrs. Margarita Nelken, Spanish nationality and admits her to the office of deputy; but with the condition that on taking the oath of allegiance she expressly state that she solicits the recognition of her nationality as a Spaniard.[38]

The discussion of Article 103 was continued on November 19. It concerned the organization and procedure of the jury. The *dictamen* left the matter to a special law. Quintana de León and others offered an amendment drafted as follows:

The people will participate in the administration of justice by means of the *Tribunal del Jurado*. Its organization and procedure will be the object of a special law. The jurisdiction of the popular court will be extended to every class of crimes.[39]

The commission accepted this text on November 18, when the author agreed to the suppression of the second sentence. The article was approved after a prolonged technical dialogue between Barriobero and Jiménez de Asúa. Barriobero's amendment provided that the jury could be suspended only in case of an officially declared civil war and would be the only competent court for the trial of crimes which were attributed to it.[40]

Article 104 originated in Article 83 of the *anteproyecto* and did not appear in the parliamentary project. Castrillo, Fernández Clérigo, and Quintana de León proposed that a precept on the Ministry of Prosecution be introduced into the constitution. The commission then drafted an article which was presented to the chamber and approved without any modifications. The article provided that the Ministry of Prosecution should be vigilant for the exact fulfilment of the laws and for the social interest. It would constitute a single body and would have the same guarantees of independence as the administration of justice.[41]

The next two articles also lacked antecedents in the pre-

---

[38] *Diario*, No. 76, 2442-2455; Mori, IV, 292-293.
[39] *Diario*, No. 71, Appendix 1.
[40] *Ibid.*, No. 73, Appendix 4, No. 76, 2441-2442.
[41] *Ibid.*, No. 77, November 19, 1931, 2480-2484; Jiménez de Asúa, 442-443.

liminary projects. The first, Article 105, provided for the organization by law of *tribunals de urgencia* (Courts of Emergency) to enforce the protection of the individual guarantees. It was introduced into the commission at the request of the Minister of Justice. Jiménez y Jiménez had presented an amendment proposing the establishment of means to avoid arbitrary arrests and irregular treatment by the police. Jiménez de Asúa successfully defended the proposal in the chamber against the attack of Barriobero and it was approved.[42]

The second article was introduced by the commission and was approved with one slight modification. The original draft declared that every Spaniard had the right to be indemnified for damages incurred through the error or crime of the judicial functionaries in the exercise of their offices, as the law should determine. The state would be responsible for the indemnity. Pascual Leone's amendment merely added the word "judicial" to clarify the "error" for which the state would be responsible.[43]

Title VII was completed with the approval of Article 106. The judiciary had not been made completely autonomous but it was well protected against the intervention of designing politicians. Individual rights were guaranteed against the abuse of justice, either arbitrary or accidental.

[42] *Diario,* No. 77, 2484-2489; Jiménez de Asúa, 443-446.
[43] *Diario,* No. 75, Appendix 4, No. 76, Appendix 12; No. 77, 2489-2491; Jiménez de Asúa, 446-449.

XX

FINANCE AND REFORM

THE DEBATE on the totality of Title VIII of the constitution was begun on November 19. In the evening of the same day a drama was staged in the *cortes* that the Commission of Responsibilities had been rehearsing since its appointment on July 13, and that the country had been awaiting with great expectation. The deputies paid little attention to the attack of Azarola on the *dictamen*. Their thoughts were concentrated on the events that were to take place that evening. Alfonso XIII was to be tried by the *cortes*. He was not to appear in person, nor did the deputies desire that he should. The republic had been founded as a result of the mistakes of the monarchy and was about to assume an aspect of permanence, consolidated by a fundamental law, now on the eve of its promulgation. An indictment of the exiled monarch would arouse patriotic fervor in the hearts of the Republicans if not in the whole country.

The gallaries were filled by 10:30 in the evening and, for the first time in many sessions, all of the deputies were assembled. Besteiro opened the session. Then the secretary read the report of the Commission of Responsibilities to a silent and attentive chamber. It was the act of accusation against Alfonso de Bórbon Habsburgo y Lorena. His reign was characterized by an inclination toward absolute power. He had accepted the constitution in a formulary manner and had not kept faith. The parliament had become a democratic fiction and the sovereignty proclaimed in the Constitution of 1876 had never been effective. After the *coup d'état* of 1923, the last vestige of the power of the *cortes* had been destroyed by its arbitrary dissolution.[1]

[1] Mori, IV, 296-298.

Alfonso was also charged with imperialism in the African wars, which had been conducted in opposition to the will of the people. He had not only instigated the campaigns but his interference had produced disaster. When the parliament investigated the Annual disaster, it had been dissolved to save the King. When a second parliament proved more energetic, Alfonso had prepared the *coup d'état*. He was held solely responsible for the suspension of the constitutional guarantees and the establishment of the arbitrary and absolute government of the dictatorship. His reign had become one of personal power.

Therefore the King was guilty of *lesa majestad*. The people were co-sovereign under the Constitution of 1876 and the King was an executor of the national will, while the parliament represented the majesty of the people. He was also guilty of military rebellion. As a result of these crimes he should be degraded from all of his dignities, rights, and titles. If he entered the national territory he would be condemned to perpetual imprisonment, and if he continued his acts of rebellion he would merit the penalty of death. All of his property in the national territory was to be confiscated.[2]

Royo Villanova and Centeno presented a *voto particular* which proposed the substitution of high treason for *lesa majestad*. The people, they declared, desired only the political death of Alfonso. He had been dethroned as a result of his perjury and attack on the national sovereignty. He should now be condemned to perpetual exile and never be allowed to hold any public office.[3]

The Count of Romanones rose to defend the ex-king. He was now known by his real name, Alvaro Figueroa. For forty years he had served the monarchy, three times as premier, innumerable times as minister. He had been president of both the congress and the senate. It was his duty to defend the King, he declared. He did not really have his heart in the task, however, for his defense could not reverse a pre-

[2] *Ibid.*, 299-303.
[3] *Ibid.*, 304-307.

determined verdict. He declared that the necessary requisites of every trial were missing and the King was accused, the crime was named, and the penalty imposed, without a proper trial.

He endeavored to answer the charges brought by the commission. He could not reply to the accusation that Alfonso had manifested inclinations toward absolute power. He merely said, "I neither admit nor deny the charge." In disputing the charge of imperialism and responsibility for events in Morocco, he declared, "The King is inviolable, the King is irresponsible, and his ministers bear the responsibility." It was mere supposition that he had brought on the Annual disaster. Three ministers had done nothing to prevent the discovery of the responsibility.[4]

He, Alvaro Figueroa, had been an implacable enemy of the dictatorship, because he knew that its inevitable result would be the fall of the monarchy. The Marqués de Estella was not the dupe of Alfonso, however, and he endeavored to prove it, by reading the telegram sent by Primo de Rivera to Muñoz Cobos. He then declared:

It was not a general who gave the signal and then submitted to the decision of the King; it was a general who, from the first moment, imposed himself on the King in a clear, final, and categorical manner.[5]

The attorney for the King attacked the Catalans. The movement leading to the *coup d'état* had begun in Barcelona. The Catalans were aware of it. They had assisted it. In any event, Alfonso could not have overthrown the dictator if he had desired to do so, and he had never exercised less personal power than under the rule of Primo de Rivera.

The King could not be convicted of *lesa majestad,* for he was majesty. He could not have led a military rebellion which was forced upon him. Alvaro Figueroa opposed the confiscation of the property of the King particularly. If Alcalá Zamora had believed all of the charges against Alfonso were true, he

[4] *Ibid.,* 314-317.
[5] *Ibid.,* 319.

would not have permitted him to leave Spain on April 14.[6] This evidence and these arguments, however, did not convince the Republicans. It was essential for their cause to believe that Alfonso was the one responsible for the dictatorship and that he should be condemned before the people of Spain.

Angel Galarza was the prosecutor for the republic. He built his case around the charges of the *ponencia* or report of the Commission of Responsibilities. He declared that Alvaro Figueroa had been unable to defend the King despite his recognized parliamentary ability. Then he proceeded to analyze the defense and combat it. It is not necessary to follow his prosecution of the case closely, for the deputies did not have to be convinced of the guilt of Alfonso. They were already prepared to render their decision. The only point of contention was the question of the penalties to be imposed.[7]

The debate continued as Ossorio y Gallardo opposed the *ponencia*. The necessary guarantees for trial and procedure were missing. The action would damage the *cortes* more than the King. He asked that the chamber reflect upon the matter. The trial was not to be considered as a juridical process but as an historic and political fact. González López pointed out that the important consideration was the necessity of adopting measures of security against the possible return of the King.[8]

Pedro Rico and other members of the Radical minority now presented an amendment to the report of the commission. They proposed that Alfonso should be declared guilty of high treason, as a juridical formula which included all of the crimes covered in the act of accusation. The republic should take over the property of the king, and any Spanish citizen could apprehend his person if he should ever reënter the national territory.[9]

[6] *Diario*, No. 77, November 19, 1931, 2505-2510.
[7] *Ibid.*, 2510-2516.
[8] *Ibid.*, 2516-2519.
[9] Mori, IV, 345.

Centeno withdrew the *voto particular* because the crime of high treason had been included in the amendment of Pedro Rico. Royo Villanova, however, refused to agree with Centeno on this procedure and maintained the *voto* alone. The crime of Alfonso, according to the agrarian deputy, was his disregard of the constitution. Majesty itself could not commit the crime of *lesa majestad*. Alfonso had failed in his duties, but not as a co-sovereign, because sovereignty was vested in the nation, according to the creed of the democratic parties under the monarchy. This was the juridical concept that had caused his dissent from the *ponencia*. He could not support the amendment because it declared Alfonso was outside of the law. No man was without the law. When Alfonso ceased to be king he became a man, and all men were protected by law.[10]

Gil Robles then spoke amid protests and continued interruptions. He could support none of the three proposals because the accusation was based on mere supposition. No sanction had been imposed on Alfonso on April 14. The people wished only to expel him from Spain. He declared that the responsibility "of the king has already been made effective by a revolution . . . after that there remains only the judgment of history."[11] Rico defended and explained his amendment, which was accepted in principle by Eduardo Ortega y Gasset, who expressed the hope that it would meet with the approval of the chamber. Alcalá Zamora and Azaña spoke in defense of the act of accusation, and the latter urged that the chamber proceed to an immediate vote. The amended *ponencia* was then approved by acclamation, amid *vivas* for Spain and the republic. Alfonso was declared guilty of high treason.

The chamber returned to the consideration of the constitution, and with the debate on Article 104 of the *dictamen* the real discussion of the eighth title began. This section of the constitution was concerned with public finance, and the

[10] *Ibid.*, 346-349.
[11] Diario, No. 77, 2522-2523; Mori, IV, 350-353.

articles were rapidly approved with but few modifications. The only problem was that raised by the representatives of the regional interests who feared lest the legality of their statutory regulations be anticipated. The deputies, however, were anxious to conclude their constitutional task.

Discussion of Article 107 of the constitution was begun on November 20. It was based on Article 104 of the *dictamen* and Article 84 of the *anteproyecto* and provided for the regulation of the annual budget. The government was to formulate the budget, the *cortes* was to approve it. The project for the general budget for the following year was to be presented on October 2, and was to be in force for one year. The juridical commission had arranged that the alterations in the budget from the preceding one and the balance of the previous year should also be presented to the *cortes*. The parliamentary commission omitted these requirements. It also deleted the juridical provisions that if the budget was not voted before the first day of the economic year, the old budget should be discussed and passed by the *cortes* for the next year.[12]

After the debate on the title as a whole the commission redrafted the article and modified the time of presenting the budgetary project. It could be presented during the first ten days of October instead of on October 2. The debate was prolonged by the amendment of Cornide, who proposed the extension of the budget of the previous year. The new draft of the commission was defeated in a nominal vote, 104-84. Another draft was composed after the acceptance of an addition proposed by Gomáriz. This provided that if the budget was not approved before the first day of the economic year, the old budget should be extended for three months. The commission added the restriction that it could not be extended longer than four months, and the article was approved on November 24.[13]

[12] Jiménez de Asúa, 449-450.
[13] *Ibid.*, 449-451; *Diario*, No. 78, November 20, 1931, 2538-2552; No. 79, November 24, 1931, 2571.

An additional article was inserted after article 107 as a result of the acceptance of the *voto particular* of Castrillo by the commission. The *anteproyecto* had provided that the parliament could not increase the credit in any article or chapter of the budgetary project except for concrete cases of general necessity and national interest. This proposal had to be signed by a tenth of the deputies and passed by a majority of two-thirds. The parliamentary commission had omitted this Article 85 of the *anteproyecto*. Castrillo and Sacristán both proposed that it be included, and the commission agreed. Article 108, as approved by the chamber, provided that any increase had to be requested by a tenth of the deputies and approved by an absolute majority of the chamber.[14]

Eleven more articles of the eighth title were approved in the session of November 24. The first was based on the *dictamen*, which was an expansion of Article 86 of the *anteproyecto*. The commission agreed to redraft the article after considering the *voto* of Castrillo and the amendments of Artigas and Sacristán. The prohibition of special funds was suppressed, and the *voto* of Castrillo was incorporated into the third paragraph. Article 109 then provided that there should be only one budget for each economic year, which should include ordinary income and expenditures. An extraordinary budget had to be authorized by the absolute majority of the *cortes*. The third paragraph required the annual examination of the accounts of the state by the Tribunal of Accounts of the Republic, which would report any ministerial infraction or responsibility to the *cortes*.[15]

Article 110, which was identical with the *dictamen* and a modification of the original *anteproyecto*, was approved without debate. The *cortes* alone approved the budget and it did not require promulgation by the president to be effective.[16] The following article was nearly identical with both of the preliminary projects. The floating debt which the

[14] Jiménez de Asúa, 451-452; *Diario*, No. 79, 2571.
[15] Jiménez de Asúa, 452-454; *Diario*, No. 79, 2572.
[16] Jiménez de Asúa, 454-455; *Diario*, No. 79, 2574.

government could incur during the economic year was to be fixed in the budget.[17] Article 112 was identical with Article 89 of the *anteproyecto*. It required that every law authorizing loans should contain the conditions of the loan, including the interest rate and the provisions for the amortization of the debt. The *cortes* might restrict these conditions as it saw fit.[18]

The deputies consumed little time in debate and passed immediately to Article 113. The budget could contain no authorization that would permit the government to exceed the expenditure provided in it, except in case of war. Expanding credits could not exist. These provisions were nearly identical with the *dictamen,* which varied in wording from the *anteproyecto*.[19] Article 114 was identical with Article 91 of the *anteproyecto* and differed from the *dictamen* in the use of *cortes* instead of *parlamento*. It was approved without debate and declared that the expenditures authorized in the budget could not be altered by the government. When the *cortes* was not in session, the government could, on its own responsibility, supplement the credit in cases of war or the avoidance of war, the maintenance of public order, public calamities, and international compromises. The procedure in these emergencies was to be determined by special laws.[20]

The addition of another article, proposed by Gabriel Franco, was defeated and the chamber then approved a new draft of Article 115. The corresponding Article 111 of the *dictamen* was nearly identical with the *anteproyecto*. No one was obliged to pay taxes not approved by the *cortes* or the corporations legally authorized to impose them. The collection of the various forms of revenue were authorized by laws in force and could be effected only through the previous authorization of the budget. The new text was drafted on the basis of an amendment offered by Corominas, and differed

[17] Jiménez de Asúa, 455-456; *Diario,* No. 79, 2574-2575.
[18] Jiménez de Asúa, 456-457; *Diario,* No. 79, 2577.
[19] Jiménez de Asúa, 457-458; *Diario,* No. 79, 2578.
[20] Jiménez de Asúa, 458-459; *Diario,* No. 79, 2578.

from the original in the use of certain phrases necessary to clarify the meaning of the article.[21]

Sacristán withdrew his proposal for an additional article, and Article 116 was approved without discussion. The variations in style between the definitive article and the corresponding articles of the preliminary projects were the result of the final revision by the commission. The law of budgets would contain only the norms applicable to the execution of the budget, which would be effective while the budget was in force.[22] A second paragraph was added to Article 113 of the *dictamen* on the proposal of the commission. The original text required the authorization of a law for the disposition of the properties of the state by the government or the issuance of bonds on the national credit. The addition declared null all operations which violated this restriction and absolved the state of any obligation to repay such bonds or the interest on them. Article 117 was approved without other modifications.[23]

The following provision, Article 118, was identical with both the *dictamen* and the *anteproyecto* and was approved after a brief debate. Galarza and Royo Villanova offered amendments, but they were withdrawn. The brevity of the debate indicated the lack of interest the articles aroused in the chamber. The approved article placed the public debt under the protection of the state. The credit necessary for the payment of interest and principal on the debt was to be included in the budget and could not be debated, while the provisions were in accord with the laws authorizing the debt. Any economic operation implying the responsibility of the treasury was given the same guarantees.[24]

The next article was drafted by the commission on the proposal of the government after the *dictamen* had been presented, and had no precedent in either of the preliminary

[21] Jiménez de Asúa, 459-461; *Diario*, No. 79, 2583.
[22] Jiménez de Asúa, 461-462; *Diario*, No. 79, 2583.
[23] Jiménez de Asúa, 462-463; *Diario*, No. 79, 2583.
[24] Jiménez de Asúa, 463-464; *Diario*, No. 79, 2583.

projects. It was briefly debated and approved. Article 119 provided that every fund of amortization should be adjusted to certain norms. The directors of the fund had full control of it, and the resources with which it was endowed had to be specified. Neither these resources nor the capital of the fund could be applied to any other end of the state. Finally, the debt or debts for the amortization of which the fund was created were to be definitely fixed. Each fund was to have its own annual budget, which required the approval of the Minister of Finance. The pertinent accounts were to be submitted to the Tribunal of Accounts, which would inform the *cortes* of any deficiency or error.[25]

Article 115 of the *dictamen* was suppressed in the chamber. It had been based on Article 98 of the *anteproyecto,* but the original text was modified by the commission to include the amendment of Corominas, another of the Radical-Socialists, and part of a third proposed by Santiago Alba. It guaranteed local and regional treasuries independence of the national budget. The latter were to have their own taxes and regulate their own budgets as provided in their respective statutes and laws. None of the regions, provinces, or municipalities could be conceded any resources of the state except as specified in the statutes or by a law approved by the absolute majority of the *cortes.* Leizaola offered a *voto particular* proposing the suppression of this article, and it was agreed by a vote of 127 to 96 in the following session.[26]

Article 116 of the parliamentary project was based on a *voto particular* to the *anteproyecto,* offered by Viñuales, Valdecasas, Pedroso, and others. It provided that imposts which were included in the budget for the income of the republic should be collected in all of Spain in the same manner and by the same officials. The establishment of local agreements or *conciertos* contingent upon these imposts was prohibited. Leizaola presented a *voto particular* asking that this article

[25] Jiménez de Asúa, 464-465; *Diario,* No. 79, 2583.

[26] Jiménez de Asúa, 465-468; *Diario,* No. 79, 2583; No. 80, November 25, 1931, 2623-2625.

be suppressed, and the Catalans also proposed one in defense of their regional interests. The commission concluded that it would be serious to abolish the existing local agreements, particularly those of the Basques, and agreed to suppress the article. The chamber approved.[27]

The final article of the eighth title was approved on November 25. It established the Tribunal of Accounts as the prosecuting organ of economic activity. This body was subjected directly to the *cortes* and exercised powers delegated by the chamber in the examination and final approval of the accounts of the state. It would be established by a special law. Any conflict arising between it and other organs of the state would be submitted to the decision of the Court of Constitutional Guarantees. The definitive Article 120 was based on the *voto particular* of Enrique Ramos to the *anteproyecto*. This proposal was considerably modified by the commission. The *dictamen* provided that the tribunal should approve the accounts of the autonomous regions and the other organisms of the republic. This aroused the Catalans, who opposed the article on the ground that Catalonia should be freed from the intervention of the tribunal. As a result of the amendment of Corominas, the disputed provision was suppressed.[28] García Valdecasas proposed an additional article prohibiting the concession of direct taxes on businesses operating in more than one region. This was defeated in an ordinary vote.[29]

The haste with which the eighth title was approved indicated the fatigue of the deputies and the absence of any provision on which there was a wide divergence of opinion. The provisions concerning the budget were very exact, and every care was taken to prevent waste or illegal expenditures. The integrity of the treasury was guaranteed and the establishment of the Court of Accounts assured that if the constitution was strongly interpreted no raids on the treasury or violation of the constitution would be condoned.

[27] Jiménez de Asúa, 468-469.
[28] *Ibid.*, 469-471; Mori, IV, 374.
[29] *Diario*, No. 80, 2637 *ff.*

Consideration of Title IX, entitled "Guarantees and Reform of the Constitution," was begun on November 26. The constitutional commission presented a new draft of the five articles and a debate on the totality of the title was produced by various proposals to reform the whole *dictamen*. The *voto particular* of Castrillo was withdrawn and for that reason does not merit analysis. The other proposals were more important in that they produced a debate before the discussion of the individual articles began.

The real debate was the result of the amendment of José Xiráu of the Catalan Left. He proposed that the Court of Constitutional Guarantees be replaced by a Council of the Republic, which was in reality a second chamber. Xiráu defended his amendment and explained the functions and method of electing his proposed council. Its first function was political. It would examine and report on all of the projects of law approved by the chamber. He considered it dangerous to have neither a senate nor the technical councils. In addition, Article 118 of the *dictamen* was a political deformity in granting the Court of Constitutional Guarantees the power to declare laws unconstitutional. The Council of the Republic would resolve this difficulty by intervening between the president and the chamber. Its second function was a delicate one. It would have cognizance over the legislative conflicts which arose between the state and the autonomous regions and among the regions. The *dictamen* offered no solution for harmonizing these conflicting interests. It was a technical and juridical impossibility for the Court of Constitutional Guarantees to act as an intervening organ in political problems. The legislative bodies of the regions would send representatives to the Council of the Republic and, in this manner, both the people and the regions would be represented. Finally, it would have a purely political function as an interventive organ.[30]

This was the last effort of the deputies who desired a sec-

[30] *Ibid.*, No. 81, November 26, 1931, 2653-2655; Mori, IV, 375-382; Jiménez de Asúa, 471.

ond chamber to introduce their concepts into the constitution. It proved a futile one. Xiráu's amendment was defeated, 144-135. The Radicals, Republican Action, the Progressives, the Federals, and the Catalan Left joined in supporting the amendment, but the Socialists and Radical-
Socialists, with the assistance of various independent deputies,
were too strong for them. A similar proposal of a National
Council, offered by Gabriel Franco, was withdrawn, and the
other efforts to amend the ninth title in a federal sense were
likewise defeated. Pí y Arsuaga, for example, asked that the
court charged with judging the president of the republic,
ministers, president and magistrates of the Supreme Court,
and the prosecutor of the republic, should be popularly
elected. But the *dictamen* as a whole was approved and the
discussion of the articles began.[31]

Article 121 of the constitution provided for the establishment of the Court of Constitutional Guarantees. Its jurisdiction extended over all of the territory of the republic, and it
was competent to pass on the constitutionality of laws; protect
individual guarantees when petitions to other authorities had
been ineffective; solve the conflicts between the state and
the autonomous regions and between the regions; examine
and approve the powers of the *compromisarios* who participated in the election of the president of the republic; assess
the criminal responsibility of the president of the republic,
the president of the council and the ministers, the president
and magistrates of the Supreme Court, and the prosecutor
of the republic. Four of these powers were attributed to the
court in Article 117 of the *dictamen,* which was based on
Article 100 of the *anteproyecto,* although the latter was different in several particulars. The commission had suppressed
the power of the court to pass on the constitutionality of
laws and statutory decrees and to determine the validity of
the election of senators and deputies to the *cortes.*[32]

The commission redrafted the original *dictamen* by adding

---

[31] Mori, IV, 392; *Diario,* No. 81, 2658-2662; Jiménez de Asúa, 471-472.
[32] Jiménez de Asúa, 472-474.

the power to pass on the constitutionality of laws and the examination and approval of the powers of the presidential *compromisarios.* The second provision had been included in Article 68. In the course of the debate the *dictamen* was further modified at the suggestion of Sánchez Albornoz. This described the possible conflicts between the state and the regions as those of "legislative competency" and "all others that may arise." Article 121 was thus approved.[33]

The following article of the parliamentary project, Article 118, was suppressed by the commission. It became unnecessary when Article 121 was modified to enable the Court of Constitutional Guarantees to decide on the constitutionality of laws.[34]

Article 119 of the *dictamen* was debated during parts of two sessions. It was concerned with the composition of the Court of Constitutional Guarantees. The two preliminary projects differed in this respect. According to the *anteproyecto,* the court was to consist of the president and two members of the Supreme Court, the president and two members of the Council of State, the president of the Tribunal of Accounts, two members elected by all of the colleges of lawyers of Spain, two members elected by the faculties of law of the Spanish universities, and a representative of each of the autonomous regions. These judges would serve for five years, and the president of the court would be elected for the same period by the judges. The *dictamen* also provided for the membership of the president and two judges of the Supreme Court, but the two judges were to be elected instead of being definitely designated in the constitution. The Council of State had been suppressed in the parliamentary project, and the representation of that body was also deleted. Two members elected by the *cortes* were to serve instead. The representative of the Tribunal of Accounts was also omitted. It was further provided that the president of the Supreme Court should serve in the same capacity in the Court of Con-

[33] *Ibid.,* 474-475; *Diario,* No. 81, 2669.
[34] Jiménez de Asúa, 475.

stitutional Guarantees. Otherwise, the composition of the courts established by the two projects was the same.[35]

A number of amendments were offered in the Cortes when this article was considered. The Minister of Justice spoke in behalf of his proposal, similar to an amendment of Basilio Alvarez, that members of the Supreme Court should not serve on the Court of Constitutional Guarantees, since one of its duties was to enforce responsibility. The commission accepted the suggested and redrafted the article. Sánchez Albornoz and Rey Mora offered amendments which coincided with the criterion of Eduardo Ortega y Gasset. As a result of the acceptance of the concept embodied in these, the qualification of autonomy was dropped from the regional representation, and all of the regions were entitled to one representative. Thus a new national entity appeared, the unorganized region.[36]

The Court of Constitutional Guarantees, according to the approved Article 122, consisted of a president chosen by the *cortes,* who might be a deputy; the president of the high consultative body of the republic as provided in Article 93; the president of the Tribunal of Accounts; two deputies elected by the *cortes;* a representative for each of the regions, two members elected by all of the colleges of lawyers; and four professors elected by all of the faculties of law of Spain.[37]

Those who had recourse to the Court of Constitutional Guarantees were specified in Article 120 of the *dictamen.* They were the prosecuting ministry, judges and courts who regarded a law unconstitutional, the government of the republic, the autonomous regions, and apprieved persons. The *anteproyecto* had provided that the entities recognized as organisms of public law might also appeal to the court, but the constitutional commission suppressed the section. The chamber accepted an amendment of Balbontín by a vote of 52-29, which expanded the phrase "aggrieved persons" to

[35] *Ibid.,* 476-478.
[36] *Ibid.,* 478-479; *Diario,* No. 82, November 27, 1931, 2712-2717.
[37] Jiménez de Asúa, 476.

read "every individual or collective personality," although the aggrieved might not have been directly offended. Article 123 was then approved.[38]

The chamber introduced Article 124, which was provided in neither of the preliminary projects. The text was modified as a result of an amendment of Sánchez Albornoz accepted by a vote of 51 to 5. It provided that an organic law should establish the immunities and prerogatives of the members of the court.[39]

The last article of the constitution provided for its reform. The *dictamen* declared that the government, a fourth of the deputies, or 25 per cent of the electors could initiate the amendment. The proposal should indicate the article or articles to be suppressed or reformed. It would then require the vote of three-fourths of the deputies to be approved. The necessity of the reform was thus agreed upon and the congress was automatically dissolved. An election would be held within sixty days and the new chamber would function as a constituent assembly to decide on the proposed amendment. After the reform was made the new chamber would act as an ordinary *cortes*. The only difference between the *dictamen* and the *anteproyecto* lay in the specification of the number of the deputies required to propose the amendment. The approval of its necessity required a four-fifths vote in the *anteproyecto*. The chamber modified the article by the suppression of the popular initiation of an amendment and the reduction of the majority for approving the proposal to two-thirds of the deputies during the first four years of the life of the constitution, and to an absolute majority after that period had passed. This modification was made at the suggestion of Alcalá Zamora. Article 125 was approved on November 27, and with its approval the constitution was completed.[40]

The brevity of the last title of the constitution is not

[38] *Ibid.*, 479-481; *Diario*, No. 82, 2723.
[39] Jiménez de Asúa, 481; *Diario*, No. 82, 2725.
[40] Jiménez de Asúa, 482-484; *Diario*, No. 82, 2726.

indicative of its importance. It established a court to protect the integrity of the fundamental law of Spain and to guarantee its permanence. It set up a method of reform that was complex enough to forestall a possible capricious modification of its liberal and social precepts. The deputies of the Constituent Cortes intended their work to endure.

XXI

THE PROMULGATION OF THE CONSTITUTION

THE CONSTITUTION had now been completed, but it had yet to receive the definitive revision in style by the constitutional commission and the final approbation of the chamber. In addition, there were several proposals of additional articles and the transitory dispositions that accompanied the promulgation, which had yet to be approved.

Terrero proposed four additional articles. One referred to the flag of the republic, was accepted by the chamber, and incorporated into Article 1. Two others, concerning the abolition of the Constitution of 1876 and the promulgation of the new constitution, were defeated as unnecessary. The fourth addition offered by Terrero proposed the postponement of the right of suffrage to women. It was almost identical with two other transitory propositions of Victoria Kent and Peñalba. These represented the last effort of the moderates to present a reaction which they considered inevitable if the women exercised the franchise.

The debate was prolonged, centering largely around Peñalba's amendment. It suggested that the right of women to vote should be effective in the first municipal elections. They could not vote in the regional, provincial, or legislative elections until after the existing *ayuntamientos* had been totally renewed. This proposal was defeated by the bare margin of four votes, 131-127. The women of Spain were thus allowed to vote in the first elections without restriction.[1]

The irrepressible Dr. Juarros also proposed an additional article. He made a final plea for the inclusion in the consti-

[1] *Diario*, No. 82, 2726-2728; No. 83, December 1, 1931, 2733-2752; Jiménez de Asúa, 485.

311

tution of obligatory physical and sexual education, pre-matrimonial guarantees, sanitary provisions, and eugenic abortion. In addition, the physicians who were appointed to the public health service should be recognized as public officials. He declared that he would not have offered these suggestions if the fundamental law had dealt only with genuinely constitutional matters. Jiménez de Asúa replied that the commission approved of his program, but it could not be considered as appropriate in the constitution. The chamber rejected the amendment.[2]

Two transitory proposals were included in the constitution. One provided that the Constituent Cortes should elect the first president of the republic by a secret vote. The successful candidate had to obtain an absolute majority of the deputies accredited to the *cortes*. If none of the candidates succeeded in obtaining this vote a second election would be held and the candidate obtaining the greatest number of votes would be elected. The proposition was approved without debate, and the variations in style between the constitutional provision and the original *dictamen* resulted from the revision by the parliamentary commission.[3]

At the conclusion of the session of December 1, Besteiro announced that the constitution was complete. It would be returned to the constitutional commission for revision before it was definitely approved. The absolute majority of the chamber would be required to sanction it.[4] The commission returned the definitive draft to the chamber on December 9. It was read and approved by a vote of 368-0. Many deputies present did not vote, but seventeen absent members asked that their votes be counted for the constitution. Besteiro then solemnly announced that the constitution was promulgated.[5]

[2] *Diario*, No. 82, 2728-2731; Mori, IV, 410-419; Jiménez de Asúa, 485-489.

[3] Jiménez de Asúa, 489-490.

[4] *Diario*, No. 83, 2557.

[5] The constitution was published in the *Diario de Sesiones*, No. 88, December 9, 1931, Appendix 1, and reprinted in Mori IV, 464-488. It also appeared in the daily newspapers. The government distributed thousands of copies of the constitution at the time of the inauguration of the permanent president

It must be understood that if anyone feels himself injured by these necessary surgical operations, he must realize that, in its last article, the constitution has indicated the norm and the juridical road by which the constitution itself can be reformed by those who count on the assent of a majority of citizens. And given this, it is necessary to proclaim very loudly that under pretense of reform of the constitution, no one can legitimately raise any banner of rebellion in Spain.[6]

He concluded wih this plea:

In short, our desire is that this constitution which we have just voted and sanctioned may be the origin of a vital impulse of the Spanish people, not only to raise themselves, but in order to contribute to this resurgence of a new humanity, which is being born amid afflictions.[7]

The *cortes* then accorded a vote of appreciation to the constitutional commission, and the session was suspended.[8]

A second transitory article had been included, on the proposal of the government. The Law of the Defense of the Republic was added to the constitution, to be effective for the duration of the Constituent Cortes, unless expressly repealed. The Commission of Responsibilities was given a transitory constitutional character until it had performed its mission of assessing responsibility for the mistakes of the monarchy. The nature of the Commission of Responsibilities has already been indicated, but it is important that the provisions of the law of October 21 be fully understood. On the very day that the constitution was approved, this law providing for the suspension of constitutional guarantees was added to it.[9]

Five days after Azaña was chosen President of the Provisional Government, he had proposed the Law of the Defense

---

of the republic. It has been translated into English in *Current History*, XXXVI, June, 1932, 374-384.

[6] Mori, IV, 461; *Diario*, No. 88, December 9, 1931, 2911.

[7] Mori, IV, 463; *Diario*, No. 88, 2912.

[8] Mori, IV, 459-463; *Diario*, No. 88, 2905-2913.

[9] Jiménez de Asúa, 490-491; Mori, IV, 459.

of the Republic, in fulfilment of the strong policy that he
had indicated he would follow. It was necessary to subdue the
extremists of both Right and Left, and this law was approved
to facilitate that policy. Nevertheless the intervening month
and a half had not been sufficient to guarantee the republic
against such attacks, and the Law of the Defense of the Republic was extended for the duration of the Constituent
Cortes. It had been strenuously attacked in parliamentary
debate by various deputies. The conservatives regarded the
law as a continuation of the old dictatorial policies, but it
was essential to the stability of the Government and the maintenance of public order that drastic measures be taken. In
addition, the extreme Right did not wish the republic to be
too strongly consolidated, and the greater the disorder, the
greater the resultant dissatisfaction with the republic. At least
this was the view that the supporters of the republic took. The
people of Spain could not be protected in their individual
and collective liberties as long as they regarded liberty as
licence. Inaction on the part of Azaña would have encouraged the Syndicalists and those who believed in direct action
to attack with impunity the government they wished to
destroy.[10]

The Law of the Defense of the Republic defined the following as acts of aggression against the republic:

1. Inciting resistance or disobedience to the laws or legitimate dispositions of authority.
2. Encouraging antagonism between the armed forces and
   the civil organizations, or inciting the former to break
   discipline.
3. Diffusing rumors which could break the credit or disturb the national order.
4. Committing or inciting acts of violence against persons
   or property for religious, political, and social motives.
5. Deprecating by act or word the institutions or organs
   of the state.

[10] *Diario*, No. 59, 1836-1837; Mori, IV, 280-282.

6. Apologizing for the monarchy or the persons representing it and using emblems or insignia allusive to either.
7. Possessing prohibited firearms and explosives illegally.
8. Suspending or stopping industries or work of any kind without sufficient justification.
9. Declaring strikes not announced eight days before, unrelated to conditions of labor, or not submitted to arbitration or conciliation.
10. Altering prices without justification.
11. Negligence or lack of zeal on the part of public officials in the discharge of their duties.

Persons committing any of the first ten acts could be jailed for a period equal to the duration of the law or fined as much as 10,000 *pesetas*. The perpetrators of the last crime would be removed or demoted.

This was the type of law which Miguel Maura would have liked to enforce, but Azaña turned it over to his Minister of Government, who was empowered to:

1. Suspend meetings or manifestations of a political, religious, or social character, when the circumstances of their convocation indicated that their celebration would disturb the public peace.
2. Close the centers or associations which were considered responsible for the acts defined as aggression against the republic.
3. Intervene in the bookkeeping and investigate the origin and distribution of the funds of any entity as defined in the Law of Associations.
4. Decree the seizure of every kind of arms and explosive substances, even of those held legally.

The Minister of Government was empowered to name a representative to enforce this law in a jurisdiction of two or more provinces. The law would be void if the Constituent Cortes adjourned without ratifying it.[11]

[11] Jiménez de Asúa, note, 491-493; Mori, IV, 280-281; *Diario*, No. 60, Appendix 2.

The various minorities had been busily engaged in speculation as to who should be the first president of the Second Spanish Republic. Alcalá Zamora had been practically ostracized for a short time after his relinquishment of the provisional presidency, but he soon recovered his popularity. He was an astute politician, and it appeared that he would receive the unanimous approval of the deputies as the new chief executive. The choice of the president lay largely in the hands of the Socialists, since they and their allies formed the largest bloc in the chamber and could swing the majority to the man they desired to elevate. The Socialists, however, were divided. Besteiro and a large section of the minority wished to remain in the opposition, awaiting developments before they assumed the responsibility of governing Spain. There were rumors that Largo Caballero and another section of the minority were inclined to accept power with all its consequences. They hoped to form a government of the Left with the aid of the Radical-Socialists and the deputies of Republican Action, the minority to which Azaña belonged. These rumors persisted despite denials from Largo Caballero.[12]

The deputies were so deeply interested in the approaching elections that they left the chamber to discuss politics in the passages. This circumstance explains, in part, the scanty attendance during the discussion of the last two titles of the constitution. They were fatigued with technical debate and personal exhibitions, their emotions had been spent on more vital issues. The election of the president of Spain, however, was a matter which aroused them from their lethargy and drew them from the tedious constitutional task. That task was now completed. Spain had a fundamental law, and the deputies could proceed to the election of the permanent executive and devote themselves to the elaboration of legislative projects and the solution of the problems which confronted them.

The election of the president was held in the *cortes* on December 10. There was great excitement as the result of the

[12] *El Sol*, November 15, 18, 21, 22, 1931.

vote was announced by Besteiro. Niceto Alcalá Zamora had received 362 of the 410 votes cast. Joaquín Pí y Arsuaga had received seven, Julián Besteiro two, Manuel B. Cossío two, and Miguel Unamuno and Gorbea one each. Thirty-five votes were blank, and twelve absent members voted for Alcalá Zamora, although their votes were not counted.[13]

On the following day the new president was formally inaugurated. The commission of the *cortes,* chosen to escort Alcalá Zamora to the chamber, went to his home with a cavalry escort at 1:30 P.M. The streets were filled with people, and they expressed themselves enthusiastically as the procession passed. It was a gala occasion, and automobiles passed through the streets scattering copies of the new constitution.

When Alcalá Zamora entered the chamber the deputies rose. The galleries were occupied by the members of the diplomatic corps in full dress, and the invited guests. Alcalá Zamora went to the presidential platform and bowed to the deputies and galleries. He then took the oath of office, in accord with Article 72:

I promise solemnly on my honor, before the Constituent Cortes, as the organ of the national sovereignty, to serve the republic faithfully, to enforce the constitution, to observe the laws, and to consecrate my activity as chief of state to the service of justice and of Spain.

Julián Besteiro, the president of the *cortes,* who administered the oath, replied:

In the name of the Constituent Cortes which elected you, and now invests you, I say to you: If you do this may the nation reward you, and if you do not, may it demand it of you.

Alejandro Lerroux conferred the Collar of the Order of Isabella the Catholic on the President amid ringing *vivas,* and Alcalá Zamora left the chamber.[14]

[13] *Diario,* No. 89, December 10, 1931, 2925-2928; Mori, IV, 489; *ABC,* December 11, 1931.
[14] *Diario,* No. 90, December 15, 1931, 2931-2933; Mori, IV, 491-492; *El Sol,* December 12, 1931; *ABC,* December 12, 1931.

The Provisional Government immediately resigned, and six days later the first government was announced to the *cortes*. After a short debate, the deputies accorded it a vote of confidence, 294-5. Manuel Azaña was President of the Council of Ministers and Minister of War. The Ministry of State was given to Luis Zulueta, and Alejandro Lerroux became leader of the opposition. The other ministers were:

Justice	Alvaro de Albornoz
Treasury	Jaime Carner
Navy	José Giral Pereira
Government	Santiago Casares Quiroga
Public Instruction	Fernando de los Ríos
Labor	Francisco Largo Caballero
Public Works	Indalecio Prieto
Agriculture, Industry, and Commerce	Marcelino Domingo

The president of the republic was a conservative who had declared himself in favor of the revision of the constitution. The ministry, however, was of the Left. Azaña was a member of Republican Action, supported by the Socialists, Radical-Socialists, and Catalans. The Second Republic of Spain was constitutionally consolidated. It had yet to consolidate Spain.[15]

The Constitution of 1931 merely indicated the direction and norms which the government of Spain would follow in the solution of the national problems. The Constituent Cortes had to formulate a great mass of complementary legislation in order that the republic, now endowed with sovereign powers and the authority delegated by the people, might become a reality instead of an ideal.

The Constituent Cortes which framed the Constitution of 1931 was essentially a heterogeneous body. The strongest *bloc* was formed by the Socialist and Radical-Socialist parties, but it would be difficult to trace any consistent dominance of this *bloc* during the framing of the constitution. It would

[15] *Diario*, No. 91, December 17, 1931, 2935-2955; Mori, IV, 496-498.

likewise be impossible to maintain that there was always solidarity between the component parties. Its principal opposition, the Republican Alliance, dominated by the Radicals, did not follow a continuous policy either. Although party discipline was mainained as a rule, the Spanish characteristic of individualism was frequently asserted, and party lines and procedure fluctuated constantly. The Catalans, Federals, and parties of the Right often held the balance in crises, the Radicals and the Socialists were not always opposed on vital issues. The doctrinaire leaders tried to keep their minorities to a constant program, but the number of the minorities, the variety of the interests involved in the various problems which arose, further emphasized the fundamental individualism of the action of the deputies.

As a result of the heterogeneity and individualism the constitution formulated by the *cortes* was a document which reflected the ideology of no single group. The Socialists succeeded in impressing it with many of their ideas, more than any other single group. Their strength in the constitutional commission enabled them to present more radical provisions than the chamber was always willing to accept. The two preliminary projects of the juridical and constitutional commissions reflected differences of opinion principally in the divergent technical and social tendencies. Both of these proposals, however, were accompanied by such a number of *votos particulares* and amendments, and these reflected the individual criteria of the deputies or groups of deputies so strongly, that compromise was necessary to reach an accord on a common formula. The problems involved were too critical and real to permit the acceptance of the ideology of a single minority or individual.

The document that finally emerged was progressive. It reflected the doctrines that had been gleaned from the study of various constitutions of post-war Europe, particularly the document that the assembly at Weimar had framed for the German *Reich*. It reflected the collective social securities that had been advocated more urgently, as the twentieth century advanced, as solutions for the social and economic ills that the complexities of modern society had produced. At the same time tradition was strong, based on the liberal doctrines of the nineteenth century. The constitution erected a strong state for the protection of the social and national welfare, but the individual guarantees and personal liberties were carefully guarded against a possible usurpation of power or suspension. The independence of the organs of government was established in such a fashion that one power could not encroach upon the prerogatives of another, while the individual was protected against the abuse of power by any organ. Above all rights, above all governmental institutions was the consideration of the social welfare. Liberty was provided, but it was a liberty without licence.

The constitution reflected, then, the ideals of the men who composed it. They tried to face and believed they were facing the reality of the infirmities of Spain which they sought to cure. In the main, they were professional idealists, university professors, and lawyers, with utopian and technical concepts. The document they framed for the young republic naturally contained their doctrinaire philosophy.

Spain was infirm, but she was strongly imbued with tradition on the one hand, and extreme radicalism on the other. The background of the constitutional drama that was enacted in the *cortes* was prophetic of the vicissitudes and violence that Spain had yet to endure. The extremists of both Right and Left were dissatisfied with a document of compromise. It was too moderate, too traditional for the Syndicalists, who believed in direct action and abstention from political activity, and the Communists, who were unrepresented in the *cortes*. Their problems were still unsolved, their demands had not been fulfilled. They continued their activity without the law and were ready, if circumstances permitted, to threaten the maintenance of order, the consolidation of the republic, and the continuance of the constitution.

The other extreme, the conservative and traditional forces of Spain, were definitely alarmed and rallied to the defense of their vested interests. The creation of a lay state, the suppression of the religious orders, and the provisions relating to divorce and education evoked the wrath of the Catholics. The agrarian and propertied interests were alarmed at the restrained but potential threat of socialization and nationalization. In short, with the resolution of the crisis caused by the resignation of Alcalá Zamora, the conservatives began a campaign for the revision of the constitution.

The government of Azaña, however, was prepared to deal with both extremes. The Law of the Defense of the Republic had been framed to enable the Minister of Government to maintain order and protect the republic against subversive attacks. The constitution guaranteed individual rights, but the Law of the Defense of the Republic indicated that the government was not going to deal lightly with opposition and obstruction designed to impede the consolidation and development of the republic.

The constitution was, in reality, too advanced for the country for which it had been designed. Spain could not leap from medievalism to twentieth-century social concepts, even to nineteenth-century liberalism, without a reaction. The vital question remained to be answered. Could idealism, moderation, and compromise stand the strain of reaction and direct action?

BIBLIOGRAPHY

The following bibliography contains only those works consulted in the preparation of this volume. It is not intended as an exhaustive bibliography of the Spanish Revolution of 1931 and its subsequent evolution. The *Bibliografía general española e hispanoamericana* lists hundreds of volumes whose titles indicate that they are pertinent to these subjects, but the aim has been to make this bibliography critical rather than an exhaustive list of titles.

I. SOURCES

A. OFFICIAL PUBLICATION

Constitución de la monarquía española. Cádiz, 1812.

Constitución de la nación española votada definitivamente por las Cortes Constituyentes en 1 de Junio de 1869. Madrid, 1869.

Constitución de la monarquía española promulgada en 30 de 1876. Madrid, 1876.

Constitución de la república española. Madrid, 1931.

Diario de sesiones de las Cortes Constituyentes de la república española. Nos. 1-91, July 14, 1931 to December 17, 1931. Madrid, 1931.

The official proceedings of the Constituent Cortes were prepared by the secretariat for daily publication. The pertinent numbers for the framing of the Constitution of 1931 contain the complete minutes of the sessions of the *cortes* and appendices which include all of the *votos particulares,* amendments, and legislative projects which were considered during the period.

Información española. Madrid, 1931.

This official monthly publication contains laws and decrees, speeches and articles by various ministers, monthly commercial statistics, and other valuable information. It represents, consequently, the view of the government in power.

B. COLLECTIONS

Abad de Aparicio, Hilario and Rafael Cornel y Ortiz, *Constituciones vigentes de los principales estados de Europa y America*. Madrid, 1863.

Volume I contains the Additional Act of 1856, the Reform of 1857, the Constitution of 1845, the Constitution of 1837, and the Royal Statute of 1834.

Martínez-Alcubilla, Marcelo, *Boletín jurídico-administrativo. Anuario de legislación y jurisprudencia. Apendice de 1931*. Madrid, 1931.

This collection is a compilation of Spanish legislation, based on the *Gáceta de Madrid,* the official organ for the publication of Spanish laws and decrees. The appendix for 1931 contains all of the decrees and laws of the Provisional Government and the Constituent Cortes for that year. It is well indexed, both chronologically and by subject.

Mori, Arturo, *Crónica de las Cortes Constituyentes de la segunda república española*. 13 vols. Madrid, 1932-1934.

This work constitutes a valuable contribution to Spanish constitutional history. It is based on the *Diario de sesiones* and its selections are well chosen and indicate the crises in the formulation of the Constitution of 1931. The first four volumes, which are pertinent to the subject, include the most important speeches in the *cortes* on warmly contested issues and some of the speeches on the economic interpellations and numerous legislative projects considered by the *cortes* during 1931. They also contain interesting anecdotes and comments not available in the official proceedings. Unfortunately, however, they do not indicate sufficiently the chronology of the evolution of the constitution and tend to stress dramatic rather than routine matters. It is necessary to consult the *Diario de sesiones* for a complete understanding of the evolution of the constitution. The author also misses the opportunity of giving more intimate historical details and anecdotes in his enthusiasm for the Second Spanish Republic.

C. COMMENTARIES ON THE CONSTITUTION OF 1931

Alcalá Zamora, Niceto, *Los defectos de la constitución de 1931*. Madrid, 1936.

This is primarily a criticism of the constitution by the president of the Provisional Government and first president of the republic, who began his campaign for the revision of the constitution upon his resignation, following the approval of the religious provisions of the constitution.

Jiménez de Asúa, Luis, *Proceso histórico de la constitución de la república española*. Madrid, 1932.

This is an indispensable work for the study of the evolution of the Constitution of 1931, prepared by the president of the Constitutional Commission of the *cortes,* who was also a member of the *Comisión Jurídica Asesora*. It traces the evolution of the constitution in the two commissions and compares the texts of the definitive constitution and the *dictamen* of the parliamentary commission article by article, indicating the pertinent article of the *anteproyecto* of the juridical commission or the *voto particular* which formed the basis for the respective articles. It is weak in chronology and presents a very personal bias by including the parliamentary speeches of the author on several articles, but is the most authentic account of the proceedings of the constitutional commission that is available. The author was Professor of Law at the University of Madrid.

Pérez Serrano, Nicolás, *La constitución española. Antecedentes. Texto. Comentarios*. Madrid, 1932.

The author of this work was an official of the secretariat of the Constituent Cortes and a former Professor of Political Law at the University of Madrid. It summarizes the earlier constitutions but is primarily a juridical analysis of the Constitution of 1931, rather than a history of its evolution.

Posada, Adolfo, *La nouvelle constitution espagnole*. Paris, 1932.

Posada, an eminent Spanish jurist, was a member of the *Comisión Jurídica Asesora*. His work is primarily a commentary on the constitution from a juridical point of view, although he includes a survey of the constitutional history of Spain from 1808 to 1931.

Royo Villanova, Antonio, *La constitución española de 9 de diciembre de 1931 con glosas jurídicas y apostillas políticas*. Valladolid, 1934.

Royo Villanova was an Agrarian deputy to the Constituent Cortes well known for his unitary and conservative views. This work presents a detailed commentary on the constitution, article by article, with excerpts from the numerous speeches and amendments offered by the author.

D. NEWSPAPERS

ABC, April 1 to December 15, 1931.

This leading monarchist newspaper in Spain was suspended during May and part of June, 1931. It contains summaries of the debates in the *cortes* and is accurate for its facts, although conservative in its editorial policy. The rotogravure section and cartoons furnish graphic material for a vivid picture of the early months of the Second Spanish Republic and the Constituent Cortes.

El Sol, April 1 to December 17, 1931.

The leading liberal newspaper of Spain also contains complete summaries of the proceedings in the *cortes*. The Spanish thirst for ideas rather than news is appeased by articles by prominent liberal intellectuals and politicians. It is valuable for its ideas, therefore, as well as for its news of the domestic and foreign affairs of Spain.

The New York Times, 1930-1931, *passim*.

This newspaper presents facts impartially when they are available, although it often tends to emphasize the colorful nature of the facts rather than the events themselves.

The Times, 1931.

This London daily is admirable for its reports on Spain and presents accurate information, although it is often rather conservative in its evaluation of events in Spain.

E. CONTEMPORARY MEMOIRS AND OPINIONS

Andrade, Juan, *La burocracia reformista en el movimiento obrero.* Madrid, 1935.

Andrade criticizes the bureaucracy directing the labor movement in Spain, charging it with the responsibility for the retrograde condition of the proletariat and holding it an obstacle to the progressive development of the laboring class.

Castrillo Santos, Juan, *Cuatro años de experiencia republicana, 1931-1935.* Madrid, 1935.

This volume is a review of the first four years of the Second Spanish Republic by a leader of the Right Republican minority. It reveals a moderate tendency, the policy of the minority in defending the Church, and its hostility toward the Socialists who dominated the Constituent Cortes.

Domingo, Marcelino, *La escuela en la república.* Madrid, 1932.

Domingo summarizes the achievements of the first eight months of the republic in the program of establishing the *escuela única,* of opening the way for talent and erasing the inequality of culture, and of reducing illiteracy through primary education.

Falcon, César, *Critique de la revolution espagnole.* Paris, 1932.

This is an extremist study of the Revolution of 1931 from the point of view that it was just beginning.

Gutierrez-Ravé, José, *España en 1931. Anuario.* Madrid, 1932.

This annual aimed to record the important events of the year. It contains much information and reproduces many decrees and documents.

International Labour Office, *Studies and Reports,* Series K, No 2. "Agrarian conditions in Spain," November 10, 1920.

This is a brief survey of agrarian conditions in Spain ten years before the Revolution of 1931. They had not been materially improved before the establishment of the Second Republic.

Matorras, Enrique, *El comunismo en España*. Madrid, 1935.

Matorras was ex-secretary of the organization for Communist youth in Spain, and supplies interesting information in regard to the weakness of the Communists in Spain in 1931, their very active propaganda and agitation, their internal schisms, and their slow development.

Maurin, Joaquín, *Hacia le segunda revolución. El fracaso de la república y la insurreción de octubre*. 2nd ed. Barcelona, n.d.

The communist leader critically evaluated the work of the Second Republic and advocated concentration on the national problems of Spain.

Mola, E., *Lo que yo supe*. Madrid, 1933.
Tempestad, calma, intriga, crisis. Madrid, n.d.
El derrumbamiento de la monarquía. Madrid, n.d.

These three volumes are the memoirs of the author's tenure as Director General of Security just preceding the Revolution of 1931.

Rodríguez Revilla, Vicente, *El agro español y sus moradores. La política agraria y la economia rural en la república*. Madrid, 1931.

This survey of the agrarian problem by a Socialist insists on the redistribution of the land and condemns the agrarian policy of the Provisional Government.

Valdivielso, José Simón, *Como se ha hundido el último Bórbon*. Madrid, 1931.

A jubilant and ecstatic pæan of victory at the success of the Republicans in the establishment of the Second Republic considers the municipal elections, presents the electoral results in Madrid, and gives details of the establishment of the republic and a personal analysis of the causes of the revolution.

Silió, César, *En torno a una revolución*. Madrid and Barcelona, 1933.

This meditative survey expresses personal opinions on the course of the revolution in Spain and revolutions in general. Its value lies solely in its expression of the opinion of one individual.

II. SECONDARY WORKS

Adán, Joaquín, *España y su crisis.* Madrid, 1933.

This volume surveys the causes of the economic depression in Spain with relation to the world crisis and makes suggestions for its dissolution.

Alcalá-Galiano, Alvaro, *La caída de un trono, 1931.* Madrid, Barcelona, and Buenos Aires, 1933. Translated by Mrs. Steuart Erskine as *The fall of a throne.* London, 1933.

This is a critical and reactionary study of the Revolution of 1931. At charges that the errors of the last ministers of the monarchy were responsible for the revolution as well as the methodical preparation of the revolutionary leaders.

Altamira y Crevea, Rafael, *Histoire d'Espagne.* Paris, 1931.

This is a brief handbook of political events in Spain through the municipal elections of April 12, 1931.

Historia de España y de la civilización española. 4th ed. 4 vols. Barcelona, 1928-1929.

This work by the eminent Spanish historian gives a complete and detailed account of the evolution of Spain from the earliest times to the beginning of the nineteenth century.

"Anonymous," *The Spanish republic. A survey of two years of progress.* London, 1933.

This work is a reactionary survey of the origin of the Second Republic and a condemnation of each of the republican leaders. They are charged with the failure to maintain order, the suspension of the constitutional guarantees in the Law of the Defense of the Republic, and the persecution of the Church and prominent conservatives.

Araujo García, Carlos, and Kenneth G. Grubb, *Religion in the republic of Spain.* (World Dominion Survey Series) London and Toronto, 1933.

The authors have made a brief survey of religious conditions in Spain from the Protestant point of view, appraising the prospect for evangelical work in Spain and supplying much general information.

Ballesteros y Beretta, Antonio, *Historia de España y su influencia en la historia universal.* 8 v. in 9, Barcelona, 1925-1934.

This is a history of Spain from the beginnings to the establishment of the Second Republic. It is profusely illustrated, a model of bookmaking, and contains extensive bibliographies.

Bertrand, Louis, and Sir Charles Petrie, *The history of Spain, 1711-1931.* London, 1934. Translated from the French by Warre B. Wells.

The last chapter considers the dictatorship and the municipal elections but contains little information on the Second Spanish Republic. The work is obviously popular and the translation is not documented.

Brandt, Joseph A., *Toward the new Spain.* Chicago, 1933.

While this volume is primarily a study of the First Spanish Republic of 1873, it compares the advent of the two republics. It is valuable for its analysis of events leading to the Second Republic and as a contribution to the history of the First Republic. It is well documented and contains an extensive bibliography.

Burgos y Mazo, Manuel de, *La dictadura y los constitucionalistas.* 4 vols. Madrid, 1934.

This work is a detailed party history of the activity of the defenders of the constitutional régime during the period of the directory.

Canals, Salvador, *La caída de la monarquía. Problemas de la república. Instalación de un régimen,* Madrid, 1931.

This account of the causes and some of the events of the establishment of the Second Spanish Republic is from a republican point of view. It has an excellent analysis of the Pact of San Sebastian.

Chapman, Charles E., *A history of Spain.* New York, 1927.

This is one of the best histories of Spain in English, based on the classic work of Altamira. It surveys the history of Spain to 1917.

Clarke, H. Butler, *Modern Spain, 1815-1898.* Cambridge, 1906.

This history of Spain in the nineteenth century was written by an Englishman who had traveled widely and lived in Spain. It is concerned principally with political events, but presents a survey of the political and constitutional evolution of Spain during the nineteenth century.

Cortes Cavanillas, Julián, *La caída de Alfonso XIII. Causas y episodios*. Madrid, n.d.

This survey of the causes of the overthrow of the monarchy from a monarchist point of view is interesting for the intimate details it gives in regard to the departure of Alfonso XIII and his family.

Echeverría, L. Martín, *Geografía de España*. 3 v. Barcelona, 1937.

This work contains valuable economic data and is an excellent survey of the subject.

García y García de Castro, Rafael, *Los "intelectuales" y la iglesia*. Madrid, 1934.

The intellectual movement in Spain is evaluated by a Catholic, through critical studies of the lives and philosophies of Sanz del Río, Pí y Margall, Giner de los Ríos, Castelar, Valera, Costa, Gumersindo de Azcárate, Ganivet, Unamuno, José Ortega y Gasset, Marañón, Fernando de los Ríos, *et al.*

Giménez Caballero, E., *Manuel Azaña*. Madrid, 1932.

This volume is an eulogistic biography of the man, his ideas, and activities.

Greaves, H. R. G., *The Spanish constitution*. London, 1933.

This is a brief analysis of the factors in the Revolution of 1931, the origin of the constitution, and the document itself. It contains a brief bibliography.

Hume, M. A. S., *Modern Spain, 1788-1898*. New York, 1903.

A brief history of Spain in the nineteenth century.

Madariaga, Salvador de, *Spain*. London, 1930. *España, Ensayo de historia contemporánea*. 2nd ed. Madrid, 1934.

This is an excellent analysis of the problems and factors that produced the Revolution of 1931, from a liberal point of view. The two editions are very similar, although the first, written for the English public, contains more detail. Unfortunately the second edition in Spanish does not continue the analysis of the problems after 1931, although the author was active in the early years of the republic as a diplomat and deputy in the Constituent Cortes.

Manuel, Frank A., *The politics of modern Spain*. New York and London, 1938.

This valuable survey of the evolution of the Second Spanish Republic, to the beginning of the Civil War, summarizes the problems of the Second Republic and traces its political evolution.

Maura Gamazo, Gabriel, *Bosquejo histórico de la dictadura, 1923-1930.* Madrid, 1930.

The author, who was persecuted under the dictatorship, has presented an able study of the directory.

Ors, Juan, *España y Cataluña.* Madrid, n.d.

This is a brief and somewhat sketchy survey of the Catalan problem presenting personal views.

Peers, E. Allison, *The Spanish tragedy, 1930-1936. Dictatorship, republic, chaos.* London, 1936.

This volume presents a conservative survey of the vicissitudes of the Second Republic from the fall of the directory to the beginning of the Civil War.

Piller, Pedro, *Problemas de la revolución social española.* Madrid, 1931.

This survey of the Revolution of 1931 presents the views of a devoted anarchist.

Prieto, Carlos, *Spanish front.* London and New York, 1936.

This is a brief survey of Spanish history to the outbreak of the Civil War, suggestive rather than complete.

Primelles, Carlos, José L. Barberán, and B. de Montenegro, *Los hombres que trajeron la república. De la cárcel a la presidencia.* Madrid, n.d.

The authors have presented short sketches of the lives of the leaders of the Provisional Government, based on standard encyclopedic material. The point of view is distinctly republican.

Reid, John T., *Modern Spain and liberalism. A study in literary contrasts.* Stanford University, California, 1937.

This work presents an evaluation of Spanish liberalism as revealed in the works of Pío Baroja and Ricardo León.

Sencourt, Robert, *The Spanish crown, 1808-1931.* New York, 1931.

This popular volume was written by an English journalist following the Revolution of 1931. It presents a conservative point of view and is sympathetic toward Alfonso XIII.

Soriano, Rodrigo, *La revolución española, 1931. Ayer y hoy.* Madrid, n.d.

Soriano has written a violent attack on the monarchy in an outburst of Latin enthusiasm and revolutionary activity. It is of little value except as it reflects the personal views of the author.

Trend, J. B., *The Origins of modern Spain*. New York, 1934.

This is an authoritative and scholarly study of the educational renaissance in Spain, which was produced by the liberal educators following the Republic of 1873. It presents a vivid picture of the work of Sanz del Río, Giner de los Ríos, Salmerón, Costa, Azcírate, and Cossío.

Tusquets, Juan, *Origenes de la revolución española*. Barcelona, 1932.

In this volume a Catholic priest alleges that the Revolution of 1931 was instigated by the Freemasons and Jews. Despite the documents presented, the work is unscientific and reveals a strong Catholic bias.

Young, Sir George, *The New Spain*. London, 1933.

This analysis of the causes and early evolution of the Revolution of 1931 was written by a secretary of the English embassy in Madrid.

Zabala y Lera, Pío, *Historia de España y de la Civilización española. Edad contemporánea*. 2 vols. Barcelona, 1930.

These two volumes continue Altamira's work through the nineteenth century to the *coup d'état* of Primo de Rivera. It is a valuable and scholarly work.

España bajo los Borbones. 3rd ed., Barcelona, 1936.

A short survey of Spanish history from 1701 to 1902.

INDEX